# EFFICIENCY INSTEAD OF JUSTICE?

# Law and Philosophy Library

VOLUME 84

http://www.springer.com/series/6210

# EFFICIENCY INSTEAD OF JUSTICE?

## Searching for the Philosophical Foundations of the Economic Analysis of Law

By

**Klaus Mathis**

*University of Lucerne,*
*Switzerland*

Translated by

Deborah Shannon

 Springer

Prof. Dr. iur. Klaus Mathis, MA in Economics
University of Lucerne
Faculty of Law
P.O. Box 7464
CH-6000 Lucerne 7
Switzerland
klaus.mathis@unilu.ch

*Translator*

Deborah Shannon
Norwich, United Kingdom
shannon@academictranslation.co.uk

ISBN 978-1-4020-9797-3     e-ISBN 978-1-4020-9798-0

DOI 10.1007/978-1-4020-9798-0

Library of Congress Control Number: 2008942998

Printed on acid-free paper

9 8 7 6 5 4 3 2 1

springer.com

# Preface to the English Edition

Following its acceptance as a doctoral dissertation by the Faculty of Law at the University of Zurich in 2003 and publication in the 'Schriften zur Rechtstheorie' series by the academic press Duncker and Humblot in Berlin, *Effizienz statt Gerechtigkeit*? (1st edn. 2004, 2nd edn. 2006) was received very favourably by a German-speaking readership. It therefore seemed worthwhile to produce an English version of the third, revised and expanded edition (2009) to make the text accessible to a wider audience.

The subject of this study is the economic analysis of law, which is examined from the perspective of philosophy of law, including a critical analysis of its philosophical foundations. The ideas with which Richard A. Posner has sought to justify the efficiency paradigm in the field of law are a central focus. Nevertheless, this scholarly appraisal of the economic analysis of law also attests to the reception of 'Law and Economics' in continental European law and culture.

First of all, I thank my excellent translator, Deborah Shannon of Norwich, UK, who has rendered the demanding German text into English with great care and accuracy. I also thank Prof. Dr. jur. h.c. Norbert Simon and Dr. Florian R. Simon, LL.M., the directors of Duncker and Humblot publishers, for their kind permission to publish an English translation.

Last but not least, I would like to express my deep gratitude to my highly esteemed doctoral supervisor Walter Ott, emeritus professor of the Faculty of Law of the University of Zurich, for having opened my eyes to the beauty of philosophy of law.

Lucerne, November 2008                                     Klaus Mathis

# Preface to the 3rd German Edition

Since the first edition of this book was published, 'Law and Economics' has taken its place in the canon of subjects taught to law students at a number of German-speaking universities, not least the University of Lucerne, where I gave the first lecture in 'Rechtsökonomie' (Economic Analysis of Law) in the autumn semester of 2007. During the same period, to my pleasant surprise, this groundwork text has been well received by students, which has given me sufficient encouragement to publish a third, revised and expanded edition.

For the present edition, the principal revisions and additions have been made to Chapters 4, 6, 7 and 9. In particular, the section on the economic analysis of liability and contract law now includes a discussion of the 'bilateralism critique' raised by Jules Coleman. Further, the chapter on utilitarianism has been expanded, and Chapter 7 now covers the later publications of John Rawls as well as Amartya Sen's important critique of the concept of primary goods. A further addition to Chapter 9 is a critical appreciation of the argument on the relationship between efficiency and justice advanced by Louis Kaplow and Steven Shavell in their book 'Fairness versus Welfare'. Finally, further examples relating specifically to 'Behavioral Economics' have been incorporated, and a closer analysis of environmental permits follows as a postscript to the Coase theorem. My assistant, Silvan Rüttimann, MLaw (Lucerne), has supported me tirelessly in this undertaking, and for that I thank him sincerely.

I also thank Prof. Dr. Paul Richli, the founding dean of the University of Lucerne, and our present dean, Prof. Dr. Regina E. Aebi-Müller, for supporting my research and teaching work. Very special thanks go to my doctoral supervisor, Walter Ott, emeritus professor of the University of Zurich, to whom I am indebted for my education in philosophy of law. Finally I am grateful to Prof. Dr. Norbert Simon and Dr. Florian Simon of Duncker & Humblot publishers for their renewed inclusion of the book in their 'Schriften zur Rechtstheorie' series, and to Ms. Birgit Müller for overseeing the printing process with her usual diligence.

Lucerne, October 2008                                                          Klaus Mathis

# Preface to the 1st German Edition

In Switzerland there is currently a heated debate concerning Zurich airport, and whether incoming flights should approach Zurich primarily from the north, as they always have, or from the south as well in future. Let us suppose that a court were asked to rule on which district incoming flights should pass over, the north or the south? And suppose that this court had to base its decision solely on the criterion of economic efficiency, where efficiency would mean maximizing the wealth of society.

In the case to be ruled on, the district north of the airport is relatively underpopulated, whereas the district to the south is very densely settled. Based on comparative property values alone, the predictable result is that noise pollution from a southern flight path would be far more detrimental to social wealth than the current northern flight path passing over sparsely populated areas. If the only concern were to maximize social wealth, the court would have to rule in favour of the northern approach. Its decision would certainly be economically efficient, but would it also be just?

This example along with the agenda declared in the title hint at the provocative nature of the question tackled in this book: 'Efficiency instead of justice?' The work is rooted in the philosophy of law and engages with an interdisciplinary theme spanning jurisprudence and economics. The subject matter is the economic analysis of law, which is itself analysed to trace its philosophical foundations. A pivotal focus is Richard A. Posner's theory of wealth maximization, which is presented at length and critically appraised.

At this point I would like to thank all those who have contributed, with valuable guidance, to the completion of this paper. In particular, I must thank my doctoral supervisor Professor Walter Ott who made this dissertation possible. Special thanks are due also to my mother, and to my father who sadly died in the spring, for their moral support while I was writing up the work.

Zurich, August 2003                                                                 Klaus Mathis

# Contents

# List of Figures

# Chapter 1
# Introduction

> STUDENT: I don't think Jurisprudence would be quite my
> line.
> MEPHISTOPHELES: Well, well, I can't entirely disagree.
> I know a bit about that discipline.
> Statutes and laws, inherited
> Like an old sickness, passed on by the dead
> Through endless generations, creeping down
> From land to land, from town to town![1]

In the USA, numerous research approaches have developed over the last few decades which apply economics to the field of law: property rights theory, transaction cost economics, public choice theory, constitutional economics and, not least, economic analysis of law.[2] These approaches rely on the economic model for their explanation of human behaviour. Today these economic theories of law are collectively known as 'Law and Economics'. Economic analysis of law is a branch of research pioneered by the Chicago School, and principally by Richard A. Posner, dealing mainly with civil law, and to some extent also with criminal law. It is based on the insights of property rights theory and transaction cost economics. Economic analysis of law is an interesting and challenging attempt to employ the concepts and reasoning methods of modern economic theory in order to gain a deeper understanding of legal problems, and to bring greater rationality to legal argumentation.[3] In the words of Ronald Coase:

> Much, and perhaps most, legal scholarship has been stamp collecting. Law and economics, however, is likely to challenge all that and, in fact, has begun to do so.[4]

Whereas economists are used to thinking in abstract models and tackling problems *deductively*, lawyers generally reason *inductively*: they solve a case by studying the legal records and the relevant judicial casuistics. Of course they also consult the law, which is codified in general abstract terms. Nowadays, however, it is no longer practical to solve legal problems using the law and juridical methods of reasoning

---

[1] Goethe, *Faust I*, 1969 ff.

[2] Cf. Richter and Furubotn, pp. 35 ff.

[3] Cf. Behrens, p. 1.

[4] Coase, 'Law and Economics', p. 254.

K. Mathis, *Efficiency Instead of Justice?*, Law and Philosophy Library 84,
DOI 10.1007/978-1-4020-9798-0_1, © Springer Science+Business Media B.V. 2009

alone, such is the diversity – not to mention ambivalence – of the precedents. The increasing reliance on case law also threatens the rationality of juridical argumentation. As Carl Christian von Weizsäcker aptly writes:

> The great lawyers of the nineteenth century were capable of abstract thinking. The present concretism of justice in jurisprudence that has grown up over decades, on the other hand, must be treated with scepticism. [...] Much would be gained if our allied discipline, jurisprudence, would arm itself with some of the analytical methods of economics.[5]

Many lawyers believe that legislative provisions and administrative acts can change the world for the better. State intervention frequently fails to achieve the desired effects, however, and often gives rise to side effects which nobody has anticipated. One reason for unintended consequences is that lawyers focus mainly on the *goals* rather than on the *consequences* of particular actions.[6] Any attention they pay to consequences is usually confined to the direct effects that occur in a specific instance. The mistake often made with this method is to assume that if a certain effect occurs in one instance, the same effect will hold for the system as a whole. This, of course, is frequently not the case.[7] Economic analysis of law therefore scrutinizes the law systematically for its effects on the efficiency of the overall economy.

The application of economic methods of analysis to law initially gave rise to fierce criticism from some lawyers. Karl-Heinz Fezer's vehement disapproval of economic analysis of law is almost legendary:

> The inevitable result of any economic analysis of law is an inauspicious course of action: the economic reduction of the complexity of law. The monocausal theoretical approach stunts the multifunctionality of the legal system. It strips the law of its essential functions. To express it even more plainly: *economic analysis of law and liberal legal reasoning are irreconcilable.*[8]

Equally unflattering is Peter Gauch's dismissal of economic analysis of law:

> As soon as we begin to dissect the law into economic data, we arrive at a law without quality. And what remains is sheer worthlessness.[9]

Calabresi and Melamed admit that economic modelling only sheds light on one specific aspect of the complex phenomenon of law. Although conceding that economic models are not always adequate, they recognize that traditional juridical method also has its flaws, and that it likewise conveys only one particular view of things:

---

[5] von Weizsäcker, p. 150. Translator's note: quotations from sources published only in German have been translated into English for convenience.

[6] Kleinewefers, pp. 86 f.

[7] Adams, p. 13.

[8] Fezer, p. 823 (author's emphasis).

[9] Gauch, p. 2.

Legal scholars, precisely because they have tended to eschew model building, have often proceeded in an ad hoc way, looking at cases and seeing what categories emerged. *But this approach also affords only one view of the Cathedral.*[10]

Posner distinguishes between positive and normative aspects of this analytical approach. The *positive aspect* of economic analysis of law is the claim that the 'common law' can best be explained as a system for increasing economic efficiency. In contrast, 'statutory law' does less to encourage efficiency although it, too, is influenced by economic principles.[11] The *normative aspect* is the demand that the legal system ought to encourage economic efficiency. This second, normative aspect, is of central interest to us. According to Posner it is the role of the law to encourage market competition and, where the market fails to work because transaction costs are too high, *to simulate the result of competitive markets.* This maximizes economic efficiency and the wealth of society – which ultimately mean one and the same thing, according to Posner.

The methods of economic analysis of law are based on the economic model of human behaviour on the one hand, and the theory of welfare economics on the other. In the first part of this book, under the sub-heading 'Economic Foundations' – the aim of which is to introduce lawyers to methods of economic reasoning – these two theories will be presented, along with some fundamental concepts of economic analysis of law (e.g. the Coase theorem). In the second part, we will turn to the philosophical foundations of economic analysis of law. Posner acknowledges the influences of Adam Smith and Jeremy Bentham, whom he thinks of as the founders of normative economics.[12] Posner subscribes to Smith's faith in the market – i.e. the idea of the 'invisible hand' – as an ideal allocation model, and to Bentham's ethical consequentialism, although what Posner wishes to maximize in this regard is not society's utility but its wealth. Seeking to legitimize his concept of *wealth maximization*, Posner – following John Rawls's contract theory – makes use of a consensus theory approach.[13] Since compulsion is applied under the law – in contrast to market transactions, which are voluntary – a social consensus is necessary to legitimize the application of the wealth-maximization principle. Adam Smith's moral philosophy, Jeremy Bentham's utilitarianism and John Rawls's theory of justice will therefore be outlined as 'Philosophical Foundations' in the second part of the book.

In the third part of the work, Richard A. Posner's theory of wealth maximization will be discussed in detail and critically appraised. It will become clear that he has revised and expanded upon his position several times, not least in response to the criticism provoked by his arguments. A further discussion of the relationship between efficiency and justice will follow. Finally, based on the insights gained, conclusions will be drawn on the function and significance of economic analysis of law within the legal system.

---

[10] Calabresi and Melamed, pp. 1127 f. (author's emphasis).

[11] Posner, *EAL 5*, pp. 26 ff.

[12] Posner, *Legal Theory*, p. 57.

[13] Posner, *Overcoming Law*, pp. 403 f.

# Part I
# Economic Foundations

# Chapter 2
# Homo Economicus

> *Economics is the science which studies human behaviour as a relationship between ends and scarce means which have alternative uses.*[1]

## 2.1 Introduction

Economic analysis of law is based on the use of the *economic model to explain human behaviour*. It thus makes use of the analytical tools of *microeconomics*. Microeconomic theory takes individual economic agents as the starting point of analysis. In contrast, the Keynesian theory which dominated economics in the mid-20th century was founded on *macroeconomic models*. That is to say, analysis was applied to the interrelationships between economic macrovariables, e.g. between interest rates and investment, the rates of unemployment and inflation, or between public spending and economic growth. Keynesian economic policy failed because of the naive belief that an economic system could be controlled like a machine. The major downfall of 'hydraulic Keynesianism' was its lack of a *microfoundation* – the fact that it was not underpinned by any theory of human behaviour. While economists in the field of macroeconomics differ on many issues, 'neoclassical' microeconomic theory is the *acknowledged tool of every economist*. The microeconomic approach is based on the economic paradigm.

## 2.2 The Economic Paradigm

The central element of the economic paradigm is *homo economicus* (economic man), the rational actor in situations of scarcity. Hence the analytical unit is the individual, whose resources are limited so that not all of his needs can be satisfied. Individuals therefore have to assess the different options and decide which will result in the optimum outcome. So human action is understood as a 'rational choice' between different alternatives.[2]

---

[1] Robbins, p. 16.

[2] Kirchgässner, *Homo oeconomicus*, p. 12.

K. Mathis, *Efficiency Instead of Justice?*, Law and Philosophy Library 84,
DOI 10.1007/978-1-4020-9798-0_2, © Springer Science+Business Media B.V. 2009

## 2.2.1 The Scarcity of Resources

The assumption of scarce resources refers to the disparity between the totality of goods that people have at their disposal to satisfy their needs, and the totality of goods that would be necessary to satisfy all of their needs completely. The resources in question are not just material goods, by any means. They may equally well be intangible in nature; such as security, for instance. Due to the scarcity of resources, the means at people's disposal are not infinite, so choices must be made in order to satisfy needs. 'Economic endeavour' thus denotes the prudent management of scarce resources.[3]

Scarcity, it follows, is a relative rather than an absolute concept. The degree of scarcity depends on the scale of needs and the quantity of resources available. It can be diminished, either by multiplying the resources or by lowering the level of expectations.[4] Essentially the phenomenon of scarcity is manifested in every facet of life: so the amount a household can spend is limited by its income, while the potential output of a construction company is limited by the materials, the equipment, and the number of workers at its disposal.[5] Limited financial resources aside, another important factor in scarcity is time, which is also limited. In principle, all human activity – even in the sphere of interpersonal relationships – is subject to the law of scarcity and can potentially be addressed by economic theory. Hence the discipline of 'economics' denotes a *method*, not a subject. Applying the economic approach to fields outside economics – as Gary S. Becker did in relation to the family and to crime – is sometimes labelled 'economic imperialism'.[6]

## 2.2.2 Methodological Individualism

The economic model of behaviour begins with the individual. Therefore it is also referred to as *methodological individualism*. Accordingly, collective decisions come about through the aggregation of decisions made by individuals – rather than from any autonomous action on the part of collectives, as seen from the standpoint of holistic theories. That said, it is still possible for individuals to behave differently in a group than they do when alone.[7] By virtue of their similar functions, social groups and systems are analysed as a whole. Nevertheless, the behavioural assumptions about individual agents remain applicable. Decisions made by collectives are viewed as the result of decisions made by all their individual members, transformed

---

[3] Kirchner, pp. 12 f.

[4] Behrens, p. 31.

[5] Schäfer and Ott, p. 56.

[6] For example in the title of a book edited by Ingo Pies and Martin Leschke: *Gary Beckers ökonomischer Imperialismus* [Gary Becker's Economic Imperialism].

[7] Cf. Olson, *The Logic of Collective Action*.

according to certain rules.[8] Hence the economic approach cannot be reconciled with an organic theory of the state which treats the state as an autonomous agent. Moreover, economic theory recognizes collective ideas of utility only where these can be derived from individual perceptions of utility.[9]

### 2.2.3 The Theorem of Self-Interest

The theorem of self-interest states that, given several alternatives, economic agents will choose the one with the best chance of maximizing their own utility. The utility derived from the different goods is described by the utility function: $U = U(x_1, x_2, x_3, \ldots, x_n)$. In other words, utility $U$ is dependent upon the different quantities of goods that can be consumed. Here the *law of diminishing marginal utility* (Gossen's first law) is generally assumed to apply. This states that the additional utility of each additional unit consumed will decline progressively with consumption, possibly even to a negative value. For example, the greatest utility is derived from the first bread roll that one consumes. The additional utility of the second and third rolls is lower, and by the fourth it is actually negative due to the discomfort of oversatiation. Figures 2.1 and 2.2 represent this phenomenon graphically, showing a utility function $U(x)$ for just one good, and the corresponding marginal utility function $U'(x)$ which, in mathematical terms, is the first derivative of the utility function. Here $x^\circ$ marks the point at which total utility is maximized and marginal utility is zero (satiation point).

---

[8] Kirchgässner, 'Ökonomie', p. 111.
[9] Behrens, p. 35.

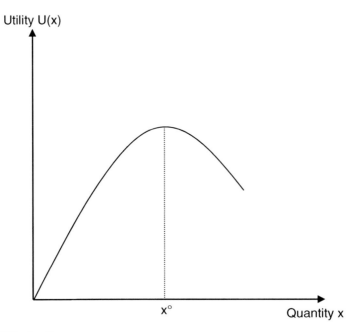

**Fig. 2.1** Utility function

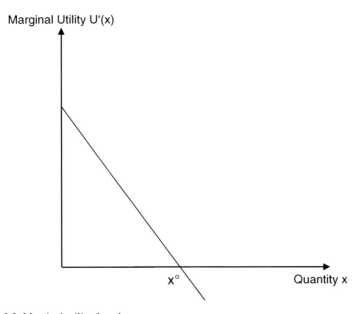

**Fig. 2.2** Marginal utility function

Economic man maximizes his own utility; in principle, the well-being of others is not his concern. But self-interested does not mean 'wolfish' towards others in the sense of '*homo homini lupus*'. Of course envy and spite are commonly encountered in reality, but then so is altruism. As a rule, however, the end effect is such that even behaviour borne of such motives serves some self-interested purpose, at least to a degree. For example, even altruistic behaviour can be explained in most cases by the fact that the individual concerned has a preference for 'good deeds' or revels in other people's good fortune.[10] According to Posner:

> [S]elf-interest should not be confused with selfishness; the happiness (or for that matter the misery) of other people may be a part of one's satisfactions.[11]

The theorem of self-interest is not morally loaded, since it states only that agents behave in accordance with their preferences.[12] The fundamental presumption is that individuals know best what is right for them (consumer sovereignty).

## 2.2.4 The Assumption of Rationality

Rationality means that in principle, individuals are in a position to act to their own advantage, i.e. to assess and evaluate their scope for action in order to maximize their own utility.[13] In modern economic theory, the idea of rationality no longer implies that the individual is like a walking computer, all-knowing and always calculating at lightning speed which of all the available options is the best.[14] As Herbert Simon puts it:

> There can no longer be any doubt that the micro assumptions of the theory – the assumptions of perfect rationality – are contrary to fact. It is not a question of approximation; they do not even remotely describe the processes that human beings use for making decisions in complex situations.[15]

Simon sees one solution to the problem in the concept of *bounded rationality*:

> A number of theories have been constructed [which] incorporate the notions of bounded rationality: the need to search for decision alternatives, the replacement of optimization by targets and satisficing goals, and mechanisms of learning and adaptation.[16]

---

[10] Cf. Kirchner, p. 13.

[11] Posner, *EAL 5*, p. 4.

[12] Kirchgässner, *Homo oeconomicus*, p. 64.

[13] Kirchgässner, 'Ökonomie', p. 110.

[14] In many economic models, however, this remains a key assumption.

[15] Simon, p. 510.

[16] Simon, p. 510. This modern-day *homo economicus* is also described as a 'resourceful, evaluating, maximizing man (REMM)'; Neumann, p. 258.

If the notion of rationality were to imply having complete information, then it would not be rational to be rational. The fact is, rationality is limited, and it limits itself. This is explained by the matter of information costs: information procurement is not a cost-free undertaking; and to be fully informed – if it were possible at all – would be unaffordably expensive. Information procurement is also subject to an economic calculus, in that the utility of each additional piece of information must be weighed up against its cost. A further difficulty is that often, the exact utility of a piece of information is only known once the information has been obtained. All the individual has to work with are expectations about the value of the information sought.

Essentially, rationality means that an individual reacts *systematically* to changes in environmental conditions, i.e. not randomly and impetuously, but equally, not adhering strictly to predetermined rules. Nevertheless, such rules can be useful since they diminish information and decision-making costs. Hence it can be rational to adhere to tried-and-tested rules in certain typical situations.[17]

Finally, note that within the economic model of behaviour with its assumption of rationality, the important and much-debated philosophical distinction between behaviour and action disappears: the behaviour of individuals is explained by the fact that they are acting rationally. This makes it possible to predict changes in behaviour in response to any change in the scope for action.[18] Moreover, no distinction is made between understanding and explanation: human behaviour is only understandable if it can be explained on the basis of the model of rational behaviour.[19]

## 2.2.5 Strict Distinction Between Preferences and Constraints

The individual's choice situation is essentially described by two elements: preferences and constraints. In economic analysis, a strict distinction is made between these two determining factors. Preferences denote people's inner motivations, constraints their external incentives. The economic model of behaviour now attempts to explain *changes in behaviour as a reaction to external incentives, i.e. changes in constraints*. Preferences are also important for explaining human behaviour but, in the short term at least, they are assumed to be constant. Consequently, they are not the decisive factor for explaining changes in behaviour.

The individual's values, which have been developed during the socialization process, are expressed in the utility function as preferences. On that basis, the individual assesses all the available options, by weighing up the advantages and disadvantages, benefits and costs of each alternative, and finally decides on the alternative that yields the highest utility subject to the given constraints. Human behaviour is interpreted as a rational choice from among the alternatives open to the individual, or in

---

[17] Kirchgässner, 'Ökonomie', p. 110.

[18] Kirchgässner, 'Ökonomie', p. 110.

[19] Kichgässner, *Homo oeconomicus*, pp. 19 f.

the language of economics: the 'maximization of utility subject to constraints under uncertainty'.[20]

The constraints limit the individual's scope for action, and hence the courses of action which represent all the possible choices. In the textbook case of a private household's consumption choices, the constraint is imposed by the amount of disposable income and the prices[21] of the consumer goods on offer.[22] Other constraints would be the time available for consumption (most important in relation to leisure activities), legal restrictions (e.g. on the consumption of prohibited drugs) or moral reservations (e.g. concerning products manufactured using child labour in developing countries).

Usually it is relatively easy to determine the constraints that govern the behaviour of particular individuals. Individuals' preferences, on the other hand, are very difficult to ascertain. Other than by means of surveys, with all their methodological difficulties, preferences can only be established indirectly. By observing individuals' behaviour, with knowledge of the constraints that apply to them, conclusions can be drawn about their order of preferences. In any case, preferences are normally far more stable than constraints and change more slowly, if at all.[23] *The assumption is that the behaviour of individuals can be systematically influenced by modifying incentives.* Any such systematic influencing of preferences is likely to be difficult, at least in the short term. This is a verifiable point: if the aim is to reduce road traffic, for instance, it is more effective to increase fuel prices than to appeal to motorists to limit their car usage.

Economics takes it for granted that the needs articulated by individuals, implicitly or explicitly, are indeed their needs. On a fundamental level, therefore, economics fails to distinguish between de facto and 'genuine' needs. This does not necessarily preclude any critical examination of preferences, however. Clearly, 'genuine' preferences can be distorted by drug consumption, by habituation and upbringing, or by political and religious indoctrination ('brainwashing'). One might also question whether the voluntary immolation of widows that still occurs in India is a true reflection of these widows' genuine preferences. It is possible that widows only agree to be burned as a result of social pressure; in that case, their behaviour would be determined by social constraints and not by distorted preferences.

So human behaviour can be influenced by modifying constraints – i.e. the conditions under which people act. This may sound revolutionary and perhaps even reminiscent of Marxism, but modern economic theory differs from Marxism in one very crucial respect: it takes the individual person with individual preferences and values as a given, and does not attempt any form of improvement. Different economic conditions will not turn self-interested people into altruists; it is more accurate to say that if external conditions change, the same people's actions will be

---

[20] Kirchgässner, *Homo oeconomicus*, p. 14.

[21] More precisely: 'relative prices', i.e. the ratio of various commodity prices to one another.

[22] See Sect. 2.4.1 below.

[23] Kirchgässner, 'Ökonomie', pp. 111 f.

different and possibly 'better'. However, this is a response to modified or improved conditions, and cannot be attributed to any 'betterment' of the people themselves.[24]

## 2.2.6 Economic Man as a Heuristic Fiction

Economics deliberately reduces the individual person to a few attributes, because it is a characteristic of economic modelling to concentrate on what is important and leave out what is less important. Economic questions and problems such as economic growth, unemployment, inflation etc. are very complex. In order to be able to analyse them scientifically, it is absolutely necessary for their complexity to be reduced.[25] This is known as the principle of *Ockham's razor*, whereby everything of secondary importance is pared away in order to obtain a simple, abstract model. By degrees, simple basic models can be concretized and refined on the *principle of decreasing abstraction*.[26] Accordingly, economic man does not stand for a rounded 'view of man' in the philosophical or theological sense, but a purely theoretical construct which is tailored to problems of an economic nature – i.e. scarcity problems in the broadest sense.[27] Thus, economic man is often called a 'heuristic fiction'; that is, a mere assumption made for the purpose of analysing economic problems.[28]

Of course, the economic approach does not set out to explain the real behaviour of a specific individual. That is a task better left to psychologists. The economist is far more interested in the behaviour of larger groups of individuals, known as 'aggregates', e.g. the behaviour of consumers or business firms. Economists look for *regular patterns* in the behaviour of the group as a whole, or at least the majority of the group under consideration. For example, it is possible to assume that individuals' behaviour will follow a normal distribution curve, and that economic theory will explain the behaviour of the average individual. In terms of distribution, the bulk of individuals cluster around the mean value, and if distribution is symmetrical, the highly variant behaviours at both extremities of the distribution cancel each other out, which is why they are of little consequence for the average.

Micro theory also provides the basis for explaining macro phenomena, which is not the contradiction it might initially appear. Indeed, if the external conditions for all individuals, or a particular group, undergo a similar change as a result of modification of a particular macro variable, the reaction of this group – not necessarily for every member individually, but certainly on average – will exhibit a regular pattern which can be explained by the individual choice calculus. For example, raising the

---

[24] Kirchgässner, 'Ökonomie', p. 112.

[25] Homann and Suchanek, p. 392.

[26] Cf. e.g. Schmidtchen, pp. 12 ff.

[27] Cf. Homann and Suchanek, p. 426.

[28] Cf. Neumann, pp. 257 ff.

price of petrol will not – *ceteris paribus*[29] – induce every single motorist to use less petrol. In the context of economics, what matters is that consumers on average will react by cutting back their consumption, so that overall the price increase effects a reduction in the quantity demanded.[30]

## 2.3 Fundamental Principles of Economics

### 2.3.1 The Law of Demand

One of the fundamental principles of economics – evident from the example just discussed – is the *inverse relationship between price and the quantity demanded*.[31] Let us consider an individual demand curve (Fig. 2.3) showing a household's demand for tomatoes: at price $p_1$ the quantity demanded is amount $x_1$. If the price of tomatoes rises to $p_2$, then normally – *ceteris paribus* – the household will reduce its demand for tomatoes to some lower amount, $x_2$. Hence, a household's demand curve plotted as a price-quantity graph will usually slope downward. Since the market demand curve for a good is plotted by aggregating all the individual demand curves, this will also be downward sloping.

Individual demand for a good does not depend solely on the price of that good, however. Other factors that influence demand are people's preference structures, income, and the prices of other goods. When one good becomes more expensive, the quantity of it demanded falls, and more of other goods are bought (the *substitution effect*); but in addition – *ceteris paribus* – the overall price level rises. If nominal income remains the same, the result is a fall in real income, and fewer goods can be bought in total (the *income effect*).

The law of demand does not apply solely to goods with explicit prices. The length of a prison sentence, for example, is the 'price' a criminal has to pay for any crime committed. Bear in mind, though, that the perpetrator only has a certain probability of being caught and sentenced. In this case, the relevant price would be the *expected value*, calculated from the length of the prison term multiplied by the probability that the penalty will indeed be imposed. Economists call such non-monetary prices *shadow prices*.[32]

---

[29] All other things being equal.

[30] Kirchgässner, 'Ökonomie', pp. 110 f.

[31] Posner, *EAL 5*, p. 4.

[32] Posner, *EAL 5*, pp. 5 f.

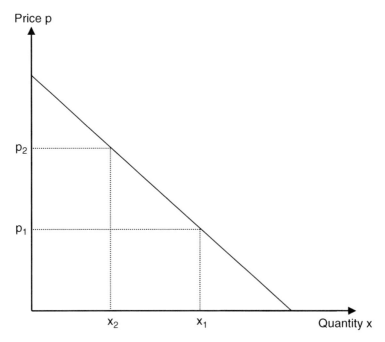

**Fig. 2.3** Demand curve

### 2.3.2 *Maximization of Utility and Profit*

Households (i.e. consumers) try to *maximize utility* under the given constraints (prices, incomes, etc.), while the equivalent challenge for business firms (producers) is to *maximize profits*. Profit is the difference between revenue and production costs. Of course, households also have to contend with costs: not just the prices of goods, but non-monetary costs such as time spent queuing at the checkout.

The economist measures costs according to the *opportunity cost principle*, i.e. in comparison with the sacrificed utility of the next-best use of the resource in question.[33] The price of one hour of leisure time, for example, corresponds to the lost income that one could otherwise have earned in that hour. The costs of a university degree are only partly comprised of tuition fees and expenditure on books; a further element is the income foregone during the period of studies. On the opportunity cost principle, a house-owner who lives in his or her own property must calculate not only the cost of maintaining the house, but also lost rental income since the house could potentially be rented out.

Both the principle of opportunity cost and the concept of shadow prices put the lie to the persistent misconception that economics is about 'money' and nothing

---

[33] Posner, *EAL 5*, p. 6.

else. Quite the opposite: *economics deals with the use of scarce resources, i.e. with real phenomena that exist irrespective of monetary categories*. Take housework; it is an economic activity even if it does not attract monetary remuneration. It gives rise to costs in the economic sense: not least, the opportunity cost of the time devoted to it. This statement applies equally to other activities that might not immediately be associated with economics:

> Sex is an economic activity too. The search for a sexual partner (as well as the sex act itself) takes time and thus imposes a cost measured by the value of that time in its next-best use. The risk of a sexually transmitted disease or of an unwanted pregnancy is also a cost of sex – a real, though not primarily a pecuniary cost.[34]

On the other hand, straightforward transfers are not – per se – costs, from an economic point of view. Supposing that the state imposes a tax of €1,000 on one person, and pays out the same amount to someone else as a transfer. From the taxpayer's vantage point, the €1,000 are private costs, but in terms of the economy as a whole, no costs are incurred because the transaction only redistributes resources rather than diminishing them in any way. However, some administrative costs are involved; moreover, the transfer has an effect on *incentives* for the people concerned.[35] Taxes can reduce taxpayers' incentives to work, while transfers can have the same effect on recipients.

Another point about the economic concept of costs is that it is *forward-looking* rather than backward-looking. The only costs that are material to a decision are future costs, not those which have been activated in the past (called 'sunk costs'). For instance, if one is at the theatre and the performance turns out to be unexpectedly dire, it is irrational to waste yet more time sitting through the rest of the show purely because one paid a lot of money for the ticket. That is now a sunk cost and cannot be reversed. On the other hand, there is still a chance to limit the non-monetary costs of the wasted time and exasperation with the show by walking out of the theatre. In reality, of course, people often take sunk costs into account when they make decisions, which is irrational behaviour. Among investors, for instance, if a share is purchased at a high price and subsequently falls, a common strategy is to buy more shares at the lower price in order to lower the acquisition price. All this really does is mask the loss from the drop in price following the first share purchase.

These examples show that the economist normally takes an *ex ante* rather than an ex post perspective. Incidentally, this is equally applicable to business profits and the calculation of business valuations. The correct method of valuing a firm is not on the basis of its acquisition value ('net asset value') but based on total anticipated net revenues, which are discounted to the present point in time ('capitalized income value').[36]

---

[34] Posner, *EAL 5*, p. 7.

[35] Posner, *EAL 5*, p. 7.

[36] Geigant et al., p. 230.

## 2.3.3 The Market Ensures the Optimum Allocation of Resources

A further fundamental principle of economics is that voluntary transactions in markets ensure that all resources are allocated to where they are most highly valued in economic terms. That is, production factors reach the place where they will generate the highest value from production, and consumer goods go to those consumers who are willing to pay the most for them. When it is impossible to bring about any further improvement by means of exchange, the allocation of resources is optimal,[37] a state of affairs known as the *Pareto optimum*.[38]

This view is rather too optimistic, however, because in reality the market does not function perfectly. Therefore the theory of *market failure* was developed. Market failure occurs when ideal market conditions do not exist (as with public goods and external effects, see below) or when economic agents restrict or even eliminate competition (e.g. through cartels or legal regulations). Moreover, fluctuations in the economy can also result from incomplete market adjustment processes. In all these cases, the economic utilization of resources is suboptimal.

The first characteristic of *public goods* is that nobody is excluded from consuming them, whether they pay anything for them or not. In addition to this *non-excludability* from consumption, public goods are also characterized by *non-subtractability* (non-rivalry) in consumption: if someone consumes a public good, – unlike, for example, a bread roll, – it does not preclude further consumption of the good by others. Classic examples of public goods are the light from a lighthouse that everyone can see, television and radio signals that everyone can receive, or a dam that protects an entire district from flooding.[39]

Public goods can also be intangible in nature. One only need think of security or political stability. These goods are not supplied on a private basis, at least not in sufficient quantities, because the producer is left to bear the bulk of the costs if consumers will not voluntarily pay their share. Because of this *free rider problem*, public goods are traditionally supplied by the state and financed from tax revenues or other compulsory deductions. Although, technically, public goods can be offered by private agents, in general it is an area where the market will fail, so it is up to the state to step into the breach and provide an adequate supply.

A similar problem is posed by *external effects* (externalities). These can occur both in the production and the consumption of goods. When external effects come

---

[37] Posner, *EAL 5*, p. 11.

[38] See Sect. 3.2.1.2.

[39] Where non-excludability is the sole characteristic, we talk about a common-pool resource (e.g. common grazing land, public highways); on this, see Hardin: 'The Tragedy of the Commons'. Where only non-subtractability (non-rivalry) applies, it is a club good (e.g. the European single market); see Buchanan: 'An Economic Theory of Clubs'. Technical means are often found to overcome the non-excludability of non-paying consumers, e.g. controlling access to roads (road pricing). Private goods which are provided by the state (e.g. state schools, state theatre) for political reasons (e.g to ensure or promote universal provision of these goods) are called meritoric goods; on this, see Musgrave: 'A Multiple Theory of Budget Determination'.

into play, private and economic costs (or utility) do not fully coincide, which results in a misallocation of resources. Motorists, for example, only bear the burden of their own vehicle and fuel costs. Meanwhile the environmental costs caused by exhaust fumes and noise are a burden on the whole community. Analysed in that way, the private costs of motoring are too low, and consequently traffic volumes are higher than the economic optimum level at true cost. Prices have an incentive and steering function in a market economy. When externalities are present, prices send out inaccurate signals. The state has the option of using taxes or subsidies to correct this kind of market failure. In environmental legislation, for instance, the 'polluter pays principle' is being imposed in the form of environmental levies. When external costs are charged to those who actually cause them, they are *internalized*.[40] Finally, it is almost inevitable that even state interventions will go wrong from time to time; in such instances, the counterpart of market failure is known as *state failure*.

## 2.4 Models of Utility and Profit Maximization

Since microeconomics relies on mathematical models to a large extent, some examples of elementary microeconomic models will now be presented and explained. Both households and business firms have to make choices in situations of scarcity. Therefore a method will be shown for determining a household's optimum consumption (household equilibrium). This model shows optimization under one constraint. Thus, what is determined is not the absolute maximum of the objective function, but a relative objective which also satisfies the constraint. For this purpose, we need to make use of differential calculus, and specifically the Lagrange method.[41] The next model to be introduced will show profit maximization under two different forms of market.

### 2.4.1 Household Maximization of Utility

A household has to decide how it will use its income to buy consumer goods. For simplicity's sake, we will restrict ourselves to a choice between two goods. Nevertheless, the findings from this simple case will also hold for *n* goods. The optimal consumption of a household, known as the household equilibrium, is the goods-quantities combination yielding the maximum utility for the given consumption expenditure. Let utility $U$ as the objective variable be dependent upon the two quantities of goods $x_1$ and $x_2$ (e.g. apples and pears). These have to be chosen in such a way that utility is maximized (the optimum combination of goods). The utility function describes the level of utility in relation to the quantities of goods consumed.

---

[40] See also Sect. 3.2.3.2 and the solution proposed by Coase, Sect. 4.3.3.2.

[41] Cf. Schumann, *Mikroökonomie*, pp. 52 ff.

Since this is the objective function, the aim is to maximize it:

$$\text{Objective function}: U = U(x_1, x_2) \qquad \rightarrow \text{max}\,.! \qquad (2.1)$$

Consumption expenditure $C$ is constrained and can be calculated from the quantities of goods and the constant prices of those goods $p_1$ and $p_2$. The budget equation is:

$$\text{Constraint}: C = C(x_1, x_2) = p_1 x_1 + p_2 x_2 = \text{const.} \qquad (2.2)$$

Now the Lagrange method requires that we use these two functions to form a Lagrangian function. This is formed by adding the objective function to the constraint equation, rearranged to equate to zero and multiplied by the Lagrange multiplier $\lambda$:

$$L(x_1, x_2, \lambda) = U(x_1, x_2) + \lambda(C - p_1 x_1 - p_2 x_2) \qquad (2.3)$$

Next we form partial derivatives with respect to the three independent variables and set the results equal to zero.

$$\partial L/\partial x_1 = L'_1 = U'_1 - \lambda p_1 = 0 \qquad (2.4)$$

$$\partial L/\partial x_2 = L'_2 = U'_2 - \lambda p_2 = 0 \qquad (2.5)$$

$$\partial L/\partial_\lambda = L'\lambda = C - p_1 x_1 - p_2 x_2 = 0 \qquad (2.6)$$

If Equations (2.4) and (2.5) are solved for $\lambda$ and equated, we arrive at the following relationship:

$$U'_1/p_1 = U'_2/p_2 \qquad \text{Gossen's second law} \qquad (2.7)$$

According to Equation (2.7), at the consumption optimum, the marginal utility divided by price is equal for both goods. This means that at the optimum, regardless of whether the last unit of money is spent on good 1 or good 2, the same utility or degree of satisfaction must result. Until this is the case, the household simply buys more of the good giving higher marginal utility per unit of money than of the good which delivers lower marginal utility per unit of money. This process is repeated until the marginal utility per unit of money is finally equal for both (or all) goods. This is the law of equalization of marginal utility (Gossen's second law). Moreover the budget constraint reappears in Equation (2.6), which ensures that this, too, is respected.

Plotted as a graph (Fig. 2.4), the household equilibrium is located at the point where the relevant utility indifference curve is tangent to the budget line. The budget line is the constraint and describes all consumption possibilities that fully utilize the total consumption expenditure. The higher the total consumption expenditure or the lower the prices, the further the distance of the budget line from the origin. The slope of the budget line is determined by the ratio of prices to one another and equals $-p_1/p_2$. Utility indifference curves represent the utility function of the

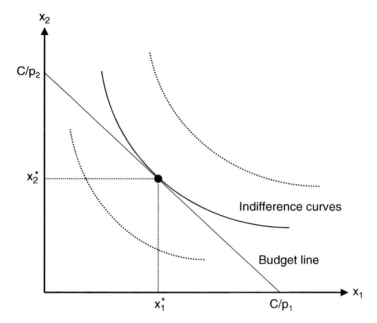

**Fig. 2.4** Household equilibrium

household and describe the goods-quantities combinations which deliver equal utility. The convexity of the curve signifies a tendency to prefer mixed consumption of both goods over consumption of just one or the other exclusively. A whole set of indifference curves exist, and the utility represented by an indifference curve increases with its distance from the origin. Therefore to determine the optimum, the relevant indifference curve is the most outlying curve that still touches the budget line.

## 2.4.2 Maximization of Profit by the Business Firm

The differential equation can also be used to represent profit maximization by a business firm. We distinguish between two forms of market: perfect competition and a supply monopoly.

### 2.4.2.1 Perfect Competition

Perfect competition is a type of market characterized by bilateral polypoly, i.e. a theoretically infinite number of suppliers and buyers, none of which is in a position to influence the price of the commodity in question. The price is determined by the intersection point of market supply and market demand. For individual market participants, it is a given, so they behave as *quantity adjusters (price takers)*. Accordingly, a business firm needs to determine the profit-maximizing quantity of output at the given commodity price and the given cost function. Profit $P$ is the difference between revenue $R$ and costs $C$, both of which depend on quantity $x$.

The profit function is thus:

$$P(x) = R(x) - C(x) \rightarrow \text{max .!} \tag{2.8}$$

To determine the extreme values (the profit maximum and the profit minimum) the first derivative must be set equal to zero:

$$P'(x) = R'(x) - C'(x) = 0 \tag{2.9}$$

$$R'(x) = C'(x) \tag{2.10}$$

Since $p$ is constant: $R(x) = px$, therefore $R'(x) = p$, and thus:

$$p = C'(x) \qquad \text{first-order condition} \tag{2.11}$$

In the perfect competition model, the first-order condition demands that *price be equal to marginal cost*. A profit maximum is only found if, in addition, the second derivative is less than zero:

$$P''(x) = R''(x) - C''(x) < 0 \tag{2.12}$$

$$R''(x) < C''(x) \qquad \text{second-order condition} \tag{2.13}$$

A firm's individual supply curve normally has a positive gradient. That is, the higher the price $p$, the greater the quantity supplied $x$. The supply curve for the market is found by aggregating the supply functions of all business firms offering the commodity in question (Fig. 2.5).

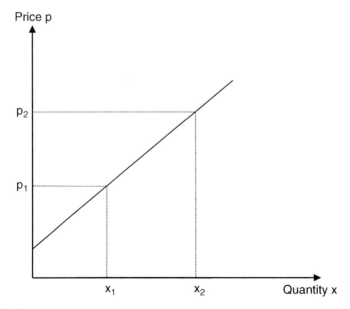

**Fig. 2.5** Supply curve

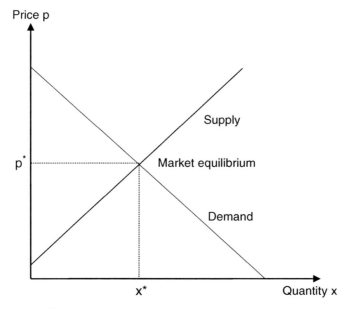

**Fig. 2.6** Market equilibrium

By combining the market supply curve and the corresponding market demand curve on one graph, the market equilibrium under perfect competition can be located at the point where the two curves intersect (Fig. 2.6).

### 2.4.2.2 Supply Monopoly

A supply monopoly consists of a single supplier and a theoretically infinite number of buyers. Subject to the given price-volume function (demand function) and cost function, this supplier must determine not only the optimal quantity but also the optimal price-quantity combination. The profit maximum can be calculated by proceeding, initially, in the same way as for the perfect competition model. Equation (2.10) can be carried forward unaltered, but because $p$ is not constant this time, Equation (2.11) cannot be formed. Marginal revenue $R'(x)$ is derived from revenue $R(x) = p(x)x$. The latter is calculated by multiplying price and quantity, whilst price in turn is dependent on the quantity supplied, in accordance with the price-volume (demand) function.

$$R'(x) = C'(x) \qquad \text{first-order condition} \qquad (2.10)$$

In the supply monopoly model, the first-order condition demands that *marginal revenue equals marginal cost*. A profit maximum is obtained if Equation (2.13) is also fulfilled:

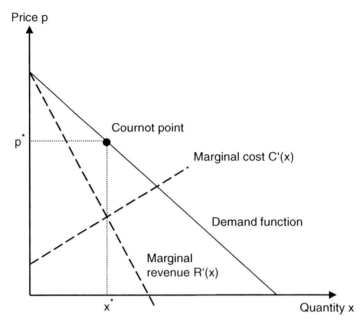

**Fig. 2.7** Supply monopoly

$$R''(x) < C''(x) \qquad \text{second-order condition} \qquad (2.13)$$

The monopoly quantity $x^*$ can be determined from a graph by locating the intersection point of the marginal revenue and marginal cost curves. The corresponding monopoly price $p^*$ can be obtained by substituting the monopoly quantity $x^*$ into the demand function. The optimal price-quantity combination is called the Cournot point (Fig. 2.7).

The common feature of these models is the technique of *marginal analysis*. In the profit-maximization model, for example, the economist does not seek to determine the total or average revenue and the total or average costs for a given quantity, but the incremental growth in revenue and costs of one more unit of output; in other words, the marginal revenue and marginal cost of each additional unit produced. As long as the marginal revenue from an additional unit exceeds the marginal cost, a marginal profit will result. Every additional unit of output that generates a marginal profit increases overall profits. On the basis of the cost and revenue function assumed, marginal profit will normally tail off beyond a certain quantity of output, decline to zero and finally become negative. Upon reaching the quantity at which marginal profit equals zero, total profit has been maximized.[42]

---

[42] Which is expressed in Equations (2.9) and (2.10). For a profit maximum, the additional condition is that Equation (2.13) must be fulfilled.

## 2.5 Critique

### 2.5.1 Unrealistic Assumptions

Psychological studies cast strong doubts on the validity of the assumption of rationality, even if allowance is made for the concept of bounded rationality.[43] Some of the other premises – such as the frequent assumption of perfect competition in markets – are likewise criticized for bearing no resemblance to reality.

In his famous essay, 'The Methodology of Positive Economics', Milton Friedman mounted a rigorous defence against criticisms of the axioms of neoclassical theory. His arguments sparked a controversy which has not abated to this day. According to Friedman, far from being empirical statements about reality, the underlying assumptions are actually *'as if'* statements. Utility maximization is not, in this view, something that individuals verifiably strive for. From the results of their actions, however, it appears exactly *as if* they did.[44] Consequently Friedman rejects any criticism of his premises. He treats a theory as a *predictive tool*, not a model of reality. Thus the power of a theory cannot be tested by the validity of its premises, but by its usefulness for testing hypotheses which have been put forward based on these theories. He goes so far as to claim that the more significant a theory, the more unrealistic its assumptions:

> Truly important and significant hypotheses will be found to have "assumptions" that are wildly inaccurate descriptive representations of reality, and, in general, the more significant the theory, the more unrealistic the assumptions [. . .].[45]

Friedman is primarily concerned with usability in the economic policy context: hypotheses should deliver usable predictions on the basis of as little concrete information as possible.[46] Posner adopts a similar stance to Friedman and emphasizes the explanatory and predictive power of economic theory. But he does not believe it necessary to test the truth of the premises as such:

> An important test of a theory is its ability to explain reality. If it does a lousy job, the reason may be that its assumptions are insufficiently realistic; but we need not try to evaluate the assumptions directly in order to evaluate it. Judged by the test of explanatory power, economic theory is a significant (although only partial) success. [. . .] Another test of scientific theory is its predictive power, and here too economics has had its share of success, most dramatically in recent years.[47]

Drawing a comparison with the natural sciences – the standard that economic theory has always aspired to – Posner shows that theories can still be very useful even if the assumptions they are based on are not completely accurate:

---

[43] Blaug, p. 232.

[44] Frank, p. 19.

[45] Friedman, p. 14.

[46] Hotz, p. 304.

[47] Posner, *EAL 5*, p. 18.

Newton's law of falling bodies is unrealistic in its basic assumption that bodies fall in a vacuum, but it is still a useful theory because it predicts with reasonable accuracy the behavior of a wide variety of falling bodies in the real world.[48]

One objection to this *instrumentalism* is that 'explanation' is more significant than 'prediction'. Friedman's methodology neither explains reality nor extends knowledge. Such theories yield no new knowledge about the causal relationships between phenomena.[49] Michael Scriven aptly comments:

[T]here certainly seem to be occasions when we can predict some phenomenon with the greatest success, but cannot provide any explanation of it. For example, we may discover that whenever cows lie down in the open fields by day, it always rains within a few hours. We are in an excellent position for prediction, but we could scarcely offer the earlier event as an explanation of the latter. It appears that explanation requires something "more than" prediction; and my suggestion would be that, whereas an understanding of a phenomenon often enables us to forecast it, the ability to forecast it does not constitute an understanding of a phenomenon.[50]

One can also argue to the effect that firms in competition with each other cannot avoid acting to maximize profits. If they did anything else, they would be eliminated from the market.[51] Seen in that light, economic man would be built into the logic of the market, and divergent behaviour would be selected out in the process of competition:

[...] note that Friedman shares the same *market optimism* as Smith. The latter, however, presupposes that even in a world *full of ignorance* about the future, companies and households can often enough make decisions which are *adequate to the situation*. He further implies that under competition, the lazy, stupid and careless but also the weak and unfortunate have only minimal chances of exercising important decision-making functions in the longer term.[52]

The counter-argument to this view is that entrepreneurs or their advisers would probably have learned economic theory in the course of their studies. This could explain why firms behave in accordance with the rules of economic theory, which would then prove to be a self-fulfilling prophecy.

## 2.5.2 The Static Nature of the Analysis

The economic approach primarily uses the method of *comparative static* analysis, which prioritizes economic exchange processes and comparison of the attendant states of equilibrium.[53] But the economy and, above all, the law are *evolutionary*

---

[48] Posner, *EAL 5*, p. 18.

[49] Cf. Pheby, p. 83.

[50] Scriven, pp. 176 f.

[51] Homann and Suchanek, p. 422.

[52] Meyer, p. 41. On Adam Smith's market optimism see Sect. 5.3.

[53] Hotz, p. 310.

in their development. Hence it is worth looking into how these developments occur and the nature of the accompanying learning processes. Indeed, economic theory struggles to describe and explain *developments*. It is good for analysing structural relationships and for comparing static states, but explaining transitional processes is not one of its strengths.

### 2.5.3 Reductionism

Another charge is that the economic approach reduces reality to a small number of purely economic parameters. But reductionism is not a dirty word for the economist, quite the contrary. Posner himself defends the restriction to essentials and the method of abstraction used in economics:

> But abstraction is of the essence of scientific inquiry, and economics aspires to be scientific. [...] Similarly, an economic theory of law will not capture the full complexity, richness, and confusion of the phenomena – criminal or judicial or marital or whatever – that it seeks to illuminate. But its lack of realism in the sense of descriptive completeness, far from invalidating the theory, is a precondition of theory. A theory that sought faithfully to reproduce the complexity of the empirical world in its assumptions would not be a theory – an explanation – but a description.[54]

The economic model of behaviour only gives predictability within a narrow subsystem of society, namely where the price mechanism can be relied upon as a mechanism of incentive and deterrence. It is true that Gary S. Becker and others integrate phenomena of social interactions such as social prestige or altruism, customs and traditions into their models. But this is always kept strictly within the model of economic man – perhaps as a variable of the utility function, as a change in relative prices, or as an additional constraint. Thus, for example, customs and traditions help to lower information costs. Of course, the construction of extended utility functions or the consideration of institutional constraints on the behaviour of individuals represent welcome signs of progress. But the attempt to describe all social phenomena solely in terms of economic categories such as utility and cost also has its shortcomings. Particularly in the analysis of law, drawing a veil over social and psychological aspects can give rise to drastically wrong conclusions. The recidivism rate of delinquents is known to depend upon their social milieu, for instance; some types of punishment may provoke prisoners to commit far more serious crimes; and in numerous cases, drug-related crimes have to do with losing the social support of a community or questioning the meaning of life.[55]

Now if aspects like these are left out of the analysis, and if this is confined to viewing individuals 'as if' they were nothing more than cost-benefit calculators, always seeking the most cost-effective alternative, then caution about any recom-

---

[54] Posner, *EAL 5*, p. 18.

[55] Hotz, pp. 305 f.

mendations derived from such analyses is certainly not misplaced. Policy informed
solely by such formulas could actually make problems worse, or shift them onto
other levels. The impacts of the legal regulatory framework or an infringement of
the law must not be reviewed solely from the perspective of a single individual; it is
essential to take account of the social context at the same time.[56]

This is the direction of more recent approaches which can be grouped under
the heading of 'Behavioral Economics'.[57] The aim of this line of research is to
critically reassess the psychological foundations of economics and to map them out
more realistically,[58] since a sounder psychological basis is likely to enhance the
explanatory power of economic models.[59]

The *prospect theory* put forward by Daniel Kahneman and Amos Tversky, following on from the work of Simon, represents a milestone which further relativizes
the *assumption of rationality*.[60] Their theory is founded on empirical observations
and describes phenomena such as how individuals perceive their profits and losses.
Kahneman and Tversky observed that individuals are prone to '*loss aversion*',
i.e. they feel a loss of € 1,000 more acutely than a € 1,000 gain. 'Prospect theory' differs from conventional 'expected utility theory' in the way that it treats the
probabilities assigned to certain events. Whereas 'expected utility theory' assumes
that decision-makers value a 50% probability of a profit at exactly 50%, 'prospect
theory' takes the line that people tend to overvalue low probabilities of gain, and to
underestimate medium and high probabilities of gain. In this connection, the concept
of '*anchoring*' can be cited as a typical example. The theory is that people often
reach probability judgements through intuition or on the basis of intransigent views
(known as 'anchors'), which are often completely arbitrary and consequently not
adequately adapted to the actual conditions.[61]

On the basis of these findings, human behaviour can no longer be called rational in the strict sense, but neither is it wholly unpredictable, completely irrational
or even random. Quite the opposite: economists can both describe and model the
forms of human rationality and irrationality, and often the theories of behavioural
economics add just one or two parameters to conventional models. By way of an
example, take the concept of loss aversion mentioned above: the loss aversion co-
efficient can be described as a quotient arising from the ratio of the marginal cost
of a loss to the marginal utility of a gain. The standard model is the special case in
which this numerical value is 1.

---

[56] Hotz, p. 306.

[57] See Mathis, 'Behavioral Economics'.

[58] It also provides better means of refuting the criticism that economists often engage in mere
'*model Platonism*', divorced from reality.

[59] On the general issue, see e.g. Camerer, Loewenstein and Rabin (eds.): *Advances in Behavioral
Economics* or Frey and Stutzer: *Economics and Psychology*.

[60] See Kahneman and Tversky: 'Prospect Theory'.

[61] On the general issue, see Kahneman and Tversky: 'Prospect Theory'.

Behavioural economics also calls into question the *theorem of self-interest*. It investigates the extent to which a quality like fairness plays a part in human behaviour. Many people do in fact stray from exclusively self-interested behaviour. There are also signs that the consideration of fairness and mutual benefits are important to bilateral negotiations and the functioning of markets. More recent studies in behavioural economics therefore attempt to explain how social, economic and legal conditions influence the inclination towards reciprocity, i.e. acting for mutual advantage.[62]

Finally, the neoclassical model of human behaviour makes the tacit and highly unrealistic assumption that *willpower* is unconstrained. Under this model, economists see behaviour as no more than a straightforward decision-making process of choosing between different alternatives. They also assume that once a decision is made, it will be swiftly and smoothly enacted. But the very concept of willpower is indication enough that the execution of a chosen course of action does not always happen automatically. In some cases we have to motivate ourselves in order to bring about the desired behaviours. Hence, people frequently mobilize their willpower to suppress or break compulsive or impulsive habits ('visceral' motivations).

George Loewenstein defines three *visceral factors*: (1) drives such as hunger and sexual desires; (2) emotions such as anger and fear; and (3) physical sensations such as pain. Although the visceral factors have important purposes for survival and procreation, they can sometimes drive us into behaviours which create conflicts with self-interest. For example, people run the risk of harm to their health in the form of obesity if they have easy access to high-calorie foods and consume them whenever they are hungry. Thus the implementation of a decision is always at the mercy of acute and intensive desires, even when people are quite capable of recognizing what is in their own interests.[63] This realization also yields useful insights in law, particularly for the economic analysis of criminality: findings in this field indicate that it can be more effective to develop strategies and concepts to help people to strengthen their willpower and support them in controlling their behaviour instead of trying to combat crime by toughening the penalties.[64] New insights from behavioural economics are therefore entering economic analysis of law under the banner of 'Behavioral Law and Economics'.[65]

---

[62] See e.g. Fehr and Fischbacher: 'Why Social Preferences Matter'; or Gintis et al. (eds.): *Moral Sentiments and Material Interests*.

[63] On this point, see Loewenstein: 'Willpower: A Decision Theorist's Perspective'.

[64] See also Sect. 4.4.3.

[65] See Sunstein (ed.): *Behavioral Law and Economics*; and Engel et al. (eds.): *Recht und Verhalten: Beiträge zu Behavioral Law and Economics*.

## 2.6 Summary

Every methodological approach has its strengths and weaknesses. What seems to be called for, therefore, is *methodological pluralism*. Analysis of a subject should be undertaken under different aspects and using a variety of methods *which complement but also relativize one another*. In this spirit, economic research can render valuable services and should not be rejected by jurisprudence, but seen as a form of enrichment.

# Chapter 3
# Efficiency Criteria

> *When an economist says that free trade or competition or the control of pollution or some other policy or state of the world is efficient, nine times out of ten he means Kaldor-Hicks efficient.*[1]

## 3.1 Introduction

Defining efficiency criteria is a traditional concern of *welfare economics*. Whereas microeconomics deals with the behaviour of individual economic agents and the workings of markets, the task of welfare economics is to develop criteria for evaluating economic policy measures and economic regulatory systems. Welfare economics has both a *positive* and a *normative* element. On the one hand it attempts to *explain* how certain economic policy measures or economic regulatory systems influence a country's economic development. On the other hand it is concerned with *evaluating* social states, i.e. finding out whether the effects triggered by a particular action are thought to have raised or lowered welfare.[2]

The clarification of this second, normative question is where welfare economics makes its real contribution. In view of this, it is confronted with a fundamental methodological problem: can normative questions ever be answered scientifically? Should science not confine itself to clarifying factual problems? The principle of *value freedom* formulated by Max Weber demands that scientists must always draw a clear distinction between explanatory and normative statements, and declare their own value judgements openly. For any logical method that leads to value-laden conclusions necessarily includes value-laden premises.[3] The propositional content of a conclusion can never be greater than the propositional content of the premises from which that conclusion is derived.[4]

---

[1] Posner, *EAL 5*, p. 15.

[2] Külp, pp. 469 f.

[3] The fact that normative judgements cannot be derived from factual statements alone is called Hume's law: 'One can't derive an "ought" from an "is".' The attempt to derive a normative judgement from a factual statement in spite of this is called the naturalistic fallacy.

[4] Külp, p. 470.

The *value-judgement problem* can be dealt with in two ways: either one declares one's own value positions clearly, as a prelude to deriving value judgements – together with other factual statements – from them. Or one attempts to find universally acceptable value premises from which, once again, evaluative conclusions as well as factual statements can be derived. The representatives of traditional welfare economics – such as Arthur C. Pigou, Vilfredo Pareto, Nicholas Kaldor and John R. Hicks – took the second route, i.e. they believed they had found welfare criteria which were universally acknowledged.[5]

Another methodological problem is posed by the *scale* used to measure individual and collective welfare. Proponents of 'old' welfare theory (e.g. Pigou) tried to measure welfare in terms of the changes in utility experienced by individuals as a result of changes in their economic situation. In so doing, they assumed that it was possible to measure utility on a *cardinal* scale. Pareto – a proponent of the 'new' welfare theory – settled for an *ordinal* concept of utility. Seen this way, an individual only compares the utility of different states (e.g. two combinations of goods) in terms of 'better', 'worse' or 'equally good' without attempting to assess utility by means of a cardinal value.[6]

## 3.2  Pareto Efficiency

Vilfredo Pareto developed a concept of efficiency for the evaluation of social states, which is based on the following three principles:[7]

(1) *Consumer sovereignty*: the preferences of individuals are autonomous and are respected as such (consequently there are no 'good' or 'bad' preferences).
(2) *Non-paternalism*: all that matters to society is the utility of individuals; the state does not require any additional consideration as an end in itself.
(3) *Unanimity*: changes of allocation require the consent of all, i.e. everyone has a right of veto.

### 3.2.1  The Concept

The terms Pareto efficiency or Pareto efficient can be used in a relative sense – to mean that state A is *Pareto superior* to state B, – or in an absolute sense – as when a certain state is designated *Pareto optimal*.

---

[5] Külp, pp. 470 f.

[6] Schumann, 'Wohlfahrtsökonomik', p. 222.

[7] Blaug, p. 125.

### 3.2.1.1  The Pareto Criterion

A Pareto superior change fulfils the Pareto criterion (the Pareto principle). This can be defined as follows:[8] any change that puts one member of society in a better position without making somebody else worse off is a Pareto improvement.[9] In contrast, a change that violates the Pareto criterion is termed Pareto inferior.

### 3.2.1.2  The Pareto Optimum

The term Pareto optimum is used to denote the state reached when one person's position cannot be improved any further except by making another person worse off. Pareto optimality is the *state in which no further Pareto superior changes are possible*.[10] Pareto-optimal efficiency is composed of three subsidiary types of efficiency which must be cumulatively fulfilled in a Pareto optimal state:

(1)  efficient production,
(2)  efficient consumption,
(3)  efficient production structure.

First of all, Pareto optimality signifies that *production is efficient*. What this means is that the production of one good cannot be increased without having to curtail production of another good. Let us assume an economy in which production is limited to just two goods, guns ($x_1$) and butter ($x_2$). A *production possibilities curve* – more generally known as a transformation curve – can be used to show all the alternative combinations of these two goods that can possibly be produced, given the available production factors.[11]

In Fig. 3.1, for example, at point A only butter is produced, at point B only guns. At points C and D, however, both goods are being produced. Because a rise in production of the one good always correlates with a fall in production of the other, the transformation curve slopes downward. Moreover, its concave curvature means that it is technically more advantageous to produce some of each good than limiting production to one only (the law of increasing opportunity costs). But production efficiency exists at all points on the transformation curve because full use is being made of the total resources available.[12] What cannot be achieved are production combinations outside the transformation curve, e.g. point E, because the available resources are not sufficient to do so. Points inside the curve, e.g. point F, represent possible production combinations, but these are inefficient because they do not exhaust the available resources.

---

[8] Baumol, p. 400.

[9] In addition to this customary definition, mention is sometimes made of a 'weak' Pareto criterion, which requires that all members of society must be made better off (evidently originated by Pareto himself). Eidenmüller, p. 48.

[10] Geigant et al., p. 695.

[11] Schäfer and Ott, p. 27.

[12] Schäfer and Ott, pp. 27 f.

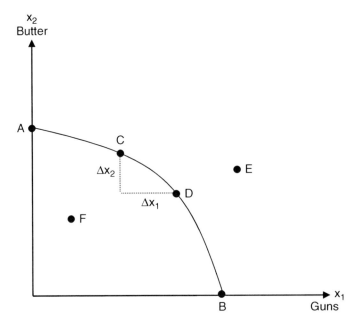

**Fig. 3.1** Transformation curve (cf. Schäfer and Ott, p. 27)

*Efficiency in consumption* can most easily be explained by means of a thought experiment attributed to Léon Walras. He imagined a situation in which goods did not have to be produced, but were already available. This is the case in a prison camp, supposing that every prisoner receives certain quantities of chocolate, cigarettes and beer. Now because the inmates' preferences for these commodities vary, they can increase their utility simply by exchanging goods. Efficient consumption is reached when no further mutually beneficial exchanges are possible. As this example shows, it is possible to increase utility even without additional production, but only for as long as perfectly efficient consumption has not been attained.[13]

Finally, Pareto efficiency also calls for an *efficient production structure*. This condition requires optimal coordination of consumption and production. If the first two conditions are met but the third is not, this is a case where production and distribution are efficient but the utility of some economic agents could still be increased by producing different quantities of the different goods, without any detriment to other agents' utility.[14]

---

[13] Schäfer and Ott, pp. 28 f.

[14] Schumann, *Mikroökonomie*, p. 268.

## 3.2.2 The Pareto Optimum and Competitive Equilibrium

Note that the three specified conditions apply regardless of the prices of goods or production factors. The assumption is made, however, that competition prevails in markets and the price mechanism functions optimally.[15] Market equilibrium with perfect competition throughout all markets in an economy – under ideal conditions, in the absence of external effects in particular – represents a Pareto optimum (the first welfare theorem). A Pareto-optimal competitive equilibrium can be derived from any given initial endowment of households with production factors. Every conceivable competitive equilibrium is Pareto optimal, and conversely, every conceivable Pareto optimum can be interpreted as a competitive equilibrium, achievable from a suitable initial endowment of the households (the second welfare theorem).[16]

So Pareto efficiency is closely linked with the conditions of the ideal market. And the Pareto criterion can only be applied where transactions are voluntary. For people have more sense than to consent to a transaction which leaves them worse off. *In the sphere of law, where the state can apply compulsion, normally the Pareto criterion, which is based on free will, is not directly applicable.*

## 3.2.3 Critique

### 3.2.3.1 The Problem of Initial Endowment

Pareto efficiency does not mean that a society is organized justly, however justice may be defined. This relates to the fact that a particular Pareto-efficient production combination can only be defined if the *initial endowment of members of society with production factors* or property rights is known. This may be illustrated with the following example.[17]

Let us assume that in country A, a few families own all the land and real capital, whilst the only resource all the other families have is their labour. Through production and exchange, a Pareto-efficient state could be achieved. In contrast, we will assume that in country B, the initial endowment with production factors is egalitarian. Here, too, a Pareto-efficient state can be attained by means of production and exchange. The states in countries A and B, whilst they are both Pareto optimal, are nevertheless very different. Whereas production in country A tends to consist mainly of luxury goods for the rich, country B tends towards the production of goods for mass consumption. It follows that both countries differ substantially in respect of income distribution and production structure.

---

[15] Schumann, *Mikroökonomie*, pp. 268 f.

[16] Schumann, 'Wohlfahrtsökonomik', p. 223.

[17] Cf. Schäfer and Ott, pp. 29 f.

Confining attention to the question of allocation – and neglecting the question of distribution – may, in the worst case, result in people starving to death under Pareto optimal conditions. According to Amartya Sen:

> A state in which some people are starving and suffering from acute deprivation while others are tasting the good life can still be Pareto optimal.[18]

When the initial endowment of resources is brought within the scope of the discussion, not one but many different Pareto-efficient states are possible. But the Pareto criterion does not explain which of these states is of greatest merit. Of course, given the same initial endowment, a Pareto-efficient state is preferable to a Pareto-inefficient state, on principle. But whether this initial endowment is 'just', one does not know. In many cases, it is tacitly assumed that the initial endowment will replicate the existing distribution of resources within a society; this implicit acceptance of prevailing conditions is, of course, a value judgement. If one also considers the problem that in some instances, certain key aspects of the initial endowment may have come about as a result of *violence, oppression or fraud* – albeit perhaps at a much earlier historical juncture – then it becomes clear how unsound it is to espouse any particular initial endowment without having subjected it to critical scrutiny.[19]

Redistribution from the rich to the poor is also impossible, according to Paretian welfare economics, because some individuals would be made worse off in comparison to the original state, in breach of the Pareto principle. The application of the Pareto criterion therefore presupposes a *basically conservative position* and favours the status quo.[20] In the words of Hans Albert:

> Any regulation which limits itself to applying the Pareto criterion reveres the status quo, because it gives every individual an unlimited veto against changes of state perceived as impairing the satisfaction of his needs.[21]

Thus, anyone who stipulates unanimity and will allow the state to go no further than bringing about Pareto improvements is advocating a doctrine of inviolable gains.[22]

### 3.2.3.2 External Effects

The concept of the Pareto optimum fundamentally assumes the production of a business firm to be determined only by the quantities of factors it deploys and the utility of households only by the quantities of goods they consume – but not by the quantities used or consumed by other business firms or households. It excludes direct dependencies between the production volumes of different firms, as well as

---

[18] Sen, *Resources*, p. 95.

[19] Albert, *Rationale Praxis*, p. 130.

[20] Bohnen, p. 100.

[21] Albert, *Rationale Praxis*, p. 130.

[22] Schefczyk and Priddat, p. 463.

interpersonal interdependencies of utility such as envy or benevolence, i.e. *external effects in production or consumption.*[23]

In reality, however, external effects (externalities) are common. Such effects occur in production and in consumption when the actions of one agent cause consequences for third parties. Depending on whether the externalities are beneficial or detrimental to the third party, they are called *positive* or *negative* external effects.[24] A further distinction is made between *technological* and *pecuniary* external effects.

*Technological external effects* arise particularly in the context of environmental pollution. Supposing that a cement factory pollutes the air and harms people's health as a result: environmental pollution generates costs for the whole economy, but these are not charged to the factory as private costs. Therefore technological externalities manage to evade the price mechanism. But if private costs are at variance with the full economic costs, the allocation of resources will be suboptimal. In our example, the factory is able to produce its cement too cheaply, because by rights the environmental costs, or the costs of preventing pollution (e.g. with a filter), ought to be borne by the factory and included in the relevant cost calculation. This *internalization* of external effects would raise the price of cement and the quantity sold would tend to fall.

Unlike the technological external effects, which the price mechanism fails to capture, *pecuniary external effects* unfold precisely by way of the price mechanism.[25] For example, if A opens a filling station directly opposite B's filling station and takes away a share of B's customers, B will suffer negative pecuniary external effects caused by A.[26] But technological external effects can also occur in market transactions, as for instance when residents living near a food store are disturbed by the noise of customers' vehicles.

External effects also occur in consumption, which can produce negative external effects in third parties as a result of envy and spite. By the same token, of course, it can produce just the opposite effect, namely when one person delights in another person's good fortune. Interdependencies of utility also result from an individual's position in society. What is significant is not just an individual's absolute position, but one's *relative position* and any *shift of position* within society. Such a shift can have an influence on the satisfaction of needs and the associated attributions of value, since it tends to go hand in hand with shifts in social power which can be very significant.[27]

*If one takes account of external effects, even the majority of free-will market transactions violate the Pareto principle because they almost always affect third parties in one way or another.*

---

[23] Schumann, 'Wohlfahrtsökonomik', p. 224.

[24] Geigant et al., pp. 267 f.

[25] Therefore internalization of pecuniary external effects is not appropriate.

[26] Posner, *EAL 5*, p. 7.

[27] Albert, *Rationale Praxis*, p. 128.

### 3.2.3.3  The Static Nature of the Analysis

The comparison of two social states using the Pareto criterion is a *static comparison*; the transition process is ignored. Hence it is problematic to interpret the result dynamically and to make legal policy recommendations on this basis. The greater efficiency of a proposed regulation A over regulation B would be a necessary but not a sufficient condition for introducing the regulation, because transition costs would still have to be borne in mind. But economic analysis frequently excludes the costs of the transition, thus tacitly assuming them to be zero. Looking at the costs of restructuring legal systems in Eastern Europe and the new federal states of post-unification Germany, this proves to be a wholly untenable assumption.[28]

Bear in mind also that in a dynamic analysis starting from a given initial endowment, there are any number of developmental paths on which a Pareto optimal competitive equilibrium can be achieved in every period.[29] Moreover, the Pareto criterion only takes account of future generations in so far as they feature in the present generation's calculations.[30]

### 3.2.3.4  The Danger of Mixing Positive and Normative Theory

In welfare economics, the Pareto optimum is often equated with a normatively-laden efficiency objective. But the use of Pareto optimality as a normative concept is extremely problematic, for originally, the Pareto optimum was used as a process criterion for *explaining* how markets worked. Over time, welfare theory turned its attention to *evaluating* how markets worked. This shift made the Pareto optimum into a result criterion. The state of efficiency defined within the framework of a general equilibrium theory was thus elevated to an ideal of efficiency, so that effectively Pareto efficiency was functioning as the reference concept for a normative analytical approach.[31] Thus, the concept of Pareto efficiency is often brought to bear with normative intentions; yet there is an abiding implication that it belongs to the terminology of positive economics.[32] This approach is highly questionable because it leads to the mixing of positive and normative theory.[33]

## 3.3  The Kaldor-Hicks Criterion

### 3.3.1  The Concept

As we have seen, the Pareto principle is based on the assumption of the *free market model*. Every market participant is free to choose whether or not to engage in market

---

[28] Koboldt, Leder and Schmidtchen, p. 379.

[29] Schumann, 'Wohlfahrtsökonomik', p. 224.

[30] Blaug, p. 125.

[31] Pies, p. 127.

[32] Cf. Blaug, p. 127.

[33] Mack, pp. 39 f.

transactions. The *law* however, is *coercive in character*. Therefore the concept of Pareto efficiency required *modification* before it could usefully be applied to law.[34]

This modification was introduced in the late 1930s when the British economist Nicholas Kaldor turned his attention to a problem which had exercised the national legislature in the previous century. The debate concerned the Corn Laws, protectionist legislation which defended British farmers from foreign competition. *The central question was whether laws should be changed to benefit the economy as a whole even if this would make a particular group worse off.*[35] This is a question of great practical significance in law, because legal decisions often have to be taken by weighing up competing interests. Nicholas Kaldor and John R. Hicks proposed a collective decision-making rule to be applied to non-Pareto-superior decisions. This rule – they believed – would only involve a weak value judgement.[36]

Kaldor argued that the abolition of the Corn Laws was a Pareto-superior change, albeit in a modified sense. The gains of a country as a whole from free trade should normally be at least great enough to allow for compensation of the grain-farmers' losses. Kaldor believed that the gainers could pay the farmers for the right to abolish tariffs and still end up with a net gain. The important thing is that the gainers would be in a position to purchase the right, i.e. they would have the means to compensate the losers, but would not necessarily have to do so. Hicks generalized Kaldor's argumentation and applied it broadly to trade barriers.[37] Today the criterion proposed by Kaldor and Hicks is formulated more generally: *a change is an improvement by the Kaldor-Hicks criterion if the gainers value their gains more highly than the losers their losses.*[38]

Kaldor and Hicks argued for *hypothetical compensation*, because in their view a change of rules was deemed legitimate if the benefits of the new rule to society outweighed its drawbacks for the disadvantaged group. This view is reminiscent of the *utility principle*, according to which it is of no consequence who gains or loses from a particular measure; the only point of relevance is the total utility to society.[39] *With the Kaldor-Hicks criterion, however, the values attached by the gainers and losers to their gains and losses are reckoned in monetary units.*

Kaldor and Hicks transformed the Pareto criterion, which had developed out of the free market model, into a tool that can also be applied in the sphere of law, which is coercive in character. So the substance of the Kaldor-Hicks test is that every new allocation of property rights is acceptable as long as the gainers' benefits outweigh the losers' disadvantages.[40]

---

[34] Fletcher, p. 158.

[35] Fletcher, pp. 158 f.

[36] Sen, *Collective Choice*, pp. 30 f.

[37] Fletcher, p. 159.

[38] Baumol, p. 402.

[39] See Sect. 6.2.2.

[40] Fletcher, p. 159.

### 3.3.2 Comparison with the Pareto Criterion

The Pareto criterion was developed to obtain a criterion for decision-making which did not rely on interpersonal utility comparisons. Nevertheless, rather than solving the problem of interpersonal comparison of utility, it simply sidestepped it. Moreover, the price of this was to render the Pareto principle applicable only to cases where nobody is made worse off, i.e. decisions to which everyone can consent. The Kaldor-Hicks criterion differs from the Pareto principle in that it is not confined to options which leave nobody worse off, but also permits those which make some people better off at other people's expense. If someone demands actual compensation, what this means is that the Pareto principle must in fact be satisfied. So the Kaldor-Hicks test does not indicate actual Pareto improvements, only *potential Pareto improvements*. One of its advantages is to dispense with the administrative overhead that would otherwise be associated with compensation arrangements.[41]

To compare the Kaldor-Hicks criterion and the Pareto principle more thoroughly, we can make use of some graphs.[42] For the sake of simplicity we will assume a society with only two members: $X$ and $Y$. In Fig. 3.2, one axis shows $X$'s utility and the other shows $Y$'s utility.[43]

We now assume that both $X$ and $Y$ have a certain utility represented by point A. According to the Pareto principle, any change is an improvement if it leads to a point in the area above and to the right of A; for example, points B, C or D but not point E, which does not satisfy this condition. At point E, whilst $Y$'s utility is greater than at the outset situation A, $X$'s utility is lower. This would violate the Pareto principle because $X$ would not consent to this change.

The next question is, does it at least satisfy the Kaldor-Hicks principle? Supposing that we asked $Y$ the maximum amount he would be willing to pay for the change from A to E, and $Y$ would be prepared to pay amount $K_y$. We would next ask $X$ how much he would be willing to pay to prevent the change from A to E. He would be prepared to spend amount $K_x$. If $K_y$ were greater than $K_x$, the Kaldor-Hicks test would be satisfied because in this case $Y$'s gain would be sufficient to compensate for $X$'s loss yet still yield a net gain for $Y$. As we know, the Kaldor-Hicks test does not require actual payment of compensation, because if compensation is paid then the Pareto principle would have been satisfied in the first place. The requirement is only for potential, not actual, compensation.

In order to represent this graphically we make use of a utility possibilities curve (PP' in Fig. 3.3). Let us assume that we begin at point F and ask ourselves what will happen if $Y$ gives a share of his wealth[44] to $X$. This could be represented as a movement to point G, where – compared with point F – $Y$ is worse off and $X$ is

---

[41] Cf. Schäfer and Ott, p. 32.

[42] After Baumol, p. 401.

[43] In this context it does not matter how utility is measured; nor do $X$'s and $Y$'s utility scales need to be comparable. It is merely assumed that utility for $X$ and $Y$ increases along the respective axes.

[44] On the term 'wealth' see more extensive discussion in Sect. 8.4.1.1.

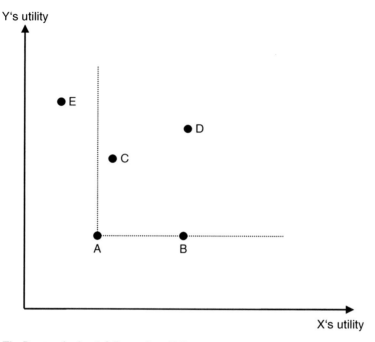

**Fig. 3.2** The Pareto criterion (cf. Baumol, p. 401)

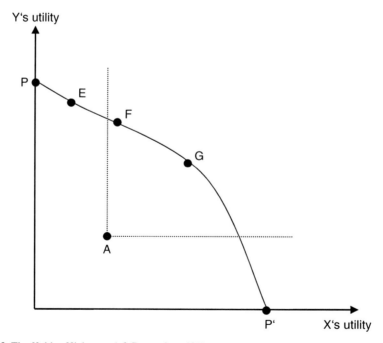

**Fig. 3.3** The Kaldor-Hicks test (cf. Baumol, p. 401)

better off. Movement to point E would represent a similar redistribution of wealth, and so on. Consequently, PP' is the geometric map of all points representing the respective utilities of $X$ and $Y$ which could result from a redistribution of wealth between $X$ and $Y$. In other words, for all movements along the utility possibilities curve, one individual's gain in wealth is always equal to the other's loss. So along this curve, social wealth is constant.

Let us now consider the change from point A to E, which – as already mentioned – violates the Pareto criterion because it represents an improvement for $Y$ but a setback for $X$. The utility possibilities curve PP' passes through point E. Points F and G also lie on this utility possibilities curve, i.e. they can be reached from E by redistributing wealth. Moreover, both points are above and to the right of point A, i.e. a movement from A to F or G fulfils the Pareto criterion.

From these considerations, it can be concluded that a movement from A to E, while it does not satisfy the Pareto criterion, certainly meets the criterion of the Kaldor-Hicks test because $X$'s loss could be at least compensated by redistributing wealth. This hypothetical compensation effects a movement along the utility possibilities curve to point F or G, both of which fulfil the Pareto criterion in relation to the starting point A. While movement from A to E initially violates the Pareto criterion, potentially it satisfies it: by redistributing wealth, points could be reached which do meet the Pareto criterion. It follows that any movement from point A to point E is a Kaldor-Hicks improvement if A is below the utility possibilities curve passing through point E.

### 3.3.3 Critique

#### 3.3.3.1 Logical Inconsistency

Tibor Scitovsky pointed out the logical inconsistency of the Kaldor-Hicks criterion in an essay written in 1941.[45] The fact is that the criterion is ambiguous, which potentially gives rise to a logical contradiction, whereby the criterion may be fulfilled for a movement from one social state A to another state B and yet, in some instances, the same may be true for a movement between the same two states in the *reverse* direction![46]

Thus, as Fig. 3.4 shows, it is possible for movement from point A to point B to represent an improvement, whilst movement from point B to point A does the same. For A lies below the utility possibilities curve RR' through B, whilst at the same time B lies below SS', the utility possibilities curve through A. This situation arises when the two utility possibilities curves intersect[47], which can occur if

---

[45] Scitovsky, pp. 77 f.

[46] Sohmen, p. 310.

[47] Baumol, p. 403.

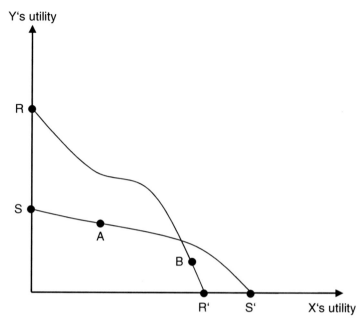

**Fig. 3.4** The Scitovsky paradox (cf. Baumol, p. 401)

(1) income distribution changes drastically in the transition from one situation to another, and if, in addition,

(2) the consumer preferences of the beneficiaries differ substantially from those of the losers.[48]

Scitovsky therefore demanded that the same situation should be evaluated as a Kaldor-Hicks improvement *in both directions* in order to be deemed superior (the double Kaldor-Hicks test or Scitovsky test).[49] The possible logical inconsistency does not render the Kaldor-Hicks criterion worthless, if supplemented with the requirement to carry out the two-way test. For projects that are relatively small in relation to the overall economy, there is only a miniscule risk that a logical inconsistency will arise.[50]

### 3.3.3.2  The Measurement Problem

Kaldor and Hicks require that the gainers should notionally be able to compensate the losers out of their gains. The unit of measurement for the potential compensation is not utility, but money. In contrast to utilitarianism, under the Kaldor-Hicks

---

[48] Sohmen, p. 310.

[49] Sohmen, p. 313.

[50] Schäfer and Ott, p. 33.

criterion it is not social utility that is maximized but wealth, i.e. the hypothetical willingness to pay for a certain resource that is about to be allocated.[51]

What needs to be asked, however, is how a court is supposed to determine the losing party's loss and the winning party's gain from a particular ruling. In economic analysis of law, Posner in particular has reformulated the Kaldor-Hicks criterion as an *auction rule*.[52] This attempts to imitate the market by auctioning off a particular right to the highest bidder. It would come into play for the allocation of a resource – e.g. the right to build an airport or prevent one from being built. Whoever is hypothetically willing to pay the highest price should be awarded the corresponding right. Under the auction rule, the interested parties themselves decide what monetary value to place on the various advantages and disadvantages. Through their willingness to pay, they themselves determine how much it is worth to them to move from one social state to another, or conversely what value they place on resisting such a move.[53]

In practice the auction rule is barely effectual, because the interested parties can claim a higher willingness to pay than if they actually had to back their bid with money (strategic behaviour). In any event, determining people's hypothetical willingness to pay creates a major information problem. According to Jules Coleman, the very idea of using the auction rule to imitate the market is utterly nonsensical. Either there is a genuine market, and no auction rule is needed, or there is no genuine market, in which case the auction rule will not work.

> Once we abandon the market, however, how are we to gather the pertinent information regarding the respective parties' willingness to pay? On the other hand, if a market exists, or can be established to determine relative willingness to pay, Posner's rule becomes otiose, since all the relevant ingredients of an exchange market are present. Posner's rule may be either otiose or unworkable.[54]

At this point, one might suggest that the auction rule could be entirely workable as a *regulatory idea*. A court could use it in the attempt to estimate roughly what losses or gains each party to a judgment might incur, depending on whether the judgment went in favour of one party or the other. Accordingly, the judgment handed down would have to ensure that the defeated party's losses could at least be compensated by the victorious party's gains. This procedure, akin to a *cost-benefit analysis*, may seem unproblematic at first glance.[55] For under this method, the advantages and disadvantages are assigned a monetary value, because they are reckoned in units of money, not in units of utility. Interpersonal utility comparisons and cardinal measurement of utility are therefore unnecessary.[56] One can object, however, that a

---

[51] Fletcher, p. 162.

[52] On Posner see Chapter 8.

[53] Schäfer and Ott, p. 34.

[54] Coleman, 'Analysis', p. 98.

[55] On cost-benefit analysis see e.g. Mishan, *Cost-Benefit Analysis*.

[56] Eidenmüller, p. 52.

*covert interpersonal utility comparison* takes place: one dollar of profit or loss has a consistent value, regardless of 'where it lands'. In terms of utility, this corresponds to the assumption of constant and equal marginal utility for all individuals. But this objection assumes a cardinal concept of utility, without which interpersonal comparison of utility is impossible.

### 3.3.3.3 The No-Compensation Problem

Whether a decision can be legitimized by demonstrating the mere possibility of compensation – the assumption made by Kaldor and Hicks – is a matter of controversy.[57] Kaldor viewed the possibility of compensation as an *objective criterion* for an increase in welfare. He believed action to be desirable in such cases, whether or not monetary compensation were made. Using this criterion, Kaldor thought, the economist was on safe ground because it was a statement of truth – provided the hypothesis is correct that every person has a preference for more utility rather than less.[58] It is seen as beyond the scope of the economist, as a scientist, to make any universally valid pronouncement on whether compensation should actually be handed over. He is not considered to be in a position to solve the problem of optimal income distribution from an 'economic standpoint'.[59] According to Kaldor:

> [I]t is quite sufficient for him [i.e. the economist] to show that even if all those who suffer as a result are fully compensated for their loss, the rest of the community will still be better off than before. Whether the landlords, in the free-trade case, should in fact be given compensation or not, is a political question on which the economist, *qua* economist, could hardly pronounce an opinion.[60]

Hicks expressly supported Kaldor's view. He too sees the possibility of compensation as a 'perfectly objective test' which can be used to reach an unequivocal judgement on the welfare gains of an action.[61] The question of whether the losers from an action should be compensated is seen as a separate issue. Similarly, Hicks considers this a matter of distribution policy, the principles of which have no claim to universal validity.[62]

The very fact that Kaldor and Hicks advance their compensation criterion as an alternative to the Pareto principle – which does not permit making any individual worse off – is indicative that they do not see the payment of compensation as a sacrosanct question. How the question is answered is *logically independent* from the viewpoint of efficiency; nothing is contingent upon an affirmative answer. This thrust might well stem from the fact that Kaldor and Hicks originally developed their criterion with reference to the Corn Laws and the abolition of protectionism. There

[57] Schefczyk and Priddat, pp. 438 f.

[58] Kaldor, pp. 549 ff.

[59] Bohnen, p. 92.

[60] Kaldor, p. 550.

[61] Hicks, pp. 108 ff.

[62] Bohnen, p. 93.

is a strong tradition of *free-trade theory* among economists. From this perspective, gains amassed thanks to protectionist measures are *illegitimate*, and need not therefore be compensated when they are subsequently lost. Thus there are no grounds for compensating farmers who suffer losses following the repeal of the Corn Laws, any more than opponents of slavery would concede that there were any grounds for compensating slave-owners following the abolition of slavery.[63]

As far as the example of slavery is concerned, one has to agree that it would be absurd if slave-owners had to be compensated for releasing their slaves. Similarly, one could conceive of land reform for the benefit of landless peasants without full, or indeed any, compensation of big landowners. The Kaldor-Hicks criterion completely eschews any necessity for real compensation. Furthermore, the gains and losses associated with the allocation of a resource are measured according to what each party is willing to pay for it. However, willingness to pay does not depend solely on individual utility, but most importantly on *ability to pay*. Since this will be lower for the poor than the rich, poor people's willingness to pay will normally be less than rich people's. It follows that under the Kaldor-Hicks criterion, the poor will generally draw the short straw, and the resource will be allocated to the rich because they can attach higher financial value to it than the poor.

Resources would thus tend to be allocated to the rich, but the poor need not be compensated for them and the rich need not pay for them. Consequently the rich would get even richer and their ability and willingness to pay would rise continually. If the Kaldor-Hicks criterion were applied in the free market, the results would be as follows: you could go on a shopping spree for whatever you liked without paying a penny, as long as you could credibly show that, of all the other people interested in the commodity, you would be prepared to pay the most *if* you had to pay. Consequently, the rich would obtain the vast majority of goods and become even richer. Their ability and willingness to pay would rise further, increasing their chances of acquiring yet more goods at no cost.

### 3.3.3.4 The Accusation of Collectivism

Being based on amounts of money derived from individual willingness to pay, the Kaldor-Hicks test avoids the problem of interpersonal comparison of utility. In its principle, however, the Kaldor-Hicks test satisfies the utility test. All that matters is the total for the whole of society; individual values make no difference as such. But monetary units take the place of utility. These express how much the individual would hypothetically be prepared to pay for the difference in utility. To quote Fletcher:

> The only difference between the utilitarian and the advocate of the Kaldor/Hicks test is that the former relies upon the standard of happiness and the latter relies on a standard implicit in a hypothetical willingness to pay for the disputed resource.[64]

---

[63] Fletcher, p. 159.

[64] Fletcher, p. 162.

Philosophically, moreover, the apparently small modification of the Pareto principle into the Kaldor-Hicks principle proves very significant: whereas the Pareto principle assumes a sovereign individual who is free to decide which transactions to enter into, and whose rights cannot be infringed without his or her consent, the Kaldor-Hicks criterion is based on the idea that every individual's rights can be curtailed if economic efficiency is improved as a result. *A principle that grants primacy to the individual is converted into a principle that puts economic efficiency first. Individualism is replaced by collectivism.*[65]

### 3.3.3.5 No Guarantee of Increased Social Utility

Another objection to the Kaldor-Hicks test is that it does not provide any guarantee of higher social utility. Let us assume that some action would make a rich person € 10 better off and a poor person € 9 worse off. The rich person could compensate the poor person in full and still profit from the transaction, which would satisfy the Kaldor-Hicks test. But now let us consider their utility: if compensation is foregone, and one makes the not entirely unrealistic assumption that marginal utility decreases as income rises, the poor person's utility loss may exceed the rich person's utility gain. A decline in social utility would result. According to Le Grand, this outcome can only be avoided by giving the rich person's utility change greater weight than the poor person's utility change. Le Grand's objection to the Kaldor-Hicks test is that it contains an *implicit value judgement*, on which basis the rich person's utility is weighted more highly than the poor person's.[66]

Since the Kaldor-Hicks test is based on monetary units rather than utility, it circumvents the awkward problem of interpersonal utility comparison – as does the Pareto criterion – and avoids the associated value judgements. But this is only possible because of the reliance on monetary units – not on utility in the utilitarian sense. The question that naturally arises is whether monetary units are an appropriate objective variable for society.[67] But Le Grand, in attempting to convert monetary units into equivalent units of utility, tacitly adopts a utilitarian stance. Hence the Kaldor-Hicks test only contains the alleged implicit value judgement when it is viewed from a utilitarian perspective and declining marginal utility of income is assumed. *However, the example cited shows that the Kaldor-Hicks test – in contrast to the Pareto criterion – cannot guarantee an increase in social utility.*

### 3.3.3.6 The Issue of Consensuality

As we know, the advantage of the Pareto criterion is that it is consensual, since it demands that nobody may be made worse off by an action. Conversely, the advantage of the Kaldor-Hicks criterion is that it is not restricted only to cases which would

---

[65] Fletcher, p. 162.

[66] Le Grand, pp. 565 f.

[67] See Sect. 8.4.4.3 for more extensive discussion.

leave nobody worse off. A single legal rule which makes some better off and others worse off has absolutely no prospect of gaining a consensus, because the new rule has asymmetrical consequences for those affected by it, who can immediately predict whether they will be among the gainers or the losers. It could be justified in the long run if the Kaldor-Hicks criterion were applied to all legal rules, and everyone expected to be both a gainer and a loser at different times in their lives, i.e. if, in the wider scheme of things, everybody could benefit from the efficiency gains achieved. So consensus could perhaps be reached about the Kaldor-Hicks criterion based on the prospect of *general compensation*. Here the possibility of participating in higher economic growth would make up for any particular instances of disadvantage.[68]

Over the long term, a law and economics approach which consistently followed the Kaldor-Hicks criterion could indeed boost productivity more rapidly than policy and law geared towards case-by-case justice. The expected faster pace of growth in real national product would benefit all social classes in the long run, while specific actions would hurt first one group and then another. This would dispense with the need for compensation in specific instances, which is also a key assumption made by Hicks.[69] This line of argumentation seems entirely credible at first glance. The following objections can be raised, however:

(1) The scale of disadvantage can be so great in some instances that 'general compensation' is not nearly enough to make up for it. For example, if countless people were consigned to starvation as the result of some action, the theoretical prospect of participating in increased economic growth would be of little comfort to them.[70]

(2) In respect of the argument that compensation would only occur over the long term, the famous pronouncement of John Maynard Keynes comes to mind: '*In the long run, we are all dead.*'[71] In any case, people normally attach higher value to an immediate and certain loss than to an uncertain gain at some time in the future. Furthermore, in a society there are always people whose chances of compensation are minimal, even in the long run.

(3) The most important argument, however, is the human need to have just treatment meted out – in specific cases and, most importantly, case by case! – to themselves and, indeed, others. The nebulous prospect of general compensation would never be sufficient reason to accept a decision in a specific instance if it were felt to be unjust. In people's minds, justice – however it is defined – has an immanent value, which is very difficult to weigh up against an increase in economic efficiency. And people's feelings are guided primarily by specific instances from their own experience, and not abstract notions like a mechanism of general compensation.

---

[68] Cf. Schäfer and Ott, p. 38.

[69] Sohmen, p. 309.

[70] Sohmen, pp. 309 f.

[71] Sohmen, p. 310.

Therefore it seems highly unlikely that a consensual basis could be established for the Kaldor-Hicks criterion.[72]

## 3.4 Summary

On closer analysis, the Pareto criterion and the principle of Kaldor-Hicks efficiency prove not to be value-free concepts. A particularly serious consideration is that both efficiency criteria contain not only weak, uncontested value judgements but also strong value judgements. Far from making analysis of normative questions superfluous, the demand for efficiency therefore has the opposite effect: it brings into sharp focus the need for closer scrutiny of the relationship between efficiency and justice. We will therefore return to this question once more at the end of the book.

---

[72] On Posner's argumentation see Sect. 8.5.2.

# Chapter 4
# Economic Analysis of Law

*[E]conomics is a powerful tool for analyzing a vast range of legal questions [...].*[1]

## 4.1 Introduction

The seminal groundwork for the economic analysis of law was done by Ronald H. Coase and Guido Calabresi. In his essay, 'Some Thoughts on Risk Distribution and the Law of Torts' (1961), Calabresi's analysis of the allocation of risks in tort law runs counter to the legal principle of fault. In 'The Problem of Social Cost' (1960), Coase developed a theorem, now named after him, which would become one of the central tenets of economic analysis of law. The conclusion of the *Coase theorem* is that the world of law should be analysed in terms of its economic impacts so as to instill a dimension of economic efficiency into legal institutions. Coase made his name not only with this theorem but also with his famous essay on 'The Nature of the Firm' (1937). In both papers, a central concept is that of *transaction costs*.[2] Another important contribution was made by Gary S. Becker who attempted to apply the economic approach to non-market areas. In his essay on 'Crime and Punishment' (1968) he made a fundamental contribution to the economic analysis of crime. Finally, Richard A. Posner's textbook, *Economic Analysis of Law* (1972), systematically analysed the law in terms of its effects on economic efficiency.

## 4.2 Concepts

### 4.2.1 Transaction Costs

Transaction costs are a key concept in economic analysis of law. The expression denotes the costs of procuring information, negotiating, executing, checking and enforcing contracts. As Coase puts it:

---

[1] Posner, *EAL 5*, p. 3.

[2] See Sect. 4.2.1.

K. Mathis, *Efficiency Instead of Justice?*, Law and Philosophy Library 84, DOI 10.1007/978-1-4020-9798-0_4, © Springer Science+Business Media B.V. 2009

In order to carry out market transactions it is necessary to discover who it is that one wishes to deal with, to inform people that one wishes to deal and on what terms, to conduct negotiations leading up to a bargain, to draw up the contract, to undertake the inspection needed to make sure that the terms of the contract are being observed, and so on.[3]

In his analysis in 'The Problem of Social Cost', Coase initially assumes a world without transaction costs, as a means of demonstrating what would happen in ideal conditions.

## 4.2.2 Property Rights

The term 'property rights' is broader in scope than 'rights of ownership'. The constitutive idea of the property rights concept is the understanding of *resources as bundles of rights*, and hence the exchange of goods as the exchange of bundles of rights.[4] Thus the question of the efficient allocation of property rights often comes within the purview of economic analysis of law.[5]

Property rights describe all the conceivable ways in which someone may utilize a resource: exploitation of the resource, alteration of its form and substance, receipt of rents, and freedom to transfer such rights to others. The concept of property rights encompasses not only private property but also state property; and restricted rights *in rem* as well as intangible property rights. *Generally speaking, property rights are defined as any legal norms which regulate the allocation of powers over resource use.* A property right is said to be extremely concentrated if all powers over a resource are held by one and the same person. On the other hand, if several people or even everyone can claim a right over the same resource, it is said to be attenuated.[6] The process of defining property rights includes regulating how they will be protected. The protection of property rights operates by way of *property rules* (affording protection of *in rem* rights) on the one hand, and *liability rules* (defining rights under liability law) on the other.[7]

### 4.2.2.1  Property Rules

Third parties may only interfere with a property right with the consent of its holder, and the holder can defend against any invasion of property rights.[8]

---

[3] Coase, 'Social Cost', p. 15.

[4] Schäfer and Ott, p. 87.

[5] Calabresi and Melamed, pp. 1090 ff.

[6] Schäfer and Ott, p. 515.

[7] Cf. Calabresi and Melamed, pp. 1089 ff.

[8] Schäfer and Ott, p. 516.

### 4.2.2.2 Liability Rules

Liability rules only give protection to property rights through a claim for damages. It is not necessary to obtain consent for such claims from the holder of the property right. Liability rules are the basis for damages claims arising from expropriation by the state, for example, or from accidents.[9]

## 4.3 The Coase Theorem

### 4.3.1 The Concept

*The Coase theorem states that where property rights are clearly allocated, and in the absence of transaction costs in a market, property rights will be exchanged until economic resources reach the place where they will be utilized most efficiently, regardless of where they were originally allocated.*[10]

The theorem consists of two claims, the hypothesis of invariance and the hypothesis of efficiency. The *invariance hypothesis* proposes that the initial endowment of property rights has no influence on the eventual allocation of resources. Market transactions ensure that property rights end up in the 'right' place, if they were not there to begin with. Furthermore, according to the *efficiency hypothesis*, the end result will always be a Pareto optimal solution.[11] *The implication of the Coase theorem is that private costs will equal social costs, since all externalities are internalized through private arrangements.*[12]

Apart from the obviously unrealistic assumption of zero transaction costs, a further assumption is that property rights have been clearly assigned to somebody at the outset. This is often not the case, especially for environmental resources.[13] From a legal viewpoint, the significance of the theorem is that it requires the law to ensure that property rights are clearly defined and unequivocally assigned. While the chosen method of assignment has an influence on income distribution, it has no effect – assuming zero transaction costs – on efficiency.

Coase had brought forth the idea for the theorem later named after him in a previous article on 'The Federal Communications Commission' (1959).[14] However, other

---

[9] Calabresi and Melamed, pp. 1106 ff.

[10] Cf. Veljanovski, 'Coase Theorems', p. 54. Note that various interpretations of the Coase theorem exist; see Cooter, pp. 457 f. and Sect. 4.3.3.3c).

[11] Siemer, p. 7.

[12] Stigler, p. 113.

[13] Who has property rights to the air, for example? Do residents have a right to fresh air or do motorists have a right to pollute the air? Similar problems are posed by emissions of other kinds, e.g. noise.

[14] Coase, Communications, pp. 23 f.

Chicago economists – including Milton Friedman and George Stigler – believed the argument to be wrong:

> Their objections centered on what George Stigler was later to term the "Coase Theorem".[15]

In his paper on 'The Problem of Social Cost', Coase therefore made an attempt to explain his argument at greater length. This paper was addressed to economists, who were struggling to grasp the paradigm shift that Coase had obviously initiated.

> I suppose this lack of comprehension represents another example, about which Thomas Kuhn has told us, of the difficulty which scientists find in changing their analytical system, or, as he puts it, in moving from one paradigm to another.[16]

Meanwhile Coase had never expected his paper to exert such a sustained influence on the discipline of law:

> It is generally agreed that this article has had an immense influence on legal scholarship, but this was no part of my intention. Law came into the article because, in a regime of positive transaction costs, the character of the law becomes one of the main factors determining the performance of the economy.[17]

Accordingly, where there are positive transaction costs, the law has a decisive role to play. Coase's initial proposition, however, is that harms are always reciprocal in nature. He goes on to develop his theorem in the framework of a model without transaction costs. Only then does he take up the question of the effects of positive transaction costs.

## 4.3.2 The Reciprocal Nature of Harmful Actions

Coase argues that harm is always a reciprocal matter. If person A harms person B, traditionally one would ask how to proceed against A. But that is the wrong question if we accept the argument that harm is *reciprocal in nature*:

> We are dealing with a problem of a reciprocal nature. To avoid the harm to B would inflict harm on A. The real question that has to be decided is: should A be allowed to harm B or should B be allowed to harm A?[18]

If the noise and vibrations from a confectioner's machinery disturb a doctor's work, for instance, and the confectioner is forced to avoid making any noise out of consideration for the doctor, this can also be construed as the doctor harming the confectioner.[19] The crucial question is, should more confectionery be produced or

---

[15] Coase, 'Law and Economics', p. 249.

[16] Coase, 'Law and Economics', p. 250.

[17] Coase, 'Law and Economics', p. 250.

[18] Coase, 'Social Cost', p. 2.

[19] The idea that both parties can always be seen as causal agents of externalities certainly has some logic, but only up to a point. Often the idea is absurd, as the following example shows. Let us assume that A shot B. A now argues in his own defence that if B had not chosen to stand in A's way as he accidentally fired the gun, B would not have been killed.

more medical services provided? Or if all the fish in a river died as a result of water pollution, the question is whether the value of the loss of fish is higher or lower than the value of the goods that the water was polluted in order to produce?[20]

## 4.3.3 The Absence of Transaction Costs

### 4.3.3.1 Negotiations Ensure an Efficient Outcome

Coase develops his argument with reference to an example involving cattle and wheat: a rancher's cattle trample a farmer's wheat fields while grazing. Obviously this is a negative external effect since the rancher is fattening his cattle to the detriment of the farmer. According to Coase the right to free grazing can be defined as one the many rights deriving from cattle ownership. It means that cattle are allowed to roam and may venture into other people's fields. On this analysis, it is up to the farmer to take his own precautions. Now one might equally invoke the right to undamaged fields as one of the rights deriving from the ownership of agricultural land. Seen in that light, it is unacceptable for cattle to graze in wheat fields. Both definitions in this case describe an identical right: from the farmer's perspective, the right to an undamaged wheat field, and from the rancher's perspective, the right to free fodder.[21]

This property right can be thought of as a right to inflict harm. If the rancher holds this right, then he is entitled to allow his cattle to graze in the wheat fields. If the farmer possesses it, the rancher has no such entitlement. According to Coase, this right to harm should be tradeable. If the rancher holds the right, the farmer should pay him for the right to harm, at a price commensurate with the scale of the potential damage. This would avert any harm to the farmer. From the rancher's viewpoint, the possibility of selling the right increases his opportunity costs of cattle herding, such that he has to consider whether it is worthwhile to persist in damaging the wheat fields. If, however, the farmer holds the right to undamaged wheat fields, he can sell the rancher the right to inflict harm, and accept the consequence of crop damage, at least by building it into the asking price for the right to inflict harm.[22]

The tradeability of the right to inflict harm means that in their own interests, both the rancher and the farmer will consider the other party's interests: Smith's principle that pursuit of self-interest increases the welfare of all (the 'invisible hand')[23] results in internalization of the external effect by voluntary agreement. Consequently, the most efficient use is made of economic resources.[24]

---

[20] Coase, 'Social Cost', p. 2.

[21] Coase, 'Social Cost', pp. 19 f.

[22] Siemer, p. 2.

[23] See Sect. 5.3.

[24] Siemer, pp. 2 f.

*The crucial point of the Coase theorem is that – in the absence of transaction costs – this result comes about by voluntary negotiations, regardless of which party was originally assigned the property rights*:

> [T]he ultimate result (which maximises the value of production) is independent of the legal position if the pricing system is assumed to work without cost.[25]

The validity of the Coase theorem in principle can be shown from the following numerical example:[26] The smoke from a factory chimney contaminates the laundry hung out to dry by five neighbours. The damage amounts to €1,000 each or €5,000 in total. The damage can be prevented in one of two ways: every household is provided with a dryer, at a unit price of €600, which costs €3,000 in total, or the factory chimney is fitted with a filter costing €1,000. It is obvious that in these circumstances, the filter is the more efficient solution, because €5,000 worth of damage can be prevented at the least cost of €1,000.

The next question is whether the most efficient solution is chosen regardless of whether the neighbours have a right to clean air or the factory has a right to pollute. If the neighbours have a right to clean air, the factory has three options (see Table 4.1): to pollute and pay €5,000 in damages, to pay for dryers for the neighbours at a total cost of €3,000, or to fit a filter for only €1,000. Obviously it will opt for the third solution as the most efficient. If on the other hand the factory has a right to pollute, the neighbours also have three options: to endure damage amounting to €5,000, to buy dryers for a total of €3,000 or to pay for a filter for the factory, costing €1,000. They too will opt for the filter as the most efficient solution.

The example shows that private arrangements always result in the most efficient solution, regardless of where the property rights are allocated.

**Table 4.1** Options for a factory emitting smoke and five neighbours whose laundry is affected

| Neighbours have a right to clean air – factory has three options: | Factory has a right to pollute – neighbours have three options: |
| --- | --- |
| (1) Pay compensation, € 5,000 | (1) Endure damage, € 5,000 |
| (2) Pay for dryers, € 3,000 | (2) Buy dryers, € 3,000 |
| (3) Buy filter, € 1,000 | (3) Pay for filter, € 1,000 |

### 4.3.3.2 Negotiation as an Alternative to State Intervention

In *The Economics of Welfare* (1932) the British economist Arthur C. Pigou demanded that in the event of externalities, the state should intervene and levy a tax

---

[25] Coase, 'Social Cost', p. 8.

[26] Cf. Polinsky, pp. 11 f.

(a 'Pigou tax'). Let us assume that sparks from a steam train set an adjacent wheat field on fire. Under the causation principle the railway would have to pay for the damage, this being a negative external effect of production. However, in the example under review, the environmental damage caused by the flying sparks is not built into the railway's calculations. Thus the social costs of the damage are greater than the private costs. In order to bring them into line with the social costs, the state should levy a tax.[27]

Pigou bases his view on a key finding of welfare theory: society's resources are always directed to their most highly valued use if individuals consider the external effects (i.e. those not affecting them personally) of their economic actions as if they were, in fact, directly affected. In other words, a Pareto optimum can only be achieved when the social costs equal the private costs of production, and of consumption.[28] With negative external effects, the social costs are greater than the private costs; with positive externalities the difference is the other way round. The alignment of private and social costs is called internalization.[29]

Coase rejects this sort of state intervention, arguing instead for *negotiated solutions* arranged between the parties affected. In the example discussed above, the railway company could compensate the farmer for the destruction of his fields, thus enabling him to cultivate his wheat somewhere else. Or, alternatively, the farmer could pay to have the locomotives fitted with some technology which prevented flying sparks. *According to the Coase theorem, from the point of view of efficiency it makes no difference who pays whom; the railway may pay off the farmer, or vice versa.*[30]

As we know, in economic terms, both parties are causal agents: if the farmer were to stop sowing wheat in the field, he would not suffer any damage. For Coase, external effects are always a reciprocal problem. If the railway is forced to compensate the farmer, then it has a loss of utility which is not necessarily of lesser value than the farmer's burnt wheat. A negotiated solution would be more constructive than a tax, because it gives due consideration to both parties' utility. However, according to Coase, such a solution presupposes zero transaction costs and clearly defined property rights:

> [I]f market transactions were costless, all that matters (questions of equity apart) is that the rights of the various parties should be well-defined and the results of legal actions easy to forecast.[31]

---

[27] Coase, 'Social Cost', pp. 28 ff.

[28] Pigou, pp. 183 ff.

[29] Cf. Schumann, *Mikroökonomie*, p. 38 and pp. 492 ff.

[30] From the point of view of *income distribution*, on the other hand, who pays whom is not inconsequential.

[31] Coase, 'Social Cost', p. 19.

### 4.3.3.3  Critique

(a) The Assumptions are Unrealistic

The first complaint concerns the theorem's restrictive preconditions: the absence of transaction costs and the clear assignment of property rights. In most cases, it is high *transaction costs* which make the internalization of external effects seem unviable to the parties involved. In reality, the costs of negotiation are likely to be very high indeed, particularly where one or even several parties must reach a unanimous agreement. Only those who expect the compensation to exceed their negotiation costs will be interested in negotiating. But even if contract negotiations are successful, further costs will be incurred to enforce contracts by means of damages payments.[32]

In the case of environmental problems, often there is *no clear assignment of property rights.* Moreover, water and air pollution are often the doing of many polluters, and are rarely attributable to a single perpetrator. But as damage of this kind can only be eliminated using complex and costly technology, state intervention is often necessary regardless.[33] Appropriate environmental policy instruments in such cases might be maximum emission limits, environmental taxes or emissions permits (tradeable pollution rights).[34] Application of the Coase theorem to this scenario does, of course, also allow for the possibility that people likely to be harmed could pay the polluters to desist from their emissions.[35] For example, water consumers in Baden-Württemberg, Germany, pay a water levy called the *Wasserpfennig* ('water penny'), in return for which farmers reduce their use of groundwater-polluting fertilizers and pesticides.[36] The debate on compensation payments from industrialized nations to certain Third World countries in the aim of preventing further deforestation of rainforests is similarly inspired by Coasean thinking.[37]

(b) Wealth and Endowment Effects Influence Allocation

The Coase theorem asserts that the final allocation will always be the same and always Pareto efficient, regardless of the assignment of property rights. It grants that the assignment of property rights will have an impact on income distribution, but this has no bearing on the allocation.

This apparent dichotomy between distribution and allocation has to be questioned, however. How property rights are assigned certainly influences the distribution of wealth. Indirectly, the *wealth effect* will indeed have some impact on allocation. This effect stems from the fact that the rich and the poor generally buy different kinds of goods. A change in distribution will alter the structure of demand,

---

[32] Schumann, *Mikroökonomie*, p. 499.

[33] Hoffmann, p. 297.

[34] See Sect. 4.3.5.

[35] Schumann, *Mikroökonomie*, p. 499.

[36] Schumann, *Mikroökonomie*, p. 500.

[37] Hoffmann, p. 297.

since demand is dependent upon income or wealth. This in turn has an influence on prices, and hence on the outcome of the allocation. Aside from this, prices may also be influenced by the *endowment effect*.[38] The supply and demand price of a commodity can differ for the same person. The observation has been made that once people have acquired an item, they are only prepared to resell it when the price offered is higher than the price they paid for it.[39]

While the final allocation, even taking all these effects into consideration, will always be Pareto optimal, it will not necessarily always be the same.[40] *Taking wealth and endowment effects into account, the efficiency hypothesis remains valid but the invariance hypothesis does not.*[41]

(c) Bargaining is Not the Same as Competition

Cento Veljanovski points out various possible interpretations of the Coase theorem, and thus the problem of talking about *the* Coase theorem at all. The two forms of interpretation he distinguishes are the *bargaining theorem* and the *competitive market theorem*.[42]

The bargaining theorem assumes two or several interested parties, who make contact with the intention of entering into a contract. The competitive market theorem, in contrast, presupposes an economic model of perfect competition. With a theoretically infinite number of parties on both sides of the market, no single player can determine the market price. Under the negotiation model, the price is the subject of negotiations. Under the competitive market model, it is simply a given and is not therefore negotiable.

According to Veljanovski, Coase mixes the two models. Although he refers to the competitive market model, Coase's examples describe personalized, bilateral transactions in which the terms of trade are negotiated to completion by the parties directly involved.[43]

> The bargaining Coase Theorem is seemingly rendered identical to the competitive market model through a semantic confusion between the common usage of the word competitive and its technical economic meaning.[44]

According to Leif Johansen, however, bargaining is a very inefficient method of decision-making:

> [B]argaining will often be an inefficient decision procedure in the sense that it tends to distort the information basis for decisions, it tends to use or waste resources in the process,

---

[38] Cooter and Ulen, p. 83.

[39] See also Sect. 8.4.4.2.

[40] See also Sect. 3.2.2.

[41] Calabresi and Melamed, pp. 1095 f.

[42] Veljanovski, 'Coase Theorems', pp. 55 f.

[43] Veljanovski, 'Coase Theorems', pp. 55 f.

[44] Veljanovski, 'Coase Theorems', pp. 62 f.

particularly by delaying decisions for reasons which are not technically necessary, it will more or less frequently lead to breakdown and failure to realize the potential gains, and threats will sometimes be carried out.[45]

An important dimension of negotiations is *strategic behaviour*.[46] For one thing, according to Veljanovski, this does not result in an unequivocal solution. Moreover, it does not usually result in an efficient outcome either – which would diametrically contradict the Coase theorem:

> Indeed if there is any theorem in such a world it is the exact opposite of the Coase Theorem. The appropriate theorem in bargaining contexts is [...]: Direct bargaining has an inherent tendency to dissipate the gains-from-trade through strategic behaviour.[47]

Where there are only two interested parties, i.e. in the case of a bilateral monopoly, the socially optimal bargaining solution is not the sole conceivable outcome. In fact, individual skilfulness at negotiation or other inequalities between the parties – inequalities which come under the heading of 'power' – can significantly alter the outcome of negotiations, compared with what would happen if power were not a factor. So, efficient allocation is by no means guaranteed.[48] Robert Cooter essentially shares this view but is not quite so pessimistic about the matter:

> Reality lies in between the poles of optimism and pessimism, because strategic behaviour causes bargaining to fail in some cases, but not in every case.[49]

By assuming zero transaction costs, Coase believes he has eliminated all obstacles – including strategic behaviour, for example – which might jeopardize an efficient outcome of bargaining; on the other hand, the apportionment of the gains from trade depends to a very major extent on the respective parties' adeptness as negotiators:

> What payment would in fact be made would depend on the shrewdness of the farmer and the cattle-raiser as bargainers.[50]

*Coase is evidently mixing the bargaining model and the competitive market model, which also appears to cast doubt on the validity of the efficiency hypothesis.* So it seems that the Coase theorem – *the* central proposition of economic analysis of law – does not itself stand up to economic analysis.

---

[45] Johansen, p. 519 (whole passage italicized in the original).

[46] Game theory addresses this matter, making a distinction between cooperative and non-cooperative behaviour.

[47] Veljanovksi, 'Coase Theorems', p. 60. Cooter calls the opposite of the Coase theorem the 'Hobbes theorem'. Cooter, p. 459.

[48] Cf. Schumann, *Mikroökonomie*, p. 499.

[49] Cooter, p. 459.

[50] Coase, 'Social Cost', p. 6.

## 4.3.4 Taking Account of Transaction Costs

### 4.3.4.1 The Choice Between Different Social Arrangements

In his subsequent explanations, Coase gives up the assumption of cost-free transactions because he believes it to be unrealistic himself. Taking transaction costs into consideration alters the outcomes of the analysis, however: rights to inflict harm would now only be traded if a positive gain could be achieved after deduction of the transaction costs. Should transaction costs really hinder an efficient allocation of property rights in the market, social arrangements of three other kinds can be considered: *amalgamation* of the interested parties into a firm; *state regulation*; or a *laissez-faire* situation.[51]

If the interested parties (the injurers and the victims) amalgamate into a firm, the external effects would automatically be internalized. Transaction costs would be reduced, but additional administrative costs would be incurred in their place for internal organization.[52] The state has to contend with similar administration costs, which is why Coase calls the state a 'super-firm'. He makes no general pronouncement on which solution will be best in a given instance; this depends on the scale of transaction costs and administrative costs. Coase believes, however, that economists and politicians had previously overestimated the benefits of state regulation.[53]

### 4.3.4.2 The Crucial Importance of Law

When transaction costs are taken into consideration, the theorem gains enormously in relevance but with precisely the opposite implications: the higher the transaction costs, the more it matters how property rights are allocated, and the greater their impact on the efficiency of an economy. If transaction costs are higher than zero – which is always the case in reality – then the law, i.e. the assignment of property rights, definitely has an influence:

> If transaction costs were zero (as is assumed in standard economic theory) we can imagine people contracting around the law whenever the value of production would be increased by a change in the legal position. But in a regime of positive transaction costs, such contracting would not occur whenever transaction costs were greater than the gain that such a redistribution of rights would bring. As a consequence the rights which individuals possess will commonly be those established by the law, which in these circumstances can be said to control the economy.[54]

This in turn can be demonstrated with reference to the numerical example of the factory and its neighbours that we used earlier.[55] Let us assume that the transaction

---

[51] Coase, 'Social Cost', pp. 15 ff.

[52] This is the subject of the article 'The Nature of the Firm'.

[53] Coase, 'Social Cost', pp. 16 ff.

[54] Coase, 'Law and Economics', p. 251.

[55] Cf. Polinsky, pp. 12 f.

**Table 4.2** Options for a factory emitting smoke and its five neighbours, taking transaction costs into account

| Neighbours have a right to clean air – factory has three options: | Factory has a right to pollute – neighbours have three options: |
|---|---|
| (1) Pay compensation, € 5,000 | (1) Endure the damage, € 5,000 |
| (2) Pay for dryers, € 3,000 | (2) Buy dryers, € 3,000 |
| (3) Buy filter, € 1,000 | (3) Pay for filter, € 1,000 + € 2,500 transaction costs = € 3,500 |

costs per neighbour were € 500, making a total of € 2,500. These are the costs incurred by the neighbours if they have to take part in negotiations and reach a joint decision.

If the neighbours have a right to clean air, the factory still has three options (see Table 4.2): to pay €5,000 in damages, to buy dryers for the neighbours for a total of €3,000, or to fit a filter for €1,000. It will opt for the filter which is the most efficient solution.

The matter takes on a different complexion if the factory has a right to pollute. In this case the neighbours have the following three options: they can endure the damage of €5,000 altogether or buy dryers for a total of €3,000. The third option consists of paying for a filter for the factory, but this option entails transaction costs because the neighbours can only reach such a decision collectively, and will have to engage in negotiations in order to do so. Taking total transaction costs of €2,500 into account, the filter solution now costs €3,500 rather than €1,000. Deterred by the prohibitively high transaction costs, the neighbours will buy themselves dryers individually.

*The example shows that in the presence of transaction costs, the original allocation of property rights can have a bearing on efficiency.* In the case discussed, it would be advantageous if the residents could be assigned a right to clean air, since that is the only basis on which the most efficient solution (fitting a filter) will be chosen. If, on the other hand, the factory has a right to pollute, the neighbours will choose a suboptimal solution (buying dryers). While this is the best possible decision in the given circumstances, there is a different way of assigning property rights which would make an even more efficient solution possible.

In this context, Coase points out the interdependence of law and economics: the reality of positive transaction costs reveals the economic functions of law. The law should provide allocation rules which reduce the necessity for subsequent transactions. Coase stresses the economic policy function of the dispensation of justice.

It would therefore seem desirable that courts should understand the economic consequences of their decisions and should, insofar as this is possible without creating too much uncertainty about the legal position itself, take the consequences into account when making their decisions.[56]

---

[56] Coase, 'Social Cost', p. 19.

*Wherever possible, property rights should be directed right at the outset to the place where they will be put to the most efficient use. If the most efficient arrangement is unknown, however, then any barriers to achieving it should be eliminated by minimizing the costs of the transfer, the enforcement of the associated rights, and the costs of application of the law.*[57]

So Coase advocates an economically reasoned system of law, which will have repercussions both for legislation and for application of the law. According to Veljanovski, the role of law from the viewpoint of economic analysis can be described in the following three ways:[58]

(1) Maximizing economic efficiency;
(2) Minimizing transaction costs;[59]
(3) When market transactions fail due to unduly high transaction costs, the law should simulate the outcome in a competitive market.[60]

Veljanovski believes only the first aim to be right, and is sceptical about the second and third. Lowering transaction costs would not guarantee efficient solutions, because the outcome of negotiations is often inefficient. Simulating the ideal market would be equally wrong, because having accepted the fact that in reality there are always transaction costs, the market outcome – ignoring transaction costs – can no longer set an authoritative standard.

> Once it is accepted that markets are costly then the competitive market outcome is no longer the relevant benchmark. The costs of using the market must also be taken into account, as must the cost of the legal system designed to replace the coordination function that would have been provided by a costless pricing system.[61]

*The efficiency objective of law consists of lowering the coordination costs of economic activities, bearing in mind that operational costs attach to both the market and the legal system. The challenge is to determine the most efficient form of institutional regulation in any given instance.*[62]

## 4.3.5 Practical Implementation by Means of Emissions Permits

Coase's bargaining solution has been put to prominent use in environmental policy – albeit in state-institutionalized form – with the creation of tradeable emissions permits.[63] Conceivable as it is to transfer certain environmental goods into private

---

[57] Siemer, pp. 82 f.

[58] Veljanovski, 'Coase Theorems', p. 68.

[59] Cf. for example Polinsky, p. 13.

[60] After Posner, *EAL 5*, p. 16. See Sect. 8.4.1.

[61] Veljanovski, 'Coase Theorems', p. 69.

[62] Veljanovski, 'Coase Theorems', p. 69.

[63] Boie, pp. 156 f.

ownership or ownership-like rights, in practice the idea of direct negotiations on
the internalization of external effects has proven to be of only limited feasibility.[64]
This is because pollution of the environment tends to involve multiple parties who
are not known to one another and who, on occasion, may figure as both polluter
and victim simultaneously.[65] Therefore the lack of information and the high transaction costs are prohibitive factors.[66] If direct negotiations are held nevertheless, a
further issue is the likelihood that coalitions will be formed, which get in the way of
Pareto-efficient bargaining solutions.[67]

*Tradeable emissions permits*, first proposed in 1968 by the Canadian economist
John Harkness Dales for the reduction of water pollution, offer a practicable alternative to direct negotiations among private parties, because they combine the theoretical idea of the Coase theorem with the exigencies of practice.[68] By specifying
clear limits and allocations, the right to use the environment is made a tradeable
commodity, thereby allowing prices for environmental resources to become established.[69] The price mechanism ensures that the reduction of emissions occurs where
the marginal costs of avoidance are lowest. To prevent unduly high transaction costs
from inhibiting the trade in these rights to use the environment, the state creates a
suitable institutional basis: a market for emissions permits.[70]

The implementation of the permit solution works as follows: the state begins
by determining the overall permitted quantity of emissions units, within the political process, and divides up this quota into a corresponding number of permits.[71]
In predetermining the absolute permissible emissions level, the state is simultaneously setting an environmental standard. Therefore the permit solution can also be
called a quantity solution with a standard-oriented approach.[72] Only holders of a
permit may emit the amount of pollutants documented therein.[73] Because the number of permits is limited, they and the permitted rights can be viewed as a scarce
resource. The pollution of the environment now has a price, which is established in
a market by supply and demand.[74]

Once the permits have been allocated, emitters whose only means of avoiding emissions are cost-intensive restructuring or reinvestment will be interested

---

[64] Wicke, pp. 242 ff.

[65] Frey, *Umweltökonomie*, pp. 111 f.

[66] Cf. Feess, p. 149.

[67] Frey, *Umweltökonomie*, pp. 111 f.

[68] Jacobs, p. 33.

[69] Diehr, p. 27.

[70] Diehr, p. 27. On the dangers of high transaction costs in a permit system, see Jacobs, pp. 90 ff.

[71] Wicke, p. 241.

[72] Jacobs, p. 33; Feess, p. 123. Environmental taxes, in contrast, are classified as price solutions.

[73] Endres, p. 110. In this context, note that controls of the volume of emissions must be carried
out.

[74] Jacobs, p. 65.

in purchasing a sufficient quantity of permits to cover their emissions volume. Generally a company will only purchase permits up to the point where the marginal costs of pollution avoidance are higher than the marginal costs of a permit.[75] Those polluters who can reduce their emissions at low cost, e.g. by fitting filter systems, will prefer some such method of avoidance over the purchase of a permit. Accordingly, these companies will make emission-avoiding investments for as long as their marginal costs of emission avoidance are lower than the marginal costs of purchasing a permit. The stipulated emissions reductions are always made by the companies which face the lowest marginal costs of emissions avoidance.[76] Through the striving of economic actors to maximize their self interest, the environment as a resource, or the right to make use of it, is allocated to those for whom it has the highest value. Because the overall costs of environmental protection are consequently minimal in macroeconomic terms, the permit solution is cost-efficient.[77]

In addition to the cost-efficiency already mentioned, the permit solution has a dynamic incentive effect and a high degree of ecological precision. The dynamic incentive effect describes the potential of an instrument to induce progress in environmental technology.[78] Since emitters can sell permits they no longer need, the permit solution is capable of stimulating the polluters' interest in discovering new methods of environmentally sound production and developing and implementing them in practice.[79] Ecological precision means the capacity of an environmental policy instrument to achieve the stipulated emissions target level exactly.[80] The permit solution is especially precise because the amount of permitted emissions is fixed. So the arrival of new emitters has no effect on the total emissions load.[81] If, despite this, the total load is felt to be too high, the state can resort to its 'open market policy' to reduce the number of environmental licenses in circulation by buying them back, either for retention or cancellation.[82] Finally, from an economic perspective, permits also satisfy the requirement of competition-neutrality because companies causing equal amounts of environmental pollution are made to bear equal financial burdens.[83]

According to the Coase theorem hypothesis of invariance, for the efficient allocation of resources it makes little difference who is originally assigned the use rights in the environmental medium subject to the external effect. Therefore the form of the

---

[75] Feess, p. 123.

[76] Endres, p. 126; Jacobs, p. 55.

[77] Jacobs, p. 55; Endres, p. 126. Whether the permit-trading solution, like Coase theorem direct bargaining, also results in Pareto efficiency depends essentially on Pareto-efficient definition of the total permissible emissions volume, i.e. the standard.

[78] Endres, p. 106.

[79] Jacobs, p. 61.

[80] Endres, p. 106.

[81] Jacobs, p. 68.

[82] Frey, *Umweltökonomie*, p. 122.

[83] Jacobs, p. 65.

initial allocation is of no consequence for the function of the system itself and for its environmental effectiveness. It does, however, make a very important difference to the competitive situation among the parties involved.[84] This being the case, the question of how use rights are allocated is nevertheless an important one in emissions trading. Under the emissions permits system, two alternative procedures are proposed for initial assignment: permits can be sold to the highest bidder ('auctioning'), or allocated based on each party's historical pollution ('grandfathering').[85] Whereas under the auction procedure the permit is allocated to the highest bidder in return for payment, under the grandfathering system the emitters receive their permits on the basis of their past needs – perhaps after deduction of a stipulated reduction target – at no cost.[86]

Under the *auctioning* approach, the parties obtain their allocation of permits by taking part in regular auctions.[87] All parties, new entrants included, are given the same opportunity to trade and each is free to determine how many permits to purchase (out of the total number to be issued). This arrangement largely circumvents the politically and legally thorny decision as to how many permits should be allocated to each party and by what criteria. So right from the outset, the permits go to where they deliver the greatest utility, which results in a relatively high level of economic efficiency.[88] Despite its great advantages, however, even this procedure has some fairly serious weaknesses. The prices arrived at by auction are often based on projected macroeconomic trends and forecast production load, but these are equally defining factors for price formation in the trading phase. This could bring a significant element of volatility into the permit market,[89] making longer-term planning a great deal more difficult for the parties involved. Furthermore, the parties may engage in collusion prior to the auctions, which has the potential to distort the market.[90]

Under the '*grandfathering*' system, on the other hand, environment users have a relatively high level of planning and legal certainty and do not incur additional costs.[91] These advantages are counterbalanced by some major disadvantages, however: companies which have made environmental investments even prior to the allocation are effectively penalized, because their reduced emissions volume entitles them to a smaller allocation of permits.[92] This type of distribution also raises difficulties for newcomer parties who enter the market during the trading period. In the

---

[84] Diehr, p. 36. On the income and welfare effects of the type of allocation, see also Perman et al., pp. 224 ff.

[85] Feess, pp. 124 f.

[86] On the various initial allocation methods, see Diehr, pp. 36 f.

[87] Diehr, p. 38.

[88] Cansier, p. 99.

[89] Boie, p. 160.

[90] Diehr, p. 39.

[91] Cansier, p. 99.

[92] Boie, p. 160.

absence of a concrete history of environmental pollution, reference must be made to supplementary criteria.[93] All in all, this ought to make the auction solution superior to a grandfathering system. For reasons of political viability, however, the latter is the allocation procedure frequently used in practice.[94]

An applied practical example of the permit solution can be illustrated by the *Kyoto Protocol*, adopted on 11th December 1997 as a supplementary protocol to the United Nations Framework Convention on Climate Change, (UNFCCC) with the objective of climate protection. The state parties to the Protocol succeeded for the first time in agreeing a binding quantitative target for the reduction and limitation of six[95] greenhouse gases.[96] The industrialized nations made commitments that, during the period from 2008 to 2012, they would reduce emissions of these greenhouse gases by an aggregated 5.2% from 1990 levels.[97] Not every signatory country has the same emissions reduction obligations; in fact, country-specific emissions targets and interaction options were negotiated with due regard to each country's developmental status.[98] The Kyoto Protocol only stipulates the binding emissions target for the signatory state parties; how this target is to be achieved in reality is left largely to the parties themselves.[99]

After the Kyoto Protocol was adopted at the 3rd Conference of the Parties to the Framework Convention on Climate Change in Kyoto, Japan, its entry into force hung in the balance for a long time because two final hurdles first had to be overcome: the Protocol had to be ratified by at least 55 countries, and between them the participating states had to account for 55% of the $CO_2$ emissions of the countries that were party to the 1992 Framework Convention.[100] After the USA's withdrawal, it was finally Russia's accession which cleared the way for the Kyoto Protocol to take force on 16th February 2005.[101] The Protocol can be seen as a milestone in international climate policy because it is the first treaty to define climate protection targets with binding force in international law and to place them within a fixed time frame.

---

[93] Diehr, p. 37.

[94] Mühlbauer, pp. 27 f.

[95] Carbon dioxide ($CO_2$, serves as a reference value), methane ($CH_4$), nitrous oxide (laughing gas, $N_2O$), hydrofluorocarbons (HFCs), perfluorocarbons (PFCs) and sulphur hexafluoride ($SF_6$).

[96] Endres, p. 260; Diehr, p. 61.

[97] Endres, p. 260; Diehr, p. 62.

[98] Mühlbauer, pp. 34 f. Thus Switzerland has an emission reduction target of −8%, Germany −21%, the United Kingdom −12.5%, Japan −7%, Russia 0% and Spain +15%. The initial allocation of emission rights was done via a modified 'grandfathering' procedure based on the 1990 emissions level, taking account of the country-specific reduction obligation.

[99] Diehr, p. 63. However, credit is not available for $CO_2$ reductions achieved by building nuclear power stations instead of, for example, coal-fired power stations.

[100] Endres, p. 261.

[101] Mühlbauer, p. 25.

The economic heart of the Kyoto Protocol is the endeavour to achieve emissions reductions as cost-efficiently as possible. To this end, the Protocol proposes three 'flexible mechanisms', the *Kyoto mechanisms*.[102] In addition to trading in emissions rights ('emissions trading'), these mechanisms are 'joint implementation' and 'clean development' (i.e. that development should be environmentally sustainable).[103]

Both the joint implementation and the clean development mechanisms serve to foster cooperation between state parties on the implementation of climate protection projects, and to enable the state parties to fulfil a share of their emission reduction obligations abroad.[104] Alongside the benefits of scaling up the transfer of environmental technology, however, the clean development mechanism also harbours the risk of what is known as '*ecocolonialism*'. To prevent industrialized countries from simply shifting the focus of environmental efforts onto developing countries whilst their domestic industries blithely continue to emit greenhouse gases, limits were imposed on the crediting of emissions reductions achieved by climate protection projects in developing countries towards industrialized countries' emissions targets.[105] The flexible mechanisms also allow several states to join forces as an emissions community in order to fulfil their obligations jointly (known as a 'bubble policy'). For example, as an emissions community the European Union has undertaken to achieve a $-8\%$ reduction in emissions; within this community, however, national reduction commitments may differ in size.[106] This makes it possible to take advantage of country-specific strengths in the reduction of particular gases.[107]

Whether tradeable permits actually lead to a reduction in emissions is questionable, at least for the time being. Indeed, probably for political reasons, some countries were not issued with any reduction targets at all. For example, by the year 2012, Russia and Ukraine only have to stabilize their emissions at the 1990 level. Yet following the political upheaval of 1990 and the collapse of their industrial sectors, these countries have actually experienced something like a 30% decline in emissions. They therefore have surplus emissions permits, which they are free to sell to other countries without any commensurate need to reduce their own emissions.[108] This is known as the '*hot air problem*' because effectively all they

---

[102] Mühlbauer, pp. 35 f.; Endres, p. 261.

[103] Endres, p. 261; Diehr, pp. 64 f.

[104] For instance, this enables the Netherlands to credit emissions reductions from financing a wind farm in Lithuania ('joint implementation') or a solar electricity plant in Brazil ('clean development') towards its Kyoto commitments. In this way, at least, developing countries are included in the Kyoto measures. Cooperation does not take place directly at governmental level, however, but between the implementing companies at the level of the concrete projects. Mühlbauer, pp. 36 f.; Diehr, p. 66.

[105] Diehr, p. 68. If, for example, $CO_2$ can be more cheaply avoided in Poland than in Germany, whilst it is cheaper to avoid $CH_4$ in Germany than in Poland, then they both have an interest in making the greenhouse gas reductions in whichever is the cheaper location.

[106] Wiesmeth, p. 13.

[107] Endres, p. 263; Diehr, p. 65.

[108] Wiesmeth, p. 262.

are selling is hot air, and consequently emissions trading actually produces a net rise in emissions.[109] Without the Kyoto Protocol, however, emissions would have escalated with a vengeance and a great deal of valuable experience of international cooperation could never have been gathered.

In December 2007, the 13th Conference of Parties to the Framework Convention on Climate Change met in Bali for new negotiations on the future of global climate policy. The aim of the talks was to agree on a road map (the Bali Action Plan) for future negotiations on the post-2012 climate policy regime. It was felt to be too soon to define concrete targets at this conference, however. A proposed reduction target of 25 to 40% of emissions was deleted from the drafted texts at the insistence of Japan and the USA. Nevertheless, important countries – including India, China and, for the first time, the USA – indicated their willingness to engage in global climate policy.

## 4.4 Applications of Economic Analysis of Law

In the following section, some selected applications of economic analysis of law will be introduced. We will begin with a detailed presentation of a model concerning tort law, a popular field in which to apply economic analysis of law. That will be followed by two shorter examples, one concerning contract law and the other concerning the economic analysis of crime.

### 4.4.1 The Incentives of Liability Rules

#### 4.4.1.1 Introduction

From the perspective of economic analysis of law, the primary function of legal rules on liability under tort law is not to ensure that compensation is awarded for any damage – the lawyer's immediate concern – but to exert an influence on the *future behaviour* of potential injurers and victims. Economic analysis is an *ex ante* analysis, whereas the legal perspective is an *ex post* analysis. When they assess an instance of damages, economists are not primarily interested in the incident that has already occurred,[110] but in those that might arise in the future. They are concerned with the *precedent effect* of the law.

Under the economic analysis of law, the goal of liability law is to minimize the social costs of accidents. In this connection, Guido Calabresi developed the argumentational device of the '*cheapest cost avoider*': the party which can avoid the damage at the lowest cost should bear the liability for the damage.[111]

---

[109] See Endres, pp. 264 ff.

[110] These costs are 'sunk' and hence no longer relevant to the decision.

[111] Calabresi, *Accidents*, pp. 136 ff.

Torts, from an economic viewpoint, are a form of non-market-coordinated competition for the use of scarce resources, and can therefore be interpreted as externalities. Since, according to Coase, it always takes at least two parties to bring about external effects (each functioning as a causal agent), an efficient liability rule should demand that both parties to an incident of damage must determine their optimal course of action by taking the full (internal and external) costs into account.[112]

### 4.4.1.2  A Model for Minimizing the Social Costs of Accidents[113]

In the model that follows, the expected social costs $C$ of an accident can be calculated from the costs of precautions taken to prevent it, and the expected damage from an accident. The precept of efficiency requires *minimization of the expected social costs of accidents*.

Let $x$ be the extent of precautions, and let one unit of precautions cost an amount $w$ of monetary units.[114] It follows that the level of precautions is computed from $wx$ which is plotted as a straight line through the origin with a positive slope of $w$. As more precautions are taken, the probability $p$ of an accident decreases, which is why $p(x)$ is a declining function. Let $A$ be the accident damage quantified in monetary terms;[115] thus, the expected value of the accident damage is $p(x)A$. We will assume that $A$ is constant so that $p(x)A$ is also a declining function. The sum of the costs of precautions and the expected value of damage gives us the function for the expected social costs:

$$C(x) = wx + p(x)A \tag{4.1}$$

In Fig. 4.1, the minimum point of this curve is at $x^*$, which represents the socially efficient level of precautions. Mathematically, the social costs of accidents are minimal when the first derivative of Equation (4.1) is equal to zero:[116]

$$C'(x) = w + p'(x)A = 0 \tag{4.2}$$

$$w = -p'(x^*)A \tag{4.3}$$

---

[112] Koboldt, Leder and Schmidtchen, p. 364.

[113] Cooter and Ulen, pp. 271 f.

[114] For the sake of simplicity, the variable $w$ is assumed to be constant. It would be unproblematic to extend the model – on the principle of decreasing abstraction – with the assumption that $w$ varies as the level of precautions increases.

[115] This is economic concept of damage which comprises diminished utility on all levels (material and immaterial) expressed as a monetary value. Damage in this economic sense extends to types of damage not covered by our normative concept of damage as well as the kind of non-pecuniary loss for which just redress may be awarded.

[116] Furthermore the second derivative must be greater than zero, i.e. $C''(x) = p''(x)A > 0$.

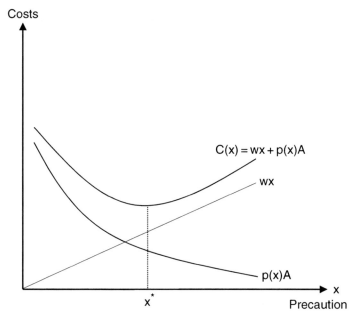

**Fig. 4.1** Social costs of accidents (cf. Cooter and Ulen, p. 271)

At the optimum, the marginal cost $w$ of an additional unit of precautions is equal to the saved marginal cost of the expected damage $-p'(x^*)A$.[117] If the level of precautions is chosen in accordance with this equation, the solution is socially efficient. *This means that precautions should be taken up to the point where the marginal damage likely to be prevented is at least as great as the marginal cost w of avoiding that amount of marginal damage. At the optimum, marginal damage and marginal cost are equally high.*[118]

### 4.4.1.3  Explanation with Illustrative Example

Let us suppose that a factory produces effluent with potentially carcinogenic effects on nearby residents. If the effluent were not treated, people's health would be harmed to the tune of €10 million. By fitting a one-stage water treatment facility costing €4 million,[119] damage to health could be reduced by €5 million.[120] By

---

[117] The superscript * stands for 'optimum'.

[118] Mathematically the marginal damages are infinitisemally small. In applied practice, however, one chooses a finite unit. Also see the following example.

[119] This corresponds to variable $w$ in Equation (4.3) (on the left of the equation).

[120] In Equation (4.3) this is seen in the expression $-p'(x^*)A$ (on the right of the equation). It is clear that it is difficult to place a value on harm to health, not least because in large part it is intangible in nature.

fitting a second stage of purification, costing another €4 million, a further reduction of health impacts amounting to €3 million could be accomplished. Fitting the first stage of purification is socially efficient: €4 million in costs compare favourably with an expected €5-million reduction in damage, resulting in a net social gain of €1 million. Investing in a second stage of purification would be inefficient, however: the expected additional reduction in damage of €3 million would give rise to additional costs of €4 million, effectively wiping out €1 million of social value.[121]

#### 4.4.1.4  Unilateral Precautions by the Victim[122]

The model presented did not specify who would take the specified precautions. Sometimes only the potential injurer can take precautions, e.g. when a surgeon operates on an unconscious patient. Sometimes, however, both the injurer and the victim can take precautions; e.g. when the manufacturer of a drug ensures its purity and the consumer sticks to the recommended dosage. The model put forward by Cooter and Ulen shows the relationship between the social costs and the precautions taken by the victim and the injurer.

The question now is what *incentives* the various liability rules exert on the behaviour of the parties involved. To answer this, we will analyse the following liability rules: 'no liability', where the victim has to bear the cost,[123] and 'strict liability', where the victim is compensated for the entire damage, regardless of fault. We will first analyse the case in which the victim alone takes precautions. The relevant costs amount to $w_v x_v$.[124]

(a) No Liability

Under the 'no liability' rule the victim himself has to bear the full cost of the expected damage, the expected value of which is $p(x_v)A$. Together with the costs of precautions, the victim's costs are:

$$C_v(x_v) = w_v x_v + p(x_v)A \qquad (4.4)$$

The victim has an interest in minimizing these costs. Equation (4.4) corresponds to Equation (4.1), so by analogy from the result of Equation (4.3):

$$w_v = -p'(x_v^*)A \qquad (4.5)$$

---

[121] One could object that both stages of treatment cost €8 million and would save an equal amount in medical costs. In fact, from the viewpoint of efficiency, this solution is on a par with the no-water-treatment option. In comparison to the solution with only one stage of treatment, however, it sacrifices €1 million of social assets. This is where marginal analysis proves its superiority to an analysis based on aggregate or average values. See also the conclusion of Sect. 2.4.

[122] Cooter and Ulen, pp. 272 f.

[123] Also known as 'victim liability'.

[124] The subscript v stands for 'victim'.

This result means that the victim is taking precautions efficiently. *If they cannot claim for damages, victims have an incentive to take a socially efficient level of precautions.*

### (b) Strict Liability

We will now discuss the second case which provides for the victim to be compensated for the entire damage. As in case (a), the cost of the victim's precautions is $w_v x_v$, and the expected loss amounts to $p(x_v)A$. But if an accident occurs, the victim receives damages $D$. Let the damages cover the whole amount of the loss ($D = A$, therefore $A - D = 0$). The victim's costs then amount to:

$$C_v(x_v) = w_v x_v + p(x_v)(A - D) \tag{4.6}$$

$$C_v(x_v) = w_v x_v \tag{4.7}$$

The victim will minimize $w_v x_v$. Because $x$ cannot be negative, the minimum point is where $x_v = 0$. The efficient solution, however, would be to behave in accordance with Equation (4.5). *Under strict liability with full compensation for damage, the victim has no incentive to take precautions, which is an inefficient outcome from society's point of view.*

### 4.4.1.5 Unilateral Precautions by the Injurer[125]

We will now consider how the incentives of the two liability rules influence the behaviour of the injurer. Firstly let us assume that the injurer takes the precautions; consequently he bears the burden of the corresponding costs $w_i x_i$.[126]

### (a) No Liability

If the injurer is not liable to pay damages, all he is responsible for are the costs of precautions $w_i x_i$. These costs are minimal at $x_i = 0$. The most efficient option, though, would be to behave in accordance with Equation (4.5). *If the injurer has no liability, he has no incentive to take precautions. This is socially inefficient.*

### (b) Strict Liability

Under this liability rule the injurer bears both the costs of precautions and the costs of any accident:

$$C_i(x_i) = w_i x_i + p(x_i)A \tag{4.8}$$

---

[125] Cooter and Ulen, pp. 273 f.
[126] The subscript i stands for 'injurer'.

The injurer will minimize these costs. Since Equation (4.8) corresponds to Equation (4.1), again by analogy from the result of Equation (4.3) it follows that:

$$w_i = -p'(x_i^*)A \qquad (4.9)$$

This result means that the injurer is taking precautions efficiently. *Since he has to compensate damage in full, this is an incentive for him to take the socially efficient level of precautions.*

### 4.4.1.6 Implications[127]

We recognize the symmetry of the results: the victim's incentives under one liability rule correspond to the injurer's incentives under the other liability rule. The implications of this are as follows: if only the victim is capable of taking precautions, the result will be socially efficient provided that this party has to bear the cost of the damage. If only the injurer is capable of taking precautions, on the other hand, then strict liability with full compensation for damage is the socially efficient liability rule.

### 4.4.1.7 Bilateral Precautions[128]

Now we will consider a case in which both the victim and the injurer can take precautions. On this basis, the social cost function is as follows:

$$C(x) = w_v x_v + w_i x_i + p(x_v, x_i)A \qquad (4.10)$$

The social costs are minimized by determining $x_v^*$ and $x_i^*$. The results of the previous analysis are equally applicable to bilateral precautions. The 'strict liability' rule with full compensation for damage induces efficient behaviour in the injurer; the 'no liability' rule does the same for the victim. In both cases, however, the other party behaves inefficiently.

Thus a dilemma arises: neither one liability rule nor the other creates incentives for socially efficient behaviour in both parties, as the possibility of bilateral precautions would require.[129] The problem cannot simply be solved by sharing the loss fifty-fifty. Both sides would then have an incentive to take some precautions, but not to the requisite extent. The outcome would thus be suboptimal.[130]

---

[127] Cooter and Ulen, pp. 274 f.

[128] Cooter and Ulen, pp. 275 f.

[129] As in Equations (4.5) and (4.9).

[130] A possible solution is to make the injurer liable for the loss in full, while the victim bears the full burden of costs from the loss. Under such a *decoupling* of loss and compensation, the injurer might have to hand over compensation to the state, for instance.

## (a) Liability for Negligence[131]

Since the liability rules discussed above did not yield a satisfactory outcome where there was a possibility of bilateral precautions, we will now examine whether liability for negligence results in a more efficient outcome. This liability rule defines a legal minimum standard of care $x^°$ with which a potential injurer must comply in order to avoid liability for damages. We set the legally required level of care at the socially efficient level ($x^° = x^*$). Now we consider the injurer's cost function. In the area of non-compliance ($x < x^°$) the injurer is liable. He bears the cost of precautions $w_i x_i$ plus the expected damage $p(x_i)A$. His cost function in the area of non-compliance is $w_i x_i + p(x_i)A$.

In the area of compliance ($x \geq x^°$) the injurer is not liable and must only pay the costs of his own precautions $w_i x_i$. In this area, therefore, the cost function is the line $wx$ in Fig. 4.2. Note the jump discontinuity in the injurer's cost function at $x^°$, which is also where the cost minimum is located. If there is a legally defined minimum standard of due care, and the injurer has to pay compensation for the full amount of damage, then he has an incentive to comply with that standard. If the legal standard of care is equivalent to the efficient level of precautions, then the behaviour of the potential injurer is socially efficient.

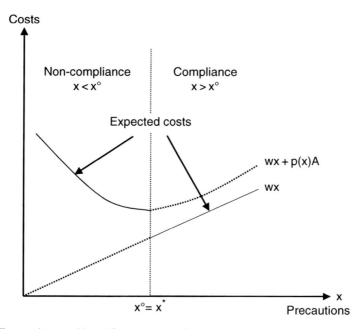

**Fig. 4.2** Expected costs with a defined standard of care (cf. Cooter and Ulen, p. 276)

---

[131] Cooter and Ulen, pp. 276 f.

The critical question now is how the potential victim behaves in this case. If the injurer can avoid liability for damages by complying with a certain standard of care, the victim will behave as under the 'no liability' rule. As we know, in that case he also has an incentive to take the efficient level of precautions. Liability for negligence thus leads to efficient behaviour, both in the injurer and the victim, as long as the legal standard of care corresponds to the efficient level.[132]

### (b) The 'Hand Rule' for Determining the Scale of Negligence

In our model of liability for negligence, we assumed that the legally defined standard of care corresponds to the efficient level. It is self-evident that an efficient outcome cannot be achieved in any other way.

In 1947 – long before the advent of the Law and Economics movement – an American federal judge named Learned Hand came up with an economic formula for determining the efficient level of care. This has passed into the literature as the *Learned Hand formula* or the *Hand rule*. The case on which he was ruling concerned whether the owner of a barge could be made liable for leaving it unattended for several hours. During this time the barge had broken free from its mooring and gone on to collide with another vessel. Judge Hand explained in his judgment:

> [T]here is no general rule to determine when the absence of a bargee or other attendant will make the owner of the barge liable for injuries to other vessels if she breaks away from her moorings. [...] It becomes apparent why there can be no such general rule, when we consider the grounds for such a liability. Since there are occasions when every vessel will break from her moorings, and since, if she does, she becomes a menace to those about her, the owner's duty, as in other similar situations, to provide against resulting injuries is a function of three variables: (1) The probability that she will break away; (2) the gravity of the resulting injury, if she does; (3) the burden of adequate precautions.[133]

In the opinion he went on to deliver, Judge Hand expressed these arguments in a mathematical formula. If $B$ represents the costs of the injurer's precautions, $P$ is the probability of damage and $L$ is the likely magnitude of damage, then there is a tortious liability for negligence wherever:[134]

$$B < P^*L \qquad (4.11)$$

The optimum level of precautions on the part of the potential injurer would thus be:

$$B = P^*L \qquad (4.12)$$

That is, the cost of avoidance corresponds to the expected value of the injury costs. Under the Hand rule, liability for negligence begins at precisely the point

---

[132] In game theory, this is known as a *Nash equilibrium*: neither party can improve its position as long the other does not change its strategy.

[133] United States v. Carroll Towing Co., 159 F.2d 169, 173 (2d Cir. 1947).

[134] Chaudhuri, pp. 79 f.

where the expected value of damage exceeds the cost of avoidance.[135] It is obvious that this economic concept of negligence sends a clear deterrent signal to potential injurers. Anyone can work out for themselves roughly whether a certain potentially dangerous activity is deemed negligent in law and will result in a tortious liability. This presumes, however, that the potential injurer is fully informed of the risk and the likely magnitude of the loss.[136]

The Hand rule in its original form is not a true marginal analysis. Nevertheless the rule is a remarkable attempt to integrate economic considerations into judicial decisions. Moreover the Hand rule can easily be translated into marginal form (the 'marginal Hand rule'). To do so, we will use the terms from our model:[137]

| Hand's term | Our term | |
| --- | --- | --- |
| B burden | $w_i$ | marginal cost of precautions |
| L liability | $A$ | (accident) damage |
| P probability | $p'(x_i)$ | marginal probability |

We can now substitute our terms into Equations (4.11) and (4.12) and obtain the following formulae:[138]

$$w_i < -p'(x_i)A \qquad (4.13)$$

$$w_i = -p'(x_i^*)A \qquad (4.14)$$

It will be instantly apparent that Equation (4.14) corresponds to our earlier Equations (4.3) and (4.9). Judge Hand may not have expressed his rule in the marginal form, but the gist of it certainly anticipates the outcome of our analysis.[139]

American courts use the Hand rule frequently to settle questions of negligence. The advantage of case-by-case application of the rule is that the standard of care can be established individually in each legal dispute, although this poses a substantial information burden for the courts. But a standard of care can also be stipulated in law. A further possibility is that courts can look to customs or best practices in the relevant field for guidance.[140]

---

[135] Chaudhuri, p. 5.

[136] Chaudhuri, p. 81.

[137] Cooter and Ulen, p. 282.

[138] $p'(x)$ is negative, because $p(x)$ is a function with a negative slope. The minus sign gives the term a positive value again.

[139] If the only concern is to assess *whether* certain behaviour – in this case, watching the barge – would have been necessary, the Hand rule in its original form will suffice.

[140] Cooter and Ulen, pp. 282 f.

### 4.4.1.8  Critique

The example of tortious liability shows the explosive force of economic analysis of law: the traditional paradigm in tort law rests on the principle of *compensation for loss*. In contrast, economic analysis is based on the *efficiency paradigm*. Under this analysis, the question is *which liability rule is socially efficient*, i.e. which rule sets the right *incentives* for both the injurer and the victim to arrive at a socially optimal level of losses in terms of the relationship between the expected cost of such losses, on the one hand, and the cost of avoidance, on the other.

H. L. A. Hart objects to this view because traditionally the question asked was not which liability rules set the right incentives, but who has the right to damages – which is a question of justice:

> This theory of incentives runs strongly counter not only to Professor Dworkin's theory that the judge must not concern himself with considerations of general utility but also with the conventional idea that liability in negligence is at least sometimes imposed as a matter of justice between the parties, on the footing that the victim of another's negligence has a moral *right* to have his loss made good by the negligent party, so far as monetary compensation can do this.[141]

Coleman levels the criticism (known as the *bilateralism critique*) that economic analysis of law is incapable of explaining the normative relationship between the injured party and the injurer: economic analysis applies ex ante analysis to hypothetical damages cases from the viewpoint of cost and risk minimization, whereas in reality a court has to rule ex post on real damages cases involving two very concrete parties who stand in a normative relationship with one another based on the case at issue:[142]

> The problem that confronts economic analysis, or any entirely forward-looking theory of tort law, is that it seems to ignore the point that litigants are brought together in a case because one alleges that the other has harmed her in a way she had no right to do. Litigants do not come to court in order to provide the judge with an opportunity to pursue or refine his vision of optimal risk reduction policy.[143]

For Coleman it is the concept of *corrective justice* that best explains the relationship between the injurer and the injured party.[144] But instead of taking its orientation from corrective justice, which is predicated on the bilateral nature of the legal relationship, economic analysis of law pursues a social goal, that of promoting efficiency.[145] In this light, according to Coleman, properties of tort law which

---

[141] Hart, 'American Jurisprudence', pp. 143 f.

[142] Coleman, *Practice*, pp. 16 ff.

[143] Coleman, *Practice*, p. 17.

[144] Similar arguments are found in Ernest J. Weinrib: *The Idea of Private Law*; Benjamin Zipursky: 'Rights, Wrongs, and Recourse in the Law of Torts'; and Martin Stone: 'On the Idea of Private Law'. On the same theme, also see Jules Coleman: 'Tort Law and the Demands of Corrective Justice'; and Stephen R. Perry: 'Comment on Coleman: Corrective Justice'.

[145] Bound up with this, according to Coleman, is the unassailable belief in the state as the engine of social change. Coleman, *Practice*, p. 344.

are obvious and intuitively transparent – like bilateralism and corrective justice – suddenly appear inexplicable and obscure.[146]

Indeed it is difficult to conceive of liability law as oriented exclusively towards the efficiency goal, ignoring the bilateral nature of the relationship between injurer and victim. Even in future, bringing about corrective justice will continue to be the primary objective of liability law. This does not preclude attempting, as a secondary objective, to bear social costs in mind and take them into account when defining liability rules, beginning perhaps with the kind of liability rule to choose: both strict liability and negligence are based on the idea of corrective justice; as we have seen in the example, however, negligence may be fundamentally superior to strict liability in terms of efficiency. The goal of any economic analysis of law must be to shed light on the effects of different regulations without demolishing the fundamental structures of liability law – like the bilateral nature of the relationship between injurer and victim – in the process.

The question as to how the relationship between efficiency and justice can be determined is one we shall return to later.[147]

## 4.4.2 Efficient Breach of Contract[148]

### 4.4.2.1 Introduction

Another area of law that can be analysed on the basis of the *Coasean framework* is contract law. Unlike the previous examples, all of which dealt with instances of damage, parties to a contract negotiate their terms so as to avoid a dispute if at all possible. Given that the parties are in a position to make provisions on any potential bones of contention in advance, one may well ask why legal rules on breach of contract are needed at all. The reason is that negotiations require a great deal of effort, and as a consequence, provisions often do not extend to every conceivable eventuality. It is therefore incumbent upon contract law, according to A. Mitchell Polinsky, to fill the gaps in contracts:[149]

> Contract law can be viewed as filling in these "gaps" in the contract – attempting to reproduce what parties would have agreed to if they could have costlessly planned for the event initially.[150]

In doing so, the rules applied should guarantee an economically efficient outcome. This means that the contracting parties' common gains from trade should

---

[146] Coleman, *Practice*, p. 21.

[147] See Chapter 9.

[148] Polinsky, pp. 27 ff. The example has been modified.

[149] From the legal viewpoint, this applies to judicial revision of contracts and dispositive legal norms, but does not hold for mandatory norms which are often motivated by sociopolitical considerations.

[150] Polinsky, p. 27.

be maximized.[151] In the example below, two different legal claims for breach of contract will be assessed under this aspect: firstly, compensation for the reliance loss (reliance damages), and secondly, compensation for the expected loss (expectation damages).

### 4.4.2.2  Breach of Contract in a Case of Double Sale[152]

Let us assume that an artist M could produce a picture for € 1, 200.[153] Buyer A wants to buy the picture which he values at € 2, 000.[154] A and M agree on a purchase price of € 1, 600, which A pays in advance.[155] In reliance on the delivery of the picture, A spends € 100 on fittings to display the picture in his apartment.[156] Buyer B is also interested in the picture and makes an offer of €2, 500 (scenario 1) or €1, 800 (scenario 2), each sum representing the picture's exact value to him.

(a) Compensation for the Reliance Loss (Reliance Damages)

If M now proceeds to breach the contract with A, the latter must be compensated so as to return him to the position as if the contract had never been made (negative contractual interest). In the present case, the reliance loss amounts to the € 100 of expenditure already incurred by A in preparation for the delivery. Since A can, of course, also demand a refund of the € 1, 600 purchase price, M must pay A € 1, 700 in total.

Since € 1, 700 is the amount that M must pay to buyer A if he breaches the contract, then an offer of € 2, 500 from B will induce him to breach it. But that is not all: M will even breach the contract if B offers him only € 1, 800. So under the alternative scenarios, M stands to make an additional profit of either € 800 or € 100. In the first case, the result is efficient: B values the picture at € 2, 500, while A values it at only € 2, 000. In the second case, however, the breach of contract is inefficient: the picture does not end up with the buyer who values it most highly, because although it is worth € 2, 000 to buyer A, it is finally purchased by buyer B who values it at only € 1, 800.

*It follows that a legal rule which only obliges the seller in breach of contract to pay reliance damages is not capable of guaranteeing an efficient outcome.*

---

[151] This implies *Pareto efficiency*, since nobody would consent to a voluntary exchange which left them worse off. Another way of expressing this is in Posner's terms: 'wealth' should be maximized. See Sect. 8.4.

[152] Polinsky, pp. 28 ff.

[153] It is a unique item, i.e. not substitutable.

[154] This corresponds to his maximum willingness to pay.

[155] This assumption is not essential but makes the numerical examples more easily understandable.

[156] In the event of non-performance by the seller, this investment is useless.

## (b) Compensation for the Expected Loss (Expectation Damages)

In awarding compensation for the expected loss, A must be put in the same position as if the contract had been performed (positive contractual interest). In this case, A would have profited as follows:[157] the €2, 000 value that he places on the picture, minus the purchase price of €1, 600 and additional expenditure of €100, gives a net amount of €300. On the principle of positive contractual interest, A has a claim for this lost profit and for his expenses (€400 in total). A can also claim a refund of the €1, 600 purchase price, so M must pay A €2, 000 in total, which coincides exactly with A's valuation of the picture.

Since €2, 000 is the amount that M has to pay to buyer A if he breaches the contract, an offer of €2, 500 from B will induce him to breach it, because this will earn him an additional profit of € 500. On the other hand, if B offers him only €1, 800, M will not breach the contract. This outcome is efficient: the product ends up with the buyer who values it most.

*A legal rule which obliges the seller in breach of contract to pay expectation damages sets the right incentives with regard to efficiency.*[158]

### 4.4.2.3   Critique

Contract law is founded on the principle that contracts must be honoured ('*pacta sunt servanda*'). It thus appears rather odd to define contract law in such a way as to create incentives for breach of contract on the grounds of efficiency. Here, again, the efficiency paradigm appears to collide with a fundamental principle of law as we know it.

The bilateralism critique against the economic analysis of liability law can equally be levelled against the economic analysis of contract law. If efficiency is elevated to the target criterion in law, it is argued, there would be no explanation for the 'privity rule' that a contract only confers rights and obligations upon the contracting parties:

> [E]ven if courts were capable of engaging in this kind of reasoning, doing so would ignore the fundamental bilateral interactional framework of contractual interactions because courts have to introduce considerations that are *not* related to the parties to the contract.[159]

Indeed, it is hard to conceive of the social goal of efficiency alone, entirely removed from the reciprocal relationship between the concrete parties to the contract,

---

[157] The concept of lost profit (*lucrum cessans*) used here depends upon how highly someone personally values a particular good. It is assessed in terms of the individual's willingness to pay rather than the market price. See also Sect. 8.4.1.1.

[158] This holds true, at least on the assumption that the contracting parties are risk-neutral (i.e. for example a €10, 000 profit at a 50% risk is valued the same as a €20, 000 profit at a 25% risk, or a sure profit of €5, 000, because the expected value of the profit in all cases is €5, 000). It further presupposes that other factors not considered in the model have no influence. Polinsky, pp. 28 f., pp. 33 ff. and pp. 59 ff.

[159] Hevia, p. 113.

as the definitive criterion in contract law. Even so, as we have seen in our example, there is nevertheless scope for taking efficiency aspects into consideration –
e.g. in determining whether expectation damages or just reliance damages should
be awarded –, without necessarily compromising the bilateral structure of the contractual relationship.

### 4.4.3  Optimal Punishment

#### 4.4.3.1  Introduction

The idea of bringing economics to bear upon the field of criminal law is nothing new.
As long ago as the 18th century, Cesare Beccaria and Jeremy Bentham developed
criteria for minimizing the social costs of crime and prosecution. In his essay 'Crime
and Punishment', Gary S. Becker instigated a revival of economic ideas in criminal
jurisprudence.[160]

#### 4.4.3.2  The Rational Delinquent

As the economic model of behaviour would have it, a person commits a crime if the
expected utility derived from it exceeds the expected costs. The utility of the crime
may be tangible (e.g. the proceeds of a robbery) or indeed intangible (as with sexual
offences). The costs arise from expenditure of various kinds (e.g. on weapons, bur-
glary tools, etc.), the opportunity costs of time dedicated to criminal activity, and the
probable costs of punishment, which are the main focus of analysis here. Essentially
a punishment is all the more of a deterrent if the probability of being arrested for the
crime is relatively high and the sentence likely to be imposed is relatively lengthy.
But it is also possible to reduce crime by increasing the opportunity costs of the time
dedicated to it. This depends heavily on the opportunities open to a potential criminal to earn an honest living. Even state programmes to combat poverty may reduce
the incentive to commit criminal offences. *Overall, measures should be defined so
as to ensure that criminal actions carry no rewards.*[161]

#### 4.4.3.3  The Optimal Crime Rate

The social costs of crime stem from the harm it inflicts, on the one hand, and the
costs of controlling crime, on the other. In Fig. 4.3, $x_0$ represents a hypothetical
crime-free state where the costs of controlling crime are commensurately high,
whereas $x_{max}$. would be a hypothetical state without any crime control measures
at all, and with a correspondingly high crime rate. *The optimal crime rate $x^*$ or,
equally, the optimal level of crime control is reached when the total social costs of
crime are minimal.*[162]

---

[160] Kunz, p. 181.

[161] Posner, *EAL 5*, pp. 242 f.

[162] Cooter and Ulen, p. 396.

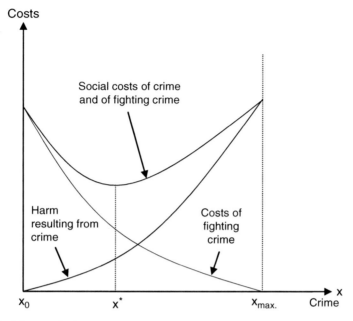

**Fig. 4.3** Social costs of crime

#### 4.4.3.4  Critique

The analysis of crime once again exposes the limitations of the economic model of human behaviour. Offenders often fail to act rationally; in fact, many crimes are committed in the heat of the moment. Aside from that, crime is a very complex phenomenon. Among other factors, the offender's *mental attitude* has a strong influence, and attitudes are partly attributable to socialization and learning processes. The economic approach concentrates on explaining behaviour as a reaction to external incentives – which is indeed its strength – whilst the mental attitudes ('preferences') of the offender are taken as given.

Because this is its strength, economic theory is capable of explaining *changes in behaviour* relatively well (for instance: why does a criminal commit more crimes in some circumstances than others?). The pivotal question of *why* someone becomes a criminal at all, though, cannot be explained adequately by this theory. So while the economic theory of crime can supply some extremely useful insights, it proves to have very limited explanatory power.

Moreover, the legitimacy of the law is integral to the effectiveness of the legal state and the legal system. The population accepts the status quo primarily on the strength of its legitimacy, rather than out of any fear of sanctions. A system of law would collapse if it could not rely on general acceptance by the public at large.[163] Constant, petty surveillance of all citizens by officials, who would themselves

---

[163] Cf. Ott, pp. 149 f.

require monitoring, is simply not feasible. *If a legal state is to function, it must be able to establish and maintain legitimacy and therefore justice. However, an efficient system of law is not automatically a just system of law.*

## 4.5 Summary

What the applications discussed have in common is that the social optimum – for the number of accidents, breaches of contract or crimes – is not zero, from the point of view of efficiency, but occurs at the point where the corresponding social costs are minimal. This statement may seem disconcerting at first, but bear in mind that even accident prevention or crime control cannot be achieved without incurring costs. Moreover, it should be reasonably straightforward – and perhaps even desirable – to analyse legal rules in terms of their incentive functions vis à vis human behaviour and social efficiency. In other words, there is no fundamental objection to a *positive analysis* of legal rules using the normative yardstick of efficiency. This positive style of analysis, however, must be clearly separated from the *normative demand* for the legal system to be defined in conformity with the efficiency principle. For this demand requires justification which economic theory itself is unable to provide. In his theory of wealth maximization, Richard A. Posner attempted to set out a justification of the efficiency objective. Before we examine this approach thoroughly, however, we first need to place it in a broader context, which is why in Part 2 we will turn our attention to the 'Philosophical Foundations'.

# Part II
# Philosophical Foundations

# Chapter 5
# Adam Smith's Moral Philosophy

> *[E]very individual [. . .] intends only his own gain, and he is [. . .] led by an invisible hand to promote an end which was no part of his intention. [. . .] By pursuing his own interest he frequently promotes that of the society more effectually than when he really intends to promote it.*[1]

## 5.1 Introduction

Adam Smith's most famous work is undoubtedly his *Inquiry into the Nature and Causes of the Wealth of Nations*[2] (1776). Here Smith casts the economy as part of a harmonious order which he refers to as a 'system of natural liberty'.[3] To explain this natural order, Smith argues for the application of the 'Newtonian method', i.e. systematic explanation of the world in terms of the fewest possible cardinal principles. For this reason, Smith has also been called the 'Newton of the social sciences'.[4] He describes the universe as a vast machine, which works in such a way that nothing is left to chance. Nature, in his view, has an internal, mechanistic order in which all elements are finely attuned to one another. It is a harmonious and manifestly beautiful work of art in every last detail. Everything in nature is believed to have a meaning and purpose; Smith's world view is *teleological*. The principal purposes are held to be the preservation and propagation of life.[5]

Smith devotes particular attention to exploring the *anthropological constants* which are revealed in everyday life.[6] People's main motivating force is deemed to be self-interest. Individuals acting for their own profit motive simultaneously contribute – as if led by an *invisible hand* – to producing the greatest possible social wealth.[7] Yet the more complex aspects of Smith's view of the world and humanity should not be glossed over. In the *Theory of Moral Sentiments*[8] (1759) he sets out

---

[1] Smith, *WN IV ii 9*.

[2] Subsequently referred to as *Wealth of Nations*.

[3] Düppen, p. 80.

[4] Medick, p. 145.

[5] Hottinger, pp. 61 f.

[6] Hottinger, p. 67.

[7] Schefold and Carstensen, p. 66.

[8] Subsequently referred to as *Moral Sentiments*.

K. Mathis, *Efficiency Instead of Justice?*, Law and Philosophy Library 84,
DOI 10.1007/978-1-4020-9798-0_5, © Springer Science+Business Media B.V. 2009

a theory of ethics in which the difficulties of human coexistence are alleviated by people's ability to sympathize with the feelings of others, and by the fact that their consciences are governed by the approval of an impartial spectator.[9] What interests Smith most about human psychology are those sensations which arise in interpersonal relationships. These human affections, feelings and passions are what he calls 'moral sentiments',[10] and he credits them with playing a greater part than reason in socialization.[11]

## 5.2 Smith's Theory of Ethics

The crux of Smith's theory of ethics is a fundamental anthropological fact, a psychological mechanism which is instrumental in constituting moral judgement: *sympathy*. It is man who must come to terms with reality, and it is *sentiment* above all which enables him to make judgements and to behave correctly. The sentiment that man feels as he lives, makes judgements and takes action in his surroundings is the root of all ethical rules. These in turn are recognized with the aid of man's reason.[12]

Smith acknowledges the moral autonomy of the individual and liberates ethics from its traditional religious bonds. He shares this outlook with the *Scottish natural law tradition* of the 18th century and, in particular, with his friend David Hume.[13] Moreover, Smith's ethics are descriptive and *empirical*: his analysis is not concerned with the question of what should be, but with matters of fact:

> Let it be considered too, that the present inquiry is not concerning a matter of right, if I may say so, but concerning a matter of fact. We are not at present examining upon what principles a perfect being would approve of the punishment of bad actions; but upon what principles so weak and imperfect a creature as man actually and in fact approves of it.[14]

### 5.2.1 Self-Interest

Self-interest, founded on self-love, and personal responsibility form the underlying foundation of Smith's system:

> Every man, as the Stoics used to say, is first and principally recommended to his own care; and every man is certainly, in every respect, fitter and abler to take care of himself than of any other person.[15]

---

[9] Schefold and Carstensen, pp. 66 f.

[10] Also called 'ethical feelings'.

[11] Patzen, p. 32.

[12] Recktenwald, pp. 37 f.

[13] Patzen, p. 29.

[14] Smith, *TMS II i V 10*.

[15] Smith, *TMS VI ii I 1*.

Accordingly, it is self-interested human endeavour which drives economic growth. Now, he points out, not only is it impossible to eliminate self-interested human endeavour, but there would be grave economic drawbacks if one were to succeed in doing so: insatiability and growth in prosperity are indivisible.[16] People's insatiable striving is based on a delusion, however; namely, the mistaken belief that happiness can be achieved through material wealth. Nevertheless, Smith considers it a good thing that nature deceives us in this way, because wealth is increased as a result.[17]

It is not just in economic life that self-interest is the motivational leitmotif. In all spheres of human action and thought – in politics, art and science, even in social and religious life – self-interested deeds are of crucial importance. However, in Smith's eyes, too much self-interest (egoism, selfishness) is as morally objectionable as too little (laziness, refusal to work).[18]

## 5.2.2 The Forces That Control Self-Interest

Four controlling forces help to counterbalance individual striving and endeavour. Only within these bounds does self-interest coincide with the common interest.

### 5.2.2.1 Sympathy and the Impartial Spectator

The first limitation on man's self-interested behaviour, according to Smith, arises from the interaction of *sympathy* or fellow-feeling and the *impartial spectator*. The very first sentence of *Moral Sentiments* makes it clear that Smith does not view humankind as purely self-serving:

> How selfish soever man may be supposed, there are evidently some principles in his nature, which interest him in the fortune of others, and render their happiness necessary to him, though he derives nothing from it except the pleasure of seeing it.[19]

Thus, according to Smith, sympathy is one of man's original sensations. Whilst man is essentially governed by self-interest, sympathy prevents him from giving free rein to this motive and sliding into unfettered egoism. In sympathy Smith sees the roots of those principles which predestine human beings to be concerned about the fate of others. Sympathy cannot be derived from self-love, so instead it must arise spontaneously. It makes its presence felt so suddenly and immediately that it takes precedence over any reflection upon self-love.[20] Sympathy, for Smith, is the ability we have inwardly to share in the thoughts and feelings of others, aided by the imagination:

---

[16] Manstetten, pp. 264 f.

[17] Smith, *TMS IV i I 10*.

[18] Recktenwald, p. 42.

[19] Smith, *TMS I i I 1*.

[20] Smith, *TMS I i I 1 ff*.

> By the imagination we place ourselves in his situation, we conceive ourselves enduring all
> the same torments, we enter as it were into his body, and we become in some measure the
> same person with him [...].[21]

The role played by sympathy in Smith's theory of ethics is to enable moral judgement. The ability to sympathize, according to Smith, is a prerequisite for any kind of moral evaluation and judgement.[22] What he means by sympathy, though, is neither substantive virtue nor any form of altruism, but the purely formal capacity that people have to empathize with one another, i.e. to imagine themselves in another person's position.[23]

The principle of the impartial spectator serves the purpose of morally qualifying both our own and other people's conduct. When we feel concern for the fate of another person, we assume the role of an external observer with the capacity to judge the other person's behaviour by imagining how we ourselves would feel in a similar situation. We refer to the same principles in order to form an opinion about our own conduct. Bear in mind, however, that this spectator is assumed to judge our deeds and feelings from a certain distance.[24]

Sympathy and the impartial spectator are references to man's social nature. But Smith knows from experience that people in general are more interested in things that affect them immediately and directly than in things that affect others. Thus a situation can easily arise where sympathy is not strong enough to monitor our own behaviour and keep it in check. For Smith, sympathy is a weaker passion than self-love.[25]

### 5.2.2.2  Social Ethical Norms

A further mechanism of control to safeguard an ordered community against the perils of self-love are social ethical norms, or 'general rules of morality' as Smith calls them.[26] Smith's derivation of these norms is not metaphysical, however, but empirical. The fact is that every society has formed general rules of ethics, determining which actions society deems acceptable and unacceptable.[27]

### 5.2.2.3  Positive Law

Yet according to Smith, even the sanctions of public approbation and disapprobation are not always powerful enough to exert sufficient restraint on people's striving for

---

[21] Smith, *TMS I i I 2*.

[22] Eckstein, p. 127.

[23] Kittsteiner, p. 45.

[24] Recktenwald, pp. 22 f.

[25] Smith, *TMS III i IV 7*.

[26] Smith, *TMS III i IV 8*.

[27] Recktenwald, p. 27.

wealth, prestige and power. This calls for an additional system of positive and state-enforceable laws.[28] It is necessary to have a *regulatory framework* with legal ground rules which regulate economic endeavour:

> In the race for wealth, and honours, and preferments he may run as hard as he can, and strain every nerve and every muscle, in order to outstrip all his competitors. But if he should justle, or throw down any of them, the indulgence of the spectators is entirely at an end. It is a violation of fair play, which they can not admit of.[29]

In order to protect human life and property, Smith argues, a system of positive laws is required. And in order to ensure that people apply and comply with the law, there also needs to be a state with the power to enforce the law.[30]

#### 5.2.2.4 Competition

Finally, the fourth limitation on self-interest – mentioned in the *Wealth of Nations* – is economic competition.[31] Smith observes that both sympathy and respect for ethical and positive rules diminish as the scope of society is enlarged – from the immediate family, to friends and acquaintances and the local community, to the nation and ultimately the global community. Thus the effectiveness of these protective mechanisms is weakened as the atmosphere becomes more impersonal. In this situation, he says, competition takes on an important protective function. The actual and potential pressure of rivalry is a constant and effective check on excessive economic striving.[32]

### 5.2.3 The Virtues

Smith cites three virtues which an impartial spectator would recognize as general rules: *prudence* to multiply one's own happiness, and *justice* and *beneficence* to multiply the happiness of others. Prudence relates primarily to individuals and the care they exercise over their own health, prosperity and prestige.[33] Justice, on the other hand, is referred to as the mainstay of a society, without which society could not function at all:

> Justice [...] is the main pillar that upholds the whole edifice. If it is removed, the great, the immense fabric of human society [...] must in a moment crumble into atoms.[34]

---

[28] Smith, *TMS II ii III 4*.

[29] Smith, *TMS II ii II 1*.

[30] Recktenwald, pp. 46 f.

[31] Smith, *WN III ii 1 ff*.

[32] Recktenwald, pp. 47 f.

[33] Schernikau, p. 15.

[34] Smith, *TMS II ii III 4*.

The most important commands of justice according to Smith, in lexical order, are:[35]

(1)  Protection of life and the person
(2)  Protection of property and possessions
(3)  Protection of contractual dues

Smith ascribes substantially less importance to beneficence than to the other two virtues. Beneficent actions – such as generosity, humanity, goodness, pity and mutual respect – should engender an atmosphere of trust in society.[36]

Smith declares that in order to exercise the three virtues, *self-command* is a necessity. Although it is the most important of the virtues, he acknowledges that it is merely instrumental in character, in that it enables the other virtues to be practised.[37]

## 5.3  The Invisible Hand

The famous metaphor of the 'invisible hand' signifies the way that self-interested action by individuals simultaneously promotes the good of society.[38] For an individual's self-interested endeavour also benefits others, as vividly expressed in what must be Smith's most frequently quoted lines:

> It is not from the benevolence of the butcher, the brewer, or the baker, that we expect our dinner, but from their regard to their own interest. We address ourselves, not to their humanity but to their self-love, and never talk to them of our own necessities but of their advantages.[39]

Smith introduces the concept of the invisible hand in *Moral Sentiments* to demonstrate that a just, i.e. egalitarian, allocation of land is not necessary: while the poor are worse off in terms of the land they have been allocated, as consumers they are almost as well off as the rich, because an invisible hand leads the rich to further the interests of society quite unintentionally:

> They are led by an invisible hand to make nearly the same distribution of the necessaries of life, which would have been made, had the earth been divided into equal portions among all its inhabitants, and thus without intending it, without knowing it, advance the interest of society, and afford means to the multiplication of the species.[40]

Smith accounts for the effectiveness of the invisible hand by pointing out that rich landowners cannot eat the unlimited amounts they produce, and are thus forced

---

[35] Smith, *TMS II ii II* 2.

[36] Schernikau, p. 17.

[37] Patzen, p. 35.

[38] Schefold and Carstensen, p. 66.

[39] Smith, *WN I ii* 2.

[40] Smith, *TMS IV i I 10*.

to hand over the greater part of their surplus agricultural production to poorer people.[41] Although trade makes it possible to exchange the surplus goods, the rich are nevertheless driven by human vanity and the need for luxury and comfort to acquire things which are not essentials of life. To produce these goods and services, the rich need craftsmen and servants. In this way, such people are also provided with money and food, even though they do not possess vast estates.[42]

Smith also uses the invisible hand metaphor in his *Wealth of Nations*. The investor, like every individual, seeks the greatest profit and thus unintentionally advances the good of society:

> [H]e intends only his own gain, and he is in this, as in many other cases, led by an invisible hand to promote an end which was no part of his intention. Nor is it always the worse for the society that it was no part of it. By pursuing his own interest he frequently promotes that of the society more effectually than when he really intends to promote it.[43]

Smith's idea of the invisible hand bears witness to an incredible optimism and faith in a system envisioned as springing from providence. On this point, Smith invokes the views of the Stoics:

> The ancient stoics were of opinion, that as the world was governed by the all-ruling providence of a wise, powerful, and good God, every single event ought to be regarded, as making a necessary part of the plan of the universe, and as tending to promote the general order and happiness of the whole: that the vices and follies of mankind, therefore, made as necessary a part of this plan as their wisdom or their virtue; and by that eternal art which educes good from ill, were made to tend equally to the prosperity and perfection of the great system of nature.[44]

Here the invisible hand is equated with 'the eternal art which educes good from ill'. In the Stoa, this is given the name Zeus or Logos. According to that philosophy, the world is created in such a way that, despite all human irrationality and imperfection, its development follows an ordered course.[45] This concept is reminiscent of Mandeville's 'private vices – public benefits' theory: anthropological vice is the engine which drives society in the right direction, while the harmful effects of vice are brought under control by the providence of nature.[46] But unlike Mandeville, Smith has no interest in justifying depraved behaviour. Instead, he has faith that human imperfection cannot disrupt the natural order.[47]

Ultimately, the idea of the invisible hand presupposes a religious faith. Smith believes that the goodness of nature will surely prevent society from degenerating into a group of inconsiderate egoists with no prospect of survival in the longer

---

[41] Smith, *TMS IV i I 10*.

[42] Trapp, Manfred, p. 129.

[43] Smith, *WN IV ii 9*.

[44] Smith, *TMS I ii III 4*.

[45] Binswanger, p. 55.

[46] Kittsteiner, p. 48.

[47] Hottinger, p. 129.

term. He compares human society to a watch, the mechanism of which works so harmoniously because its maker designed it accordingly:

> The wheels of the watch are all admirably adjusted to the end for which it was made, the pointing of the hour. All their various motions conspire in the nicest manner to produce this effect. If they were endowed with a desire and intention to produce it, they could not do it better. Yet we never ascribe any such desire or intention to them, but to the watch-maker [...].[48]

Smith – like his teacher Francis Hutcheson – was an optimistic adherent of *deism*, which assumes the existence of a creator somewhere beyond the world. But once the world has been created, God no longer interferes in the laws of nature because he has arranged all things to develop harmoniously towards an ultimate destiny which is positive for humankind.[49]

But why does self-interest apparently have the effect that Smith describes? The mechanism of the invisible hand presupposes a state in which all men are dependent on the services and products of others, i.e. a state of general *division of labour*. Where production is based on the division of labour, people are always working for one another, i.e. for the market, and not just for themselves. The reciprocal exchange of work does not come about because people have somehow realized that they must render services to their fellow men, but because the market economic system compels everyone to render such services in order to support themselves. Thus individual virtue is dispensable as a motive, because beneficence is now socially institutionalized.[50]

Smith's idea of automatic advancement of the common good expresses the thought that economic endeavour should be evaluated in positive terms for two reasons: on the one hand, it promotes individual self-realization, and on the other hand it also benefits society, so that self-interest simultaneously fulfils a social function.[51]

## 5.4  Critique

### 5.4.1  The Adam Smith Problem

What is meant by the Adam Smith problem is the seemingly irreconcilable conflict between the apparently altruistic moral philosophy in *Moral Sentiments* and the seemingly egoistic theory of the *Wealth of Nations*.

---

[48] Smith, *TMS II ii III 5.*

[49] Düppen, p. 73.

[50] Trapp, Manfred, pp. 126 f.

[51] Düppen, p. 85.

The Germans, who, it seems, in their methodical manner commonly read both, the Theory
of Moral Sentiments and the Wealth of Nations, have coined a pretty term, Das Adam Smith
Problem [. . .].[52]

In reality, however, the problem was not that the Germans had read both books.
Quite the opposite: to begin with they only assimilated the *Wealth of Nations*, barely
taking notice of *Moral Sentiments*. The lack of interest in Smith's moral theory was
rooted in the German idealist philosophers' indifference to it. Only the Historical
School really engaged with Smith's theory of ethics and 'discovered' the famous
Adam Smith problem.[53] This can be stated as follows: many of the rules of economic
behaviour put forward in the *Wealth of Nations* seem to presuppose that egoism
in economic life dominates all other human motives. Since Smith was later to be
known as the founder of the 'Classical School', he was often viewed as the originator
of ideas which were not his own but were properly attributable to other classical
economists such as Jean-Baptiste Say or David Ricardo.[54] This led to narrow and
abridged interpretations of Smith which created the impression that his *Wealth of
Nations* was contradictory to his *Moral Sentiments*.

Since then, all manner of attempts have been made to explain the apparent contradiction in Smith's thinking. The 'reversal hypothesis' was the claim that Smith's
stay in France prompted him to take up the ideas of French materialism, which
subsequently left their mark on the *Wealth of Nations*. But the reversal hypothesis
proved to be unsound. Firstly, Smith had conceived and lectured on the fundamental
ideas of *Wealth of Nations* long before his trip to France. Secondly, the later editions
of the *Moral Sentiments*, published after the trip to France, do not point to a change
of mind.[55] The 'aspect' hypothesis was the claim that in *Moral Sentiments,* Smith
wanted to depict human nature in its sympathetic essence, whereas in *Wealth of
Nations* he intended to present its self-interested behaviour. Patzen points out that
this ruse resulted in a division of facts which were, essentially, indivisible. Finally,
the 'is-ought' hypothesis proposes that in *Moral Sentiments,* Smith was describing
how people should be, and in *Wealth of Nations*, how they really are.[56]

According to Recktenwald, on closer examination the Adam Smith problem turns
out to be a phantom, for in *Moral Sentiments*, Smith never intended 'sympathy' to
mean benevolence or even altruism. The sole function of sympathy in his work
is to explain our ethical judgement and so to build a bridge to our fellow human
beings. The motives of our actions are something else altogether. Self-interest certainly numbers among these motives but, Recktenwald argues, this must not be confused with selfishness. The impartial spectator disapproves of a surfeit or a deficit

---

[52] Viner, p. 201.

[53] Recktenwald, pp. 56 f.

[54] Patzen, p. 24.

[55] Recktenwald, p. 57.

[56] Patzen, pp. 25 f.

of self-interest. Thus the purported conflict between *Moral Sentiments* and *Wealth of Nations* is shown to stem from a misinterpretation.[57]

The fact is, self-interest is emphasized not only in *Wealth of Nations*, but also in *Moral Sentiments*. Sympathy is entirely compatible with egoism and, on that score, *Moral Sentiments* actually begins by stating that even those who consider man to be egoistic through and through cannot deny the presence of sympathy.[58] The apparent contradiction dissolves completely if we also call to mind that moral sentiments carry most weight in respect of *immediate personal contacts*, a subject dealt with mainly in *Moral Sentiments*. In *Wealth of Nations*, on the other hand, the main emphasis is on the coordination of the *impersonal transactions* necessitated by national or global markets, and where self-interest is checked by competition more than by sympathy.[59] On this analysis, Smith's two major works are to be interpreted as a unified whole; they are not in any sense fundamentally contradictory; rather, they complement one another.[60]

## 5.4.2 The Impartial Spectator

The impartial spectator is an inner judge who assumes the function of the conscience. This judge represents humankind. As a representative of human society, the impartial spectator is created in God's image; a kind of demigod, in other words.[61] Man, as an observer of himself, examines the compatibility of his own ends with the ends of others. Compelled by social life, man critically assesses his own affections and interests – an endeavour that marks man out as a moral being.[62] There are obvious parallels with Kant's categorical imperative – to act so that the maxims of your will might also be the principle of a universal law – in the adoption of generalization as a formal principle. By analogy, Smith's imperative of behaviour could be formulated as follows: act in such a way that all – both outsiders and you yourself – can approve of your behaviour. And whether this conduct meets with approval is a matter for the impartial spectator, the conscience.[63]

According to Smith, moral judgements about our own actions are formed as a reflex of society's attitudes, and are primarily learned in childhood through the influence of parents, teachers and schoolmates. The totality of attitudes which accumulate in our consciousness over time operate, to some extent, as a second self which scrutinizes the natural self's plans and actions. Smith's explanation of the

---

[57] Cf. Recktenwald, pp. 57 ff.

[58] Smith, *TMS I i 1 1*

[59] Fischermann, p. 5.

[60] Hottinger, p. 47.

[61] Trapp, Manfred, p. 87.

[62] Trapp, Manfred, pp. 92 f.

[63] Hottinger, p. 118.

emergence of the conscience is thus similar to the Freudian theory of the 'superego'. This, again, is a second self which is constructed as a reflex to attitudes in the social environment – especially parental attitudes – and which performs the role of a censor, censoring the desires and actions of the natural self, the 'ego'. However, Freud's superego proves to be a single-minded, repressive authority, intent upon preventing urges from seething out of control, whereas Smith's impartial spectator is capable of expressing approval and disapproval in equal measure.[64]

The impartial spectator represents a basic facet of human experience, namely the knowledge that one's dependency upon the other members of the community imposes an obligation to be considerate. However, the spectator does not prescribe any specific behaviour; in fact it goads man into critical self-examination. In the course of this process, the judgement of others is taken into consideration. Of course, the judgement of others should not be understood as the ultimate authority on moral issues, but as forming the departure point for critical reflection. Man – prompted by his fellow human beings – engages in a process of self-examination, with the purpose of proving his worth as a social being through voluntary insight.[65] According to Smith, the impartial spectator undergoes an exchange of roles by imagining himself in other people's situations. Rawls envisages a similar process in his theory of justice, whereby the individual in the original position puts himself in different people's roles. The problematic aspect of this procedure is that it is a monological method, so there is a danger that one is simply generalizing from one's own thoughts to the whole of society. The alternative is to use models in which real discourse takes place between a variety of people.[66]

### 5.4.3 *Individual Versus Collective Rationality*

Smith's metaphor of the invisible hand expresses the idea that the pursuit of self-interest promotes social prosperity at the same time. The question to be answered, however, is how accurate this hypothesis really is. Using *game theory* it is possible to analyse whether self-interested, rational behaviour on the individual level leads to outcomes which are collectively optimal. The best-known game structure is the *prisoners' dilemma*.

The prisoners' dilemma is a game which reflects the cooperation problem, by setting up a *dilemma structure* which prevents cooperative solutions. The prisoners' dilemma is based on the rules for turning State's evidence in American law: two prisoners are held in separate cells and given no opportunity to collude on how they will behave. They are accused of having jointly committed some crime, but there is no conclusive evidence against them. The state prosecutor makes both prisoners the following proposal: if one of them confesses, he will be set free while the other will

---

[64] Raphael, pp. 54 ff.

[65] Trapp, Manfred, pp. 94 f.

[66] See Sect. 7.4.5.

**Table 5.1** Prisoners' dilemma pay-off matrix

|              | A confesses          | A denies              |
|--------------|----------------------|-----------------------|
| B confesses  | both 10 years        | A 12 years, B freed   |
| B denies     | A freed, B 12 years  | both 2 years          |

be sentenced to 12 years' imprisonment. If both confess, both will be sent to jail for 10 years. If both deny their guilt, each will be sentenced to two years' imprisonment for illegal possession of a firearm. Thus, both players have a choice between two strategies: 'confession' or 'denial'.[67] The pay-off matrix in Table 5.1 sets out the possible options.

The best strategy for the two prisoners collectively is for each to deny the crime and settle for two years' imprisonment for illegal possession of a firearm instead. These prison terms, added together, produce the lowest total number of years in prison. This would be the *strategy of cooperation*. As the following discussion will show, however, the dominant strategy for each prisoner individually is 'confession', regardless of how the other player behaves: if B confesses, it is best for A to confess too, because this will result in a 10-year rather than a 12-year prison term. But even if B denies the crime, it is better for A to confess because he will then be freed. It follows that he will select the *strategy of defection* in every case. Since the game progresses symmetrically, the same applies to player B. Thus the 'confession/confession' strategy combination is the game's only *Nash equilibrium*.[68] The dilemma of the players is that behaviour which is rational individually results in an outcome which is not rational collectively: in the 'denial/denial' solution, both players have a way of improving upon the Nash equilibrium. Assuming *non-collaborative, strictly rational behaviour*, it is not possible for the players to achieve the Pareto-efficient solution (denial/denial). This can only be realized if the players are prepared to behave cooperatively, which requires that they resist the *free rider option*[69] of 'confession'. On the assumption of rational behaviour, however, this is unlikely, even if the players see through the dilemma structure. Cooperative behaviour only makes sense from the players' point of view if it is reciprocal. For simultaneous decisions, this presupposes that the players can assure one another that they will play cooperatively. But any such assurance lacks credibility, for rational players will confess, and both players make the assumption that the other will act rationally.[70]

In the example cited, the dilemma was expressed in its most acute form because direct collusion between the two players was ruled out. Communication seems to be at least a necessary condition for a cooperative solution. Let us therefore assume that *communication is allowed*, and that the prisoners promise one another not to

---

[67] Osterloh and Tiemann, p. 323.

[68] See the end of Sect. 4.4.1.7a.

[69] Also see the explanatory notes below.

[70] Geigant et al., p. 304.

confess. Even so, it remains questionable whether they will be motivated enough to stick to the agreement. Cooperation depends on *trust* in one's counterpart.[71]

In a *one-round game*, players do not have the opportunity to determine the trustworthiness of their opposite number.[72] Consequently they face a decision under *uncertainty*, where uncertainty means the absence of a critical decision-making criterion. Another determining factor is the players' risk-affinity. One possible rule is the optimistic *maximax rule*, whereby one stakes everything – as gamblers do – on the maximal maximum, i.e. the best possible eventuality. But another possibility is the pessimistic *maximin rule*, which is to anticipate the worst possible outcome whilst trying, within that, to end up as well off as possible – like a person buying insurance. If we apply these rules to the prisoners' dilemma, we obtain the *same result* as in the original example: both will confess. The optimist who relies on the other player's promise, and seeks to make himself as well off as possible within this situation, will exploit the privilege of turning State testimony to renege on the agreement with his accomplice and confess. The pessimist, on the other hand, will anticipate his opposite number's dishonesty and assume that he will confess; he, too, will have no choice but to confess, because otherwise he will receive the maximum penalty. The strategy of defection proves rational, regardless of whether one's attitude is optimistic or pessimistic. It makes no difference whether one considers the other person to be honest or dishonest, either; in a game with only one round, non-adherence to the agreement is always the dominant strategy.[73]

Naturally one of the prisoners could credibly convince the other that he is prepared to kill him if he ever finds out he has been betrayed. This eventuality changes the pay-off matrix, however; a different decision results but this is certainly not a case of direct cooperation.[74] A different scenario again is the *iterative prisoners' dilemma*: the same game is repeated a number of times in a row. Here the players can test their counterpart's cooperativeness and trustworthiness using the *tit for tat strategy*. In round one, the first player signals his willingness to cooperate. If the other player returns his cooperation in round two, the first player continues to cooperate, but any defection in round two will be punished likewise by withdrawing cooperation in round three.[75] Over time, a relationship of trust can develop, with the result that both players make cooperation their core strategy. Nevertheless, if one player suddenly decided to defect, the other player would immediately punish him with non-cooperation in the following round. Normally this prompts a return to cooperative behaviour.

---

[71] Locher, p. 60.

[72] In our example one could object that as accomplices, the pair would know each other's trustworthiness. Here, however, it is assumed that this is not the case. And as is shown, in a game of only one round, the honesty of the other party plays no part in determining what the dominant strategy is.

[73] Höffe, *Politische Gerechtigkeit*, pp. 422 f.

[74] Locher, p. 60.

[75] Axelrod, p. 12.

For a *finite number of rounds*, though, cooperation is gainsaid by the following argumentation: in the last round, players have a greater incentive to defect because punishment is no longer possible. Even in the penultimate round, players might have no further incentive to cooperate, since both anticipate that the other will defect in the final round. The same can then be said of the third from final round, and so on; by backward induction, defecting behaviour can be rolled back to the very first round. Conversely, this argumentation cannot be applied to games with an *indeterminate number of rounds*. In realistic conditions, players are not usually in a position to know when the final interaction between them will take place. Therefore, when the number of rounds is indeterminate, cooperation can develop.[76]

So far, we have only based the discussion on two players. Of course, cooperation is also possible among *several people*. Moreover, an implicit assumption was made that no costs were attached to negotiations, i.e. that *no transaction costs* would arise – or *cooperation costs*, as it would be more accurate to call them in this instance. Any such cooperation costs would also have to be included in the pay-off matrix. Cooperation itself can only take place if the cooperation gain exceeds the cooperation costs, which are comprised of the expense of seeking cooperation partners and then negotiating, implementing and checking the whole arrangement. These costs rise with the number of participants, but tend to yield better returns when many rounds are to be played.[77]

The prisoners' dilemma makes the basic structure of many economic cooperation problems transparent. The most important example of this is the *free rider problem* in relation to *public goods*. Since nobody can be excluded from consuming public goods, a rational, self-interested individual will make no contribution to producing such a good, but will opt for the free rider strategy of consuming the good without making any input to its production.[78] The structure is familiar from the prisoners' dilemma: individually rational behaviour will result in non-supply of the public good, and this holds true even if it could be supplied Pareto efficiently. Consequently, individually rational behaviour leads to collectively non-rational outcomes.[79]

Now we could argue that it is obvious to rational people that cooperative behaviour will pay off. For if we think about it, there are only two relevant choices: universal cooperation or universal defection, cooperation being more advantageous for everyone. However, this argument ignores the real crux of the dilemma: the pay-off of cooperation becomes all the greater as more and more people cooperate. *But as more people cooperate, the free rider option becomes more worthwhile, as well.* And if everyone else is cooperating, then of course it makes defection an especially attractive option. Therefore a situation of universal cooperation can only be ensured by making appropriate and enforceable rules. From the prisoners' dilemma, we can

---

[76] Axelrod, p. 9.

[77] Locher, p. 60.

[78] See also Sect. 2.3.3.

[79] Geigant et al., pp. 304 f.

gain fundamental insights into how rules work and the *necessity for rules*, which may help us to arrive at better rules.[80]

Karl Homann views social morality as another public good, the production of which places the actors concerned in the prisoners' dilemma. Due to the collective nature of the problem, there is only one way out: the collective solution. He points out that an appropriate moral and legal regulatory framework should enable society to overcome dilemma situations, and prevent the community from collectively harming itself. However, there are also socially desirable dilemma structures: between companies in competition with one another, it is virtually a necessity to uphold the prisoners' dilemma, since it prevents them from conspiring with one another not to compete. Cooperation by means of cartels is not socially desirable in this instance. The role of competition authorities is to ensure that companies cannot eliminate the dilemma situation of competition.[81] These considerations show that the imperfection of the invisible hand can only be evened out by a visible hand, namely regulatory intervention by the state.

---

[80] Cf. Locher, p. 64.

[81] Homann, p. 78.

# Chapter 6
# Jeremy Bentham's Utilitarianism

> *[I]t is the greatest happiness of the greatest number that is the measure of right and wrong [. . .].*[1]

## 6.1 Introduction

Utilitarianism (from Lat. *utilis*: useful) is a tendency within normative ethics which has developed, principally in the English-speaking world, into a complex instrument for the empirical-rational justification of norms. To the idealistic philosophers in the German-speaking world, on the other hand, the empiricist approach of utilitarian ethics remained a closed book for the most part. This can be put down to the overpowering influence of Kant. In contrast to Kantian ethics based on duties and convictions, utilitarianism is a pure *ethic of results*. How an action is evaluated depends not on the motives of the actor but solely on the consequences of the action concerned.[2]

The origins of utilitarian thinking go back to antiquity (Plato, Aristotle and Epicurus), and are also found in mediaeval times (Thomas Aquinas) and the early modern period (in particular, David Hume, Claude-Adrien Helvétius and Cesare Beccaria). Of prime importance is Jeremy Bentham, whose work *An Introduction to the Principles of Morals and Legislation* (1798) laid the foundation of *classical utilitarianism*. Other seminal works of classical utilitarianism were John Stuart Mill's essay 'Utilitarianism' (1861) and Henry Sidgwick's publication *The Methods of Ethics* (1874).

## 6.2 Utilitarianism as a Normative Ethical Theory

### 6.2.1 Utilitarianism as a Teleological Theory

Utilitarianism – like eudemonism or hedonism – is a *teleological* ethical theory, which is the contrary of a *deontological* theory. A deontological theory of ethics, such as Kant's moral philosophy, comprises a system of norms which are credited

---

[1] Bentham, *FG, Preface*.

[2] Düppen, p. 2.

K. Mathis, *Efficiency Instead of Justice?*, Law and Philosophy Library 84, DOI 10.1007/978-1-4020-9798-0_6, © Springer Science+Business Media B.V. 2009

with absolute and unqualified validity. Acting in accordance with a deontological orientation means considering these rules alone, regardless of what consequences the action may entail.[3]

Utilitarians view this as a reality-blind *rule fetishism* which disregards not only the vicissitudes of life but also human needs. For the utilitarian, analysis of the consequences of actions is central to moral thinking. Utilitarianism measures the moral quality of an action by the quality of its *consequences*, not by its conformity to rules. Accordingly, actions should be judged according to whether they are useful on the basis of their consequences.[4] Hence, utilitarianism is also called a *consequentialist* theory of ethics.

Actions or rules for action are not adjudged right or wrong on their own account, but by reference to their consequences for the people they affect.[5] However, if the ethics of all actions are judged by their consequences alone, it means that there are no good or bad actions per se. It also implies that the intentions which underlie these actions are of no importance. Nor is there any such thing as a good or bad motive per se. A motive is only bad if it gives rise to an action with adverse consequences.[6]

## 6.2.2  The Utility Principle and the Felicific Calculus

Bentham begins his principal work *An Introduction to the Principles of Morals and Legislation* with the assertion that both our *is* and our *ought* are determined by pleasure and pain.

> Nature has placed mankind under the governance of two sovereign masters, pain and pleasure. It is for them alone to point out what we ought to do, as well as to determine what we shall do. On the one hand the standard of right and wrong, on the other hand the chain of causes and effects, are fastened to their throne.[7]

Next, Bentham introduces the *principle of utility*, which applies not only to private individuals but also to the government:

> By the principle of utility is meant that principle which approves or disapproves of every action whatsoever, according to the tendency which it appears to have to augment or diminish the happiness of the party whose interest is in question: or, what is the same thing in other words, to promote or to oppose that happiness. I say of every action whatsoever; and therefore not only of every action of a private individual, but of every measure of government.[8]

---

[3] Kersting, *Einführung*, pp. 95 f.

[4] Kersting, *Einführung*, p. 96.

[5] Höffe, *Ethik*, p. 10.

[6] Hottinger, pp. 259 f.

[7] Bentham, *IPML I 1*.

[8] Bentham, *IPML I 2*.

According to Höffe, the corresponding *utility test* can be formulated as follows:

> That action or action rule is morally right, the consequences of which are optimal for the welfare of all parties affected.[9]

Likewise, Bentham talks about the principle of 'the greatest happiness of the greatest number'[10] or 'the greatest happiness or greatest felicity principle'.[11] According to Bentham, the 'principle of the greatest happiness of the greatest number' is a better term than the 'principle of utility' because it more clearly expresses the substance of the principle.[12]

But the utility principle or the principle of the greatest happiness of the greatest number was not originated by Bentham. A similar form of words occurs even earlier, in Beccaria's *dei delitti e delle pene* (1764):

> la massima felicità divisa nel maggior numero[13]

It is likely that Bentham took the idea of the utility principle from the English translation of Beccaria's book, which appeared in 1767.[14] But he could equally have borrowed it from Helvétius, who was also a major influence on Bentham's thinking. In *De l'homme* (1772) the following formulation of the principle is found:

> le bien du plus grand nombre[15]

The originator of the utility principle is acknowledged to be Francis Hutcheson, the teacher of Adam Smith. As early as 1725, in *An Inquiry into the Original of our Ideas of Beauty and Virtue*, he wrote:[16]

> that Action is the best, which procures the greatest Happiness for the greatest Number, and that, worst, which, in like manner, occasions Misery.[17]

But nobody else has supported the utility principle as vehemently as Bentham, whilst also attempting to use it as a basis for a comprehensive theory of society.[18] The utility principle represents the crux of Bentham's entire theory of ethics, and can be traced in various forms through all his writings.[19] For Bentham, the rightness

---

[9] Höffe, *Ethik*, p. 11.

[10] Bentham, *FG, Preface*.

[11] Bentham, *IPML I 1, Note*.

[12] Bentham, *IPML I 1, Note*.

[13] Beccaria, p. 8. The literal meaning of the Italian is 'the greatest happiness *divided by* the greatest number', which suggests utilitarianism based on average utility (see Sect. 6.2.4.2), but this was translated less precisely into English as 'the greatest happiness of the greatest number'. Hottinger, p. 254.

[14] Hottinger, p. 254.

[15] Helvétius, *De l'homme IV 11*.

[16] Hottinger, p. 255.

[17] Hutcheson, p. 164.

[18] Düppen, p. 107.

[19] Hottinger, p. 254.

of the utility principle is self-evident because it is instilled in man by nature. He grants that proving this is impossible, but also unnecessary; it certainly cannot be refuted.[20] The utility principle, according to Bentham, is the sole ethical principle. The inference of this claim to absoluteness is that all other ethical principles must be wrong.[21] In particular, it precludes the existence of any *human rights* which could prevail over the utility principle.[22] According to Bentham, natural rights stem from mere wishful thinking and hence they are nothing but rhetorical nonsense:

> In proportion to the want of happiness resulting from the want of rights, a reason exists for wishing that there were such things as rights. But reasons for wishing there were such things as rights, are not rights; – a reason for wishing that a certain right were established, is not a right – want is not supply – hunger is not bread. [. . .] *Natural rights* is simple nonsense: natural and imprescriptable rights, rhetorical nonsense, – nonsense upon stilts.[23]

Under the *felicific calculus*, the *gratification value* of an action results from the difference between the pleasure and pain it causes to all parties affected. According to the utilitarian theory of ethics, obligatory moral directives for conduct cannot be obtained by means of pure deduction. What is needed in the first instance is *empirical knowledge*; that is, knowledge of the consequences of an action and the meaning of these consequences for the welfare of society. Thus the utilitarian theory of ethics is firmly rooted in reality.[24] According to Bentham, the utility of an action can be determined precisely by making reference to seven criteria. The key indicators for the measurement of pleasure and pain are their:

(1)  Intensity
(2)  Duration
(3)  Certainty or uncertainty
(4)  Propinquity or remoteness
(5)  Fecundity
(6)  Purity
(7)  Extent

'Extent' refers to the number of people affected by the action.[25] For the calculation of utility, the nature of the pleasures and pains concerned makes no difference. Bentham analyses the different utilities quantitatively, not qualitatively.[26] In contrast, John Stuart Mill introduced a qualitative analysis of utility.[27] In doing so, however, Mill distanced himself methodologically from pure utilitarianism,

---

[20] Bentham, *IPML I 11 f.*

[21] Hottinger, p. 278.

[22] Hottinger, p. 276.

[23] Bentham, *AF Art. II 9 f.*

[24] Höffe, *Ethik*, p. 12.

[25] Bentham, *IPML IV 4.*

[26] Hottinger, p. 258.

[27] Mill, 'Utilitarianism' II 9.

because in order to judge utility qualitatively he requires an additional criterion.[28] In Moore's words:

> It is plain that if you say "Colour alone is good as an end", then you can give no possible reason for preferring one colour to another. Your only standard of good and bad will then be "colour"; and since red and blue both conform equally to this, the only standard, you can have no other whereby to judge whether red is better than blue. [...] If we do really mean "Pleasure alone is good as an end", then we must agree with Bentham that "Quantity of pleasure being equal, pushpin is as good as poetry".[29]

### 6.2.3 Utilitarianism Depends on a Theory of Value

In claiming that morality depends on the consequences of an action, utilitarianism presupposes knowledge of how good or bad consequences can be recognized. That is, it requires a theory about a suitable criterion for assigning something a 'value', so that it can be designated as 'good' or 'bad'.[30] For an action is not useful in its own right, but only with reference to something else. In view of that, utilitarianism needs a theory of value which defines the scale of utility, so that the utility generated can be measured. So utilitarianism is a combination of consequentialism, on the one hand, and a value theory on the other; the latter specifies the objective to be attained by making utility judgements.[31]

According to Bentham and J. S. Mill, utilitarianism itself takes up a value theoretical position in which the fulfilment of human needs – human *happiness*, in other words – is held to be the highest value. Thus the goal is the maximum satisfaction, or the minimum frustration, of needs.[32] For Bentham, human happiness is whatever the people concerned believe it to be. The means for achieving happiness cannot be determined a priori. Knowledge of happiness, of the means to maximize happiness, and the form of action most conducive to it, is a matter of experience alone. Utilitarianism can also be combined with other value theories, however. Which particular value theory is chosen ultimately does not matter. Utilitarianism itself possesses no criterion which would make it possible to make a rational choice among competing value theories.[33]

### 6.2.4 Forms of Utilitarianism

As classical utilitarianism was refined, it branched out into a number of different variants.

---

[28] Hottinger, p. 385.

[29] Moore, *PE III 48 III*. 'Pushpin' was a game played by children.

[30] Hoerster, p. 13.

[31] Cf. Kersting, *Einführung*, pp. 96 f.

[32] Höffe, *Ethik*, pp. 10 f.

[33] Cf. Kersting, *Einführung*, pp. 96 f.

### 6.2.4.1  Act and Rule Utilitarianism

One can distinguish between the original form of utilitarianism, *act utilitarianism*, and a modified version of it, *rule utilitarianism*. The modified version was developed in response to criticism of certain dubious consequences of act utilitarianism, the principles of which would decree that, in specific cases, humans could be deprived of fundamental rights, political opponents could be tortured, treaties broken, fraud perpetrated, secrets betrayed or indeed innocent people killed.[34]

In act utilitarianism, the utility principle is applied to every single action. Rule utilitarianism, on the other hand, follows a two-stage process. Firstly, one asks about the overall utility of a rule which dictates certain actions.[35] The relevant question is, 'What would the consequence be if everyone acted that way?' An individual action which breaks a rule is held to be morally wrong even if the consequences of that action should be good in a specific instance. The idea is to obviate the need to examine, each and every time, whether the consequences of breaking a particular promise or condemning a certain innocent person will be good or bad. Instead, the question is whether a rule that 'promises need not be kept' or 'innocent people may be condemned' produces good or bad consequences.[36] The attractiveness of rule utilitarianism is that while on the one hand – like act utilitarianism – it is geared towards the satisfaction of human needs, on the other hand, like deontological ethics, it satisfies our intuitive inclination to judge ethical behaviour on the basis of rules.[37]

But rule utilitarianism gives rise to certain problems so that, not infrequently, even a rule utilitarian is forced to measure certain actions in terms of the utility principle directly. Firstly, it is not possible to make an exhaustive list of rules to which all actions can be assigned. New constellations of possible actions arise constantly, which will not be covered by any rules devised hitherto. For purely practical reasons, too, in everyday life it makes sense to keep the list of rules relatively limited. One possible solution is to apply the utility principle directly to all cases which are not covered by a rule. Secondly, in specific instances, following a rule can lead to quite absurd outcomes. In order to avoid this, the rule utilitarian has no choice but to permit adjunct use of the utility principle itself, in addition to the rules, for case-by-case judgements, and to give this principle priority over the rules whenever it is blatantly contravened by following them. Thirdly, cases are likely to arise in which two or more rules come into conflict. Here, too, the most plausible solution is to solve the conflict by applying the utility principle directly.[38]

---

[34] Mackie, p. 174.

[35] Seelmann, p. 188.

[36] Höffe, *Ethik*, pp. 30 f.

[37] Hoerster, p. 24.

[38] Hoerster, pp. 25 ff.

### 6.2.4.2  Total and Average Utilitarianism

A further question is whether total or average utility is to be maximized. In a population of a stable size it makes no difference which of the two values is maximized. Only with a variable population size does the distinction become significant. For example, we could compare two different ways of behaving, one of which would lead to a state in which the great majority of the population lives only a moderately happy life, whereas the other resulted in an extremely happy life for a small minority of people. In the first case, total utility is greater; in the second, average utility is higher.[39]

### 6.2.4.3  Happiness and Preference Utilitarianism

In classical utilitarianism, morally correct actions were those which set out to maximize happiness, joy or pleasure. For preference utilitarianism, on the other hand, – a variant propounded only in the 20th century by such figures as G. E. Moore, John C. Harsanyi or Peter Singer – the criterion is the maximum satisfaction of interests, desires or preferences. No distinction between the two is apparent as long as everyone is interested in exactly those things which make them happy. But they diverge when ex ante evaluations (preferences) and ex post evaluations (happiness) fail to coincide, i.e. when the satisfaction of an individual's interest is not in that individual's (long-term) interests.[40]

The reason for this is that preferences can be cognitively and emotionally 'distorted', irrational and self-destructive. They may be the expression of 'false' needs, the satisfaction of which does not make a person any happier. Often we do not know what is best for us, and even if we do know, we frequently lack the willpower and hence the means of controlling the preferences that determine our behaviour. Then there are preferences about these preferences, which are known as second-level preferences. Smokers, for example, often have a second-level preference for wanting to stop smoking, but generally this is not strong enough to subdue the first-level preference.[41]

### 6.2.4.4  Subjective and Objective Utilitarianism

Another discussion point is the question of whether there are objective criteria for defining what is utility-generating. The difference between Jeremy Bentham and John Stuart Mill has already been mentioned: Bentham entrusts all evaluations of happiness to a personal, subjective assessment and makes no distinction on qualitative criteria, which garnered him the reproach that his utilitarianism was a *'pig*

---

[39] Mackie, pp. 159 f.

[40] Cf. Birnbacher, 'Ökonomie', pp. 72 ff.

[41] Birnbacher, 'Ökonomie', p. 73.

*philosophy*'.[42] By contrast, Mill is convinced that qualitative distinctions are possible on the basis of 'objective' criteria. From his viewpoint, therefore, there are higher and lower pleasures. In Mill's wake there were various attempts to formulate objective criteria on the qualitative differentiation of utility. James Griffin talks about objective and subjective attempts to define well-being:

> By "subjective", I mean an account that makes well-being depend upon an individual's own desires, and by "objective" one that makes well-being independent of desires.[43]

Derek Parfit makes a similar distinction and in this connection discusses 'objective list theories':

> [C]ertain things are good or bad for us, whether or not we want to have the good things, or to avoid the bad things.[44]

In his example, happiness would come about if an individual possessed a number of elementary goods or capabilities – defined without reference to his desires – which can be universally derived from anthropological constants and objectively formulated in a list: so anyone who had such assets as wealth, good friends, health and one or two other things would be happy, regardless of how he actually felt.[45]

A similar line is taken by David O. Brink in his '*objective utilitarianism*'. For Brink, some things – particular characteristics and abilities, interpersonal relationships and, indeed, life itself – are valuable irrespective of psychological states:

> [A] valuable life consists in the possession of certain character traits, the exercise of certain capacities, and the development of certain relations with others and to the world, and that the value of such a life is independent of the pleasure it contains and whether or not this sort of life is desired or would be desired in some preferred epistemic state.[46]

Moreover Brink takes the view that we do not attribute value to certain things because we desire them, but the converse: we desire them because we think them valuable.[47] Yet he is unable to provide a convincing justification of why certain things should be intrinsically valuable.[48]

### 6.2.4.5  Positive and Negative Utilitarianism

A further distinction relates to the question of whether one should try to bring about good consequences in every situation (positive utilitarianism), or merely avoid

---

[42] The same accusation was thrown at the Epicureans of antiquity: that their theory was only fit for pigs. *Wolf*, p. 48.

[43] Griffin, p. 32.

[44] Parfit, p. 493.

[45] Gesang, *Verteidigung*, p. 28.

[46] Brink, p. 221.

[47] Brink, p. 225.

[48] Elsewhere Brink comes out in favour of rule utilitarianism. Brink, pp. 256 ff., esp. p. 258. For a critique of rule utilitarianism, see Sect. 6.2.4.1 above.

negative consequences (negative utilitarianism).[49] Karl R. Popper argues for attaching greater weight to the reduction of negative utility (pain) rather than the promotion of positive utility (pleasure), his intent being to counteract any redistribution of utility from the worse-off to the better-off.[50]

Rainer W. Trapp's 'justice utilitarianism' pursues a similar line to Popper's.[51] According to Trapp, utility should be weighted with the help of utility parameters, while the motives of actors should be noted and assessed with reference to a merit parameter. Where motives are morally reprehensible, the actor's utility gain will be given correspondingly little weight. In a similar way, a distribution parameter can be used to weight utility according to its effects on the distribution of income, in the aim of preventing excessive inequality of income distribution.[52] The question that arises, though, is whether such a weighting of utility, – which, it must be remembered, is based on non-utilitarian principles of justice, – does not violate a fundamental principle of utilitarianism; namely, that the sole decision-making principle is the quantitative aggregation of utility.[53]

## 6.3 Critique

An essential strength of utilitarianism is that its assessment of actions often coincides with generally accepted moral convictions and intuitions. The prime objection to utilitarianism, according to Hart, is that it does not take the *distinction between people as individuals* seriously and is thus incapable of guaranteeing their *basic rights*.[54] Kant staunchly rejects utilitarianism and ascribes the highest priority to justice:

> [W]oe to him who creeps through the serpent-windings of utilitarianism to discover some advantage that may discharge him from the justice of punishment, or even from the due measure of it, according to the Pharisaic maxim: "It is better that one man should die than that the whole people should perish".[55]

The following are the individual points of criticism that can be levelled against utilitarianism:

---

[49] Hoerster, p. 19.

[50] Birnbacher, 'Utilitarismus', p. 26.

[51] See Trapp, Rainer W., *'Nicht-klassischer' Utilitarismus*, esp. pp. 310 ff.; and id., 'Politisches Handeln', pp. 73 f.

[52] Gesang, 'Gerechtigkeitsutilitarismus', pp. 19 ff.

[53] Cf. Seelmann, p. 189.

[54] Hart, 'Utility', pp. 200 ff.

[55] Kant, *Science of Right*, p. 453.

### 6.3.1 The Boundary Problem

In many respects, delimiting the radius of beings affected by an action is not straight-forward: which beings are meant? Just all the human beings affected, or all the sentient beings affected, i.e. animals as well? And even if one only includes people, other questions still arise: is it only people who are alive today who matter, or should future generations also be considered? How can one estimate how many people this might be?[56]

On the other hand, the openness of utilitarianism to all people and all sentient beings can also be seen in a positive light: utilitarianism harbours great sociopolitical potential in that it urges us to give regard to the well-being of other groups, such as immigrants or people living in poor countries. Since utilitarianism allows for an analysis which embraces not just human beings but all living creatures capable of feeling pleasure and pain, it implies the possibility of animal welfare for reasons over and above the purely anthropocentric.[57] Hence it is no coincidence that Bentham was the first to formulate obligations towards animals on a theoretical level:[58]

[T]he question is not, Can they *reason*? nor, Can they *talk*? but, Can they *suffer*?[59]

The prohibition of animal torture therefore follows directly from the utilitarian principle, according to which happiness is to be maximized and suffering minimized. Moreover, utilitarianism holds out the possibility of demanding global justice, and of making decisions which take into consideration the interests of future generations.[60]

### 6.3.2 The Information Problem

As an empirical theory of ethics, utilitarianism suffers from the limitation of empirical knowledge. Every action is bound up with an infinite sequence of consequences, which people, because of our limited cognitive capacities and our uncertainty about future events and developments, are incapable of predicting. Each of us individually must be guided by our own experiences, and these vary from one individual to another. To that extent, moral judgement under utilitarianism depends on the experience of the person making the judgement. Therefore the calculation of consequences can also turn out to be wrong. Furthermore, there is a risk that living generations will not take the interests of future generations into account sufficiently, or indeed at all.[61]

---

[56] Mackie, p. 159.

[57] Höffe, *Ethik*, p. 41.

[58] Birnbacher, 'Natur', p. 118.

[59] Bentham, *IPML17 I 4*, note b.

[60] Gesang, *Verteidigung*, p. 135.

[61] Kersting, *Einführung*, pp. 98 f.

### 6.3.3 The Problem of Quantification and Utility Comparison

Utilitarianism presupposes a utility calculus, according to which one can measure and compare the utility that different things provide. Even if Bentham's assumption that all satisfaction values could be quantified in cardinal terms was quickly abandoned, utilitarianism must hold fast to the postulate of measurability and compatibility in principle. But once quantification has been unmasked as an illusion, how should one weigh up the enjoyment gained from a night at the opera against the utility of a fast-food consumer, or the frustration of a redundant worker against the pleasure of a shareholder who makes a higher return on capital as a result?[62]

According to Henry Sidgwick, even the *intrapersonal* comparison of utility (comparison of utility from the viewpoint of a single person) raises various problems: firstly, any quantitative estimation of a sentiment is a matter of imprecision per se. Secondly, the following difficulties arise: if the sensations to be compared are present simultaneously, then they are difficult to separate from one another because interference can take place between the two. If the sensation is not actually present, it must be conjured up with the aid of the imagination. Such a sensation is particularly difficult to assess, especially when it has never actually occurred and may very well only occur in the future. Thirdly, the strength of the sensation can be influenced by the deliberate act of reflecting upon it and trying to quantify it. The constant search for the maximization of pleasure can thus tend to weaken the pleasure actually experienced – a circumstance which Sidgwick called 'the paradox of egoistic hedonism'.[63] When it comes to the *interpersonal* comparison of utility (comparison of utility between several people) the problems intensify because we have little or no knowledge of the inner experience of other individuals. Assessing other people's feelings thus remains a highly speculative pursuit.[64] The effective impossibility of interpersonal utility comparisons is the main objection to the technical practicability of a utilitarian theory of ethics.

In practice, attempts are made to quantify the social value of projects with the help of *cost-benefit analyses*, but no cardinal measurement of utility, in the strict sense, is possible. On the other hand, a person might well be in a position to rank alternatives *ordinally* in relation to their utility, i.e. to produce a *rank order* of preference: for instance, A is better than C, but C is better than B. In a democracy, collective decisions based on such individual orders of preference are usually taken by means of the *majority rule*.[65] But even this procedure does not necessarily guarantee logically consistent decisions, as Condorcet's *voting paradox* shows. This can be illustrated by means of a simple example in which three voters are required to

---

[62] Cf. Kersting, *Einführung*, pp. 100 f.

[63] Sidgwick, pp. 134 ff.

[64] Sidgwick, p. 148.

[65] The majority rule is only a very rough reflection of the utility principle, however.

choose between three alternatives.[66] Let us suppose that the individuals' orders of preference are as follows (Table 6.1):

**Table 6.1** Order of preference for three voters choosing between three alternatives

| Voter | Order of preference | | | | |
|-------|---|---|---|---|---|
| I   | A | > | B | > | C |
| II  | C | > | A | > | B |
| III | B | > | C | > | A |

Under a majority vote, A will beat B by two votes to one, and B will beat C, also by two votes to one. On the grounds of logic (the law of transitivity), the consequence should be that A would beat C. However, a direct vote on options A and C results in the paradoxical outcome that C beats A by two votes to one. Where the paradox of *cyclic majorities* occurs, it is impossible to determine a clear winner. Consequently, the outcome can be influenced by the sequential order in which the alternatives are presented.[67]

Kenneth J. Arrow came up with mathematical proof that no voting process based on ordinal preferences results in a transitive social order of preferences.[68] However, Arrow's *impossibility theorem* does not imply that ordinal orders of preference will necessarily give rise to logical inconsistencies. All it says is that unstable voting outcomes cannot be ruled out with certainty.[69]

## 6.3.4 The Confusion of Is and Ought

Bentham couples 'is' and 'ought' in a highly problematic way: pleasure and pain are supposed to determine both how man acts, and how he should act.[70] Methodologically, therefore, pleasure and pain are ascribed a double function: as descriptive elements in relation to the basic structure of human motivation, and as normative elements in the sense of criteria for moral rectitude.[71] Apart from that, the idea that man's 'is' and 'ought' are exclusively determined by pleasure and pain is somewhat cheerless. Smart demonstrated this strikingly with his example of the 'pleasure machine'.[72]

Let us assume that a simple device were invented to stimulate the pleasure centre in the brain. People could use this as a direct means of creating their own pleasure – in place of the indirect means that are currently used, such as personal relationships,

---

[66] Frey and Kirchgässner, p. 147.

[67] Frey, *Politische Ökonomie*, p. 96.

[68] Arrow, esp. pp. 46 ff.

[69] Frey, *Politische Ökonomie*, p. 97.

[70] Bentham, *IPML I 1*; see Sect. 6.2.2 above.

[71] Höffe, *Ethik*, p. 16.

[72] Smart, p. 20.

sport, sexuality, reading books, listening to music, making conversation, etc. This would be an instant means of multiplying happiness, understood as the excess of pleasure over pain. But would this be a desirable state of affairs? The intuitive answer has to be no, although for a utilitarian, the question could well prove a very awkward one. However, J. S. Mill takes the view that it is better to be an unhappy Socrates then a happy fool:[73]

> It is better to be a human being dissatisfied than a pig satisfied; better to be Socrates dissatisfied than a fool satisfied.[74]

Mill justifies his viewpoint with the fact that he sees not only a quantitative but also a qualitative difference between different pleasures, and prefers the higher form of pleasure to the lower. The fundamental question raised is whether or not we have the freedom to form and shape our moral system in such a way that it fosters what we consider valuable.[75]

### 6.3.5 Responsibility for Others' and One's Own Actions

Bernard Williams objects that utilitarianism does not discriminate between responsibility for one's own choice of actions, and refraining from an action under constraints imposed by the actions of others (negative responsibility).[76] He illustrates this with an example:[77]

In the course of an expedition, Jim arrives in a small South American town. In the marketplace, twenty Indians are lined up against a wall. Facing them is a group of armed soldiers. Their captain approaches Jim and explains to him that the twenty Indians have been picked at random to be killed, in order to deter the population from further protests. Since Jim is a respected visitor from a foreign country, the officer is pleased to grant him, as a guest, the privilege of killing one of the Indians himself. If Jim agrees, the rest of the Indians will be freed because of the special circumstances. Otherwise, all twenty Indians will be killed, as originally intended. Given their plight, the Indians against the wall and the rest of the villagers beg Jim to accept the captain's offer.

What should Jim do? From a utilitarian perspective, Jim ought to kill one Indian in order to save the lives of the other nineteen. Williams argues that it makes a difference whether he carries out the killing himself or whether it is done by somebody else, because we are all directly responsible for our own actions, but not so directly

---

[73] Mackie, pp. 186 f.

[74] Mill, 'Utilitarianism' II 6.

[75] Mackie, pp. 186 f.

[76] Williams, p. 58.

[77] Williams, pp. 61 f.

for how others behave. The analysis must take account of Jim's personal integrity and not just the common good.[78]

## 6.3.6  Individual Versus Social Welfare

One thing illustrated by the example of Jim is that utilitarianism calls for the person taking action to be extremely altruistic. This person may not maximize their own utility, but must give priority to the utility of society.[79] Admittedly, the utility of the individual actor also counts towards social utility, but this is no guarantee that both measures require the same action. Often an individual would have to act against his own interests, which may well be too much to ask.[80]

According to Bentham, pleasure and pain are the only drivers of human action, which means that psychological egoism is justified on an individual level. The utility principle, on the other hand, requires that the happiness of all the people affected should be maximized. Here the egotistical motivation structure opposes the altruistic norm. According to Otfried Höffe, the committed utilitarian is therefore in a tragic situation: his motivation structure conspires against his ability to behave in accordance with the demands of the utility principle.[81]

Adam Smith introduced the idea of harmony between private and public welfare with the metaphor of the invisible hand.[82] According to Bentham, the utility principle is primarily a tool for government, which is intended to alleviate the conflict between private and public welfare by means of state intervention.[83] With his felicific calculus, Bentham wants to provide politics with the appropriate set of instruments.[84] Williams, by contrast, thinks it a naive, almost absurd, idea that society would allow itself to be governed by a utilitarian elite. In his view, assumptions should not be based on ideal observers, but should anticipate the actions of non-ideal actors.[85]

## 6.3.7  The Problem of Distributive Justice

A major weakness of utilitarianism is manifested in its indifference to income distribution. The emphasis on total collective utility wholly disregards how it is actually

---

[78] Williams, p. 62.

[79] Fletcher, p. 145.

[80] Cf. Mackie, pp. 163 ff.

[81] Höffe, *Ethik*, p. 16.

[82] See Sect. 5.3.

[83] Hottinger, pp. 297 ff.

[84] Höffe, *Ethik*, p. 17.

[85] Williams, p. 105.

distributed. For example, let us suppose that two alternative actions will bring about the same total of collective utility. One action would effectively share this utility between a small number of people, while the other action would share it between many, or even all, people. From the utilitarian point of view, both actions are of equal value.[86]

The conflict between the utility principle and distributive justice – already pointed out by Bentham – is not as crass as it may initially seem, because distribution can make a difference even under utilitarianism. In terms of utility, it is not necessarily trivial how – for instance – one hundred apples are divided among one hundred people. According to the law of diminishing marginal utility, the consumption of the first apple will give more pleasure than the consumption of the third or fourth, and once a certain number have been eaten, the marginal utility of a further apple is likely to be negative because over-consumption can easily induce nausea.[87] Consequently, society's utility could be increased – at least under a static analysis – if income were distributed more equally. The loss of utility caused by taking a dollar away from a millionaire should be significantly smaller than the utility gain that results from giving a dollar to a beggar. But when it comes to dynamic analysis – in other words, an analysis of consequences over time – this form of argumentation has major shortcomings. The negative incentives of egalitarian income distribution could impact upon work habits, resulting in a drastic decline in economic output. This in turn would impair welfare.[88]

Thus there is scope for taking income distribution into account within utilitarianism, if the principle of utility is combined with the theory of declining marginal utility. But this does not alter the fact that distributive justice is subordinate to the objective of the greatest possible social happiness.[89]

## 6.3.8 The Problem of Basic Rights

The most important reproach against utilitarianism is that it does not take the *distinction between persons* seriously and is incapable of guaranteeing their basic rights. Utilitarianism views society in terms of an model of an individual person: society as a whole is conceived of as a large-scale, utility-maximizing egoist and cannot recognize the distinction between persons, either morally or legally.[90] A utilitarian does not therefore view each person as an individual endowed with *inalienable rights*. But Bentham believed that utilitarianism did not lead to a violation of elementary human rights, because he trusted that any such violation would result in a decline in social utility. Here, too, he based his assumptions on the law of diminishing marginal

---

[86] Kersting, *Einführung*, p. 101.

[87] Cf. Höffe, *Ethik*, pp. 45 f.

[88] See Sect. 9.4.3.

[89] Hottinger, p. 277.

[90] Cf. Kersting, *Einführung*, p. 102.

utility: if an individual has a certain amount of existential happiness taken away, the value of the individual's loss would not be balanced out by awarding that happiness to another individual who is already happy.[91]

The catch in this argumentation is that it does not completely solve the problem of the violation of fundamental rights. It impossible to say with certainty that there will never be cases where it would indeed pay off, in terms of the utility gained by other members of society, to violate one individual's fundamental rights. It follows that it would be permissible to oppress or discriminate against minorities – even to the extent of infringing elementary human rights – as long as this improved things for the majority and increased the sum of collective happiness. A society built on slavery or feudalism, a police state or a military state would be not only permissible but even morally justified – as long as it maximized welfare – even if it entailed extreme intrusion into the freedom of individual citizens, or extreme economic and social inequalities.[92]

Act utilitarianism even permits the killing of an innocent person, in some circumstances, if this increases social welfare. As an example, consider a case from the southern states of the USA in which a black man was condemned to death although the court knew him to be completely innocent of the crime of which he was accused. Only thus was it possible to restrain an angry white mob from attacking a black settlement and killing numerous people. On balance, collective utility was positive: many people were saved with the sacrifice of one innocent person.[93]

The maxim of the end supposedly justifying the means is a self-evident fact for utilitarians. This applies equally to 'means' such as lies, breach of trust and fraud; and indeed torture and murder. Social welfare must be maximized by carrying out the felicific calculus, however dire the situation.[94] In response to this stock objection, some modern advocates of utilitarianism assert that rule utilitarianism produces no such untenable results. The rule that even the innocent may be punished if necessary would make everyone so afraid of being punished without due cause that rational planning of life would be rendered practically impossible. Overall, this would engender more harm than utility, so there are also utilitarian grounds for arguing that innocent people should not be punished. But in no way does this dispose of the main shortcoming of utilitarianism. In reality, there are many conceivable cases in which the regular punishment of innocents would increase overall social utility: for example, the unjust punishment of an excluded minority.[95] While cases like that may well be rare, they are significant enough that they cannot simply be ignored in the hope that they will never actually arise.

The cardinal weakness of utilitarianism goes back to its subordination of the 'right' to the 'good', i.e., the subjugation of law, justice and human dignity to

---

[91] Hottinger, pp. 275 f.

[92] Höffe, *Ethik*, p. 45.

[93] Seelmann, pp. 187 f.

[94] Kersting, *Einführung*, p. 98.

[95] Seelmann, p. 188.

considerations of usefulness. If utilitarianism really wants to avoid this problem, it must relativize its cardinal principle of utility with superordinate principles of justice.[96] According to the prevailing intuition of justice, the idea of justice demands that every individual must be sacrosanct, and this may not violated even in the endeavour to maximize social welfare. This was Sidgwick's reason for introducing the principle of fairness as a corrective principle to utilitarianism. Rawls built upon that same fundamental principle of fairness in developing his theory of justice.[97]

---

[96] Kersting, *Einführung*, pp. 101 ff.

[97] Höffe, *Ethik*, p. 45.

# Chapter 7
# John Rawls's Theory of Justice

> *Justice is the first virtue of social institutions [...]. Each*
> *person possesses an inviolability founded on justice that even*
> *the welfare of society as a whole cannot override.*[1]

## 7.1 Introduction

John Rawls's *theory of justice* is an attempt to reconcile calculated self-interest with basic rights. In order to define generally consensual principles of justice, in his *A Theory of Justice* (1971) Rawls goes back to classical theories of the *social contract*. He makes reference to Locke and, most particularly, to Rousseau and Kant but not to Hobbes, whose sovereignty theory he rejects.[2] However, Rawls is concerned not with the question of how to legitimize power but with how to shape a state in accordance with the principle of justice. The leitmotif of his theory is *justice as fairness*.

Rawls's approach is interdisciplinary: in making use of economic choice theory, he combines ethics with the methods and concepts of economics.[3] He maintains that principles of justice can be derived on the basis of rational self-interest. However, Rawls believes that this can only take place in a special situation of choice which is characterized by equality and freedom. He assumes a rational, self-interested person but introduces into his thought experiment a *veil of ignorance*: the parties in the original condition do not know what position in society they will occupy. Therefore they are forced to envisage themselves in every possible social role. The goal of Rawls's conception is to create an institutional framework for a pluralistic society, which is justified in terms of contract theory, founded on a basis of consensus, and which protects citizens in their basic rights but, beyond that, allows them to decide freely how to arrange their lives and which goals to pursue. Moreover, Rawls augments his liberal model with the dimension of the social state.[4]

In his later works, 'Political Liberalism' (1993) and 'Justice as Fairness – A Restatement' (2001), Rawls considers that in retrospect it was a mistake to have

---

[1] Rawls, *TJ*, p. 3.

[2] Höffe, *Rawls*, p. 18.

[3] Höffe, *Rawls*, pp. 7 f.

[4] Höffe, *Rawls*, p. 6.

K. Mathis, *Efficiency Instead of Justice?*, Law and Philosophy Library 84,
DOI 10.1007/978-1-4020-9798-0_7, © Springer Science+Business Media B.V. 2009

designated his approach to justification as a part of rational choice theory,[5] thereby creating the impression that his theory was founded on a Hobbesian understanding of the social contract. For this reason, Rawls no longer describes people in the original position merely as '*rational*' but also as '*reasonable*'. According to Rawls, individuals have the ability to form, verify and rationally pursue a conception of goodness. Given that they also possess a sense of justice, their relationship to society's conception of justice is one of responsibility:

> [W]hat should have been said is that the account of the parties, and of their reasoning, uses the theory of rational choice (decision), but that this theory is itself part of a political conception of justice, one that tries to give an account of reasonable principles of justice. There is no thought of deriving those principles from the concept of rationality as the sole normative concept.[6]

Rawls takes up this distinction between 'rational' and 'reasonable' from the work of W. M. Sibley. Sibley states that when reasonable people make decisions, the consequences of the decision for others are a relevant consideration:

> (1) Knowing that a man is rational, we do not know what ends he will aim at in his conduct; we know only that, whatever they are, he will use intelligence in pursuing them. (2) Knowing, however, that a man is disposed to act reasonably, where others are concerned, we may infer that he is willing to govern his conduct by a principle of equity, from which he and they can reason in common; and also that he will admit data concerning the consequences of his proposed actions upon their welfare as per se relevant to his decisions. This disposition is neither derived from, nor opposed to, the disposition to be rational. It is, however, incompatible with egoism; for it is essentially related to the disposition to act morally.[7]

Reasonableness, for Rawls, ensures that people have a definite reciprocal relationship which enables them to interact with one another fairly:

> Reasonable persons, we say, are not moved by the general good as such but desire for its own sake a social world in which they, as free and equal, can cooperate with others on terms all can accept. They insist that reciprocity should hold within that world so that each benefits along with others.[8]

The upshot is that the parties behind the veil of ignorance are interested in fair cooperation *to the advantage of all*.


## 7.2  Justice as the First Virtue of Social Institutions

In keeping with the philosophical tradition going back to Plato and Aristotle, Rawls places *justice above all other virtues*: thus, the 'right' comes before the 'good'. Rawls challenges teleological concepts of ethics, and specifically utilitarianism, an

---

[5] Rawls, *JF*, § 23.3, p. 82 n. 2.

[6] Rawls, *JF*, § 23.3, p. 82 n. 2.

[7] Sibley, p. 560.

[8] Rawls, *PL*, p. 50.

approach which strives for the greatest possible happiness for the greatest number of people, or the maximum average utility. In its place, he puts forward his own moderately deontological concept. Rawls criticizes utilitarianism – which he himself once supported – because it does not take account of the *distinction between persons* in the sense of their autonomy as individuals:

Utilitarianism does not take seriously the distinction between persons.[9]

Respect for the person, and the principles of justice which express such respect, should not be construed only as a means to an end, but in his view should flow directly into the formation of moral judgements. Furthermore, Rawls is critical that under utilitarianism the distribution of income in itself is of no importance. This equates to *indifference towards issues of distribution*.[10]

The problem of utilitarianism, he argues, is that individual liberty is subordinated to collective welfare. This would mean that slavery or feudalism, class-based and caste societies, indeed even police or military states would not only be acceptable but actually to be welcomed on moral grounds, if the form of society concerned would generate the maximum total or average utility. In an uncompromising rejection of any form of slavery, serfdom or caste system, Rawls views basic *human rights* as universally valid. In his view, personal rights take priority over collective utility,[11] because every person possesses a certain inviolability stemming from justice, which must not be allowed to be overridden, even for the sake of the welfare of society as a whole.[12]

Utilitarians tend to defend themselves with the argument that it is highly unlikely that any infringement of justice would bring about collective advantages. As soon as the existential minimum is secured, they say, interest in personal freedom far exceeds interest in material wealth. Consequently, only in extreme cases can human rights violations, such as restriction of personal liberty, be offset by benefits to the majority.[13] But even if this argument were right, one fundamental difference still remains: for the utilitarian, the institutionalization of basic rights is a question of individual preferences and their aggregation into one total measure of collective utility; in other words an analytical-empirical matter. For Rawls, on the other hand, basic rights are an unconditionally valid, normative precept, which expresses the human need to treat one another not merely as means but as ends in themselves:

[T]he principles of justice manifest in the basic structure of society men's desire to treat one another not as means only but as ends in themselves.[14]

---

[9] Rawls, *TJ*, p. 24.

[10] Kliemt, p. 99.

[11] Höffe, *Rawls*, pp. 15 f.

[12] Rawls, *TJ*, p. 3.

[13] Höffe, *Rawls*, p. 17.

[14] Rawls, *TJ*, p. 156.

Rawls concedes that the utilitarian who correctly applies utilitarian principles can certainly end up advocating institutional state guarantees of basic rights, and will in fact normally do so. His criticism is that utilitarianism only supports respect for the individual in a derivative form: it does not assume the inviolability of the person at the level of judgement formation but, at best, provides a rationale for why individuals should be institutionally endowed with inviolable personal rights. Rawls's disapproval of teleological concepts follows in the liberal, Kantian tradition. He wholly accepts that aspects other than justice, e.g. efficiency or stability, are also necessary for a viable society. While justice cannot be considered a sufficient condition, it is certainly a necessary one and an absolute priority. However efficient and stabilizing laws and institutions may be, if they are unjust they must be changed.[15]

## 7.3  The Thought Experiment

The situation of choice is constructed by Rawls in such a way that a completely de-individualized person defines the principles of justice. Without knowledge of his natural abilities or his place in society, this person will be oriented towards the primary social goods which are significant to everyone. These primary goods denote the non-material and material conditions on which all people depend to live their lives:

> [T]he basic structure of society distributes certain primary goods, that is, things that every rational man is presumed to want. These goods normally have a use whatever a person's rational plan of life.[16]

Rawls lists the following as primary social goods:[17]

(1)  the basic liberties (freedom of thought and liberty of conscience, etc.),
(2)  freedom of movement and the choice of occupation,
(3)  powers and prerogatives of office and positions of responsibility,
(4)  income and wealth,
(5)  and the social bases of self-respect.

Although, according to Rawls, it is the responsibility of individuals how they wish to live their lives, at the same time society has a duty to ensure that everyone has the opportunity to lead a good life, i.e. all members of society must be provided with the liberty and means to pursue their individual life plans. Within this societal framework of a just basic structure, which is guaranteed through the provision of primary goods, the individual life plans themselves are irrelevant as long as they do not conflict with other individuals' life plans.

---

[15] Höffe, *Rawls*, p. 9.
[16] Rawls, *TJ*, p. 54.
[17] Quoted after the list in Rawls, 'Primary Goods', pp. 165 f.; see also Rawls, *TJ*, pp. 54 and 80.

It should also be pointed out that the just institutions need not facilitate all conceivable life plans. An important feature of the primary goods is that they do not depend on the specific preferences and goals of members of society. Just because someone has especially high standards or a preference for luxury goods does not legitimately entitle that person to claim more primary goods. On the contrary, everyone must scale down their claims in the interests of justice, so that this can be realized for the whole of society. According to Rawls, the list of primary goods must therefore be defined *objectively* and must not be left at the mercy of subjective preferences:

> Desires and wants, however intense, are not by themselves reasons in matters of justice. The fact that we have a compelling desire does not argue for the propriety of its satisfaction any more than the strength of a conviction argues for its truth.[18]

### 7.3.1 The Original Position

The 'original position' which Rawls constructs as the setting for the codification of the social contract is not envisaged as a factually possible nor indeed a historical event, but a fictive one; hence it is solely a representational means within the theoretical framework.[19] This is based on a *thought experiment* which serves the purpose of legitimizing a just system of law and government. The aim of Rawls's justification strategy is for the parties to formulate principles of justice so as to express a conception of justice which would be generally accepted in the real world as a well-considered judgement. In Rawls's contract-theoretical approach, the construct of the original position represents an attempt to give the principles of justice a deductive foundation.[20]

### 7.3.2 Anthropological Premisses

Rawls sets certain premises for the parties in the original position as a logical precondition for the generation of the principles of justice. These premises take the form of carefully coordinated conditions and restrictions:[21]

(1) In the original position, the parties have a *consistent system of preferences*. They have rational, long-term life plans, i.e. they have interests which they wish to protect.
(2) In the original position the parties are *mutually disinterested* and not prepared to sacrifice their interests for others. They are not determined by love or hate

---

[18] Rawls, 'Primary Goods', p. 171.

[19] Tugendhat, p. 17.

[20] Rawls, *TJ*, p. 162.

[21] Rawls, *TJ*, pp. 112 ff.

or envy, but rather by the aim of receiving the greatest possible amount of primary goods.

(3)  The parties know the general conditions for the application of justice; they have *general knowledge* about society.

(4)  The parties have a *sense of justice* which is also known to all parties. This should ensure that the principles of justice are understood and can be used as a reference for action.

The restrictions are:

(1)  The parties are subject to the limitation of the *veil of ignorance*, i.e. they do not know any details of their life plans, nor of their attitude to risk, their class, status, position in society or natural talents. The parties are equally unaware of which generation they belong to, which makes them a kind of 'timeless person'.[22]

(2)  Coalitions are not permitted.


## 7.3.3 The Veil of Ignorance

The 'veil of ignorance' is the crucial and wholly original premiss in the construction of this original position. Rawls uses this means to force those concerned to think impartially and to take up a universal point of view. It is a device which he employs successfully to outwit the rational egoists. One could also say that the parties enter into a reversible exchange of roles. Thus, in his proposed theory, Rawls reduces the moral argumentation to a *means-end rational calculus of interests*. However, it must be emphasized that this thought experiment concerns a single individual. Neither an *actual nor a fictive discourse takes place*; the process is purely *monological* and can be carried out mentally by an individual person. It can also be done without the need for the elements of game theory, involving competing yet interdependent decision makers.[23]

To ensure that the decision will not be taken to the advantage of the self or the group, decision-makers are equipped with general knowledge – for instance, matters of economic, social, political or psychological relevance, i.e. sociological knowledge. But this is not complemented with knowledge about the particular external conditions. Individual decision-makers know neither their economic or social position, nor their natural talents and abilities; so, for example, they do not know whether they will live their lives as rich or poor, gifted or mentally handicapped, male or female, black or white. Any special considerations of this nature are omitted from the basis for decision-making. The veil of ignorance gives an operational definition to the core of justice, which is impartiality.[24]

---

[22] Rawls, *TJ*, pp. 118 ff.

[23] Höffe, *Rawls*, p. 22.

[24] Höffe, *Rawls*, p. 20.

### 7.3.4 The Maximin Choice Rule

Of the three forms of rational action – decision-making under certainty, under risk, and under uncertainty – the most difficulties are implicit in the latter option. Whilst a clear decision-making rule exists for decisions under certainty ('maximize your utility') and under risk ('maximize the expected value of your utility'), for decisions under uncertainty – i.e. when even the probabilities of events are unknown – a variety of decision-making criteria are possible. Some of the possibilities are the risk-seeking maximax rule ('maximize the maximal, i.e. the best possible situation') or the risk-averse maximin rule ('maximize the minimal, i.e. the worst possible situation'). These rules come originally from mathematical choice theory. The maximin rule is extremely pessimistic while the maximax rule is extremely optimistic. In the words of Gérard Gäfgen:

> Someone who adheres to the maximax rule will never take out an insurance policy, but will quite probably play the lottery; someone who sticks to the maximin rule will never play the lottery but will gladly take out an insurance policy.[25]

Rawls argues in favour of the maximin rule; he asserts that the parties, facing a rational choice under uncertainty, will compare the alternatives to establish the worst possible outcomes (minima) of each, prior to choosing the least-worst option (the maximal minimum). The assumption is made that the parties in the original position will operate according to this rule in choosing the principles of justice.[26] Rawls thus assumes people in the original position to be particularly *risk averse* – a presupposition about human nature which may be very plausible but for which no further justification is offered.

### 7.3.5 The Four-Stage Sequence

Starting from the original position with the veil of ignorance in full effect, Rawls sets out a *four-stage process*, during which social rules are made increasingly specific in four sequential steps, i.e. the veil of ignorance is successively lifted.[27]

(1) In the first stage, the two *principles of justice* are determined by choice in the original position, under the complete veil of ignorance.[28] All that is known are general facts about sociological theories and the conditions under which justice will be applied.

(2) In the second stage, the parties convene in a constitution-making assembly. The veil of ignorance is partially lifted. As yet, the participants know nothing about individuals but possess theoretical knowledge about their specific society and

---

[25] Gäfgen, p. 383.

[26] Rawls, *TJ*, pp. 132 ff.

[27] Rawls, *TJ*, pp. 130 ff.

[28] On the principles of justice, see Sect. 7.3.7 below.

its members. In the light of this extended knowledge, the parties choose a just *constitution* specifying rules of procedure which should facilitate just and effective laws.

(3) The veil of ignorance is lifted further so that just *legislation* can be codified. The participants should possess the knowledge of the representative legislator, who again knows nothing about his own person. The object of consultations on this level, in particular, is the application of the difference principle (the second principle of justice)[29] in economic and social policy.

(4) In the final stage the veil of ignorance is wholly removed. Everyone now knows all the facts, specifically their particular interests and details of the historical context. The rules are now applied to *concrete instances* as they arise.

## 7.3.6  The Reflective Equilibrium

In the first three stages, the parties go through a revolving thought process until they have arrived at the *reflective equilibrium*. What this means is the following: a formulation of principles, set up hypothetically for theoretical purposes, is tested in a thought experiment to determine its acceptance in the fictive original position. It is constantly modified as necessary, in an iterative process, until it attains complete acceptance.

## 7.3.7  The Two Principles of Justice

In the original position, the individual behind the veil of ignorance decides upon two principles of justice: the liberty principle and the difference principle.[30] The liberty principle is an egalitarian distributive principle with regard to non-material primary goods; the difference principle is a non-egalitarian distributive principle, which takes special account of the least well-off in terms of endowment with primary material goods.

### 7.3.7.1  The First Principle of Justice: The Liberty Principle

According to Rawls's theory, the parties in the original position have a list of conceptions of justice to choose from, and choose the greatest possible liberty as the *first principle*. This states that:

> Each person is to have an equal right to the most extensive total system of equal basic liberties compatible with a similar system of liberty for all.[31]

---

[29] See Sect. 7.3.7.2 below.

[30] Rawls, *TJ*, pp. 130 ff.

[31] Rawls, *TJ*, p. 266.

The *first priority rule* (the priority of liberty) states that the basic liberties can only be limited for the sake of liberty, if less extensive liberty strengthens the overall system of liberties for all, and if less than equal liberty can be accepted by all.[32] Rawls defines and lists the following basic liberties:[33]

- Political liberties (rights to vote and to occupy public office),
- Freedom of speech and assembly,
- Freedom of thought and liberty of conscience,
- Personal liberty (inviolability of the person),
- The right to personal property,
- Protection from arbitrary arrest and imprisonment.

Here, Rawls operates on the following hypotheses:

(1) Such a list can be defined *conclusively*. Liberties which are not contained in this list – by the converse logic – do not enjoy the special priority of the basic liberties.
(2) These basic liberties are equal for all. To that extent, the core of this approach is egalitarian, moderately relativized by the second principle of justice.

Rawls's concept of liberty is centred on political and economic freedom of action. These freedoms together form an overall system.

### 7.3.7.2  The Second Principle of Justice: The Difference Principle

The difference principle states that:

Social and economic inequalities are to be arranged so that they are both:

(a) to the greatest benefit of the least advantaged, consistent with the just savings principle, and
(b) attached to offices and positions open to all under conditions of fair equality of opportunity.[34]

The second principle of justice regulates the distribution of income and assets and the arrangement of organizations in which differences of power and responsibility come to bear. Inequalities are only permissible where they improve the lot of the least advantaged members of society.

The principle applies to the distribution of the primary social and economic goods, a category in which Rawls particularly subsumes the powers and prerogatives of office, income and wealth, and the social bases of people's self-respect. Fundamentally, these primary goods are to be distributed equally, although this requirement may be waived if an inequitable distribution works to every

---

[32] Rawls, *TJ*, p. 266.

[33] Rawls, *TJ*, p. 53.

[34] Rawls, *TJ*, p. 266.

person's advantage and provided that access to the sought-after positions remains open to all.[35]

For application of the difference principle in practice, however, a suitable scale or index is required whereby the different types of primary goods (social opportunities and powers, economic prospects and the social conditions for self-respect) can be aggregated into a single variable. Here Rawls resorts to the simplifying assumption that the various types of primary goods are generally found to correlate positively with one another, and consequently people are either better or worse off on all dimensions of socioeconomic distribution of goods. Having thus simplified the problem, he can use the income distribution ranking as an index because, by his assumption, the other social and economic primary goods will correlate positively with this.[36]

Finally, it should be pointed out that the *just saving principle* also features as a constraint within the difference principle. Rawls thereby brings into play not only *intra*generational but also *inter*generational justice. When it comes to intergenerational justice, saving fulfils a very important function: the accumulation of a real capital stock serves the purpose of establishing and maintaining a *just system over time*. Rawls's definition of capital is not limited to mechanical capital, such as industrial plant and machinery, but also extends to intellectual and cultural assets.[37] Once the necessary capital base has been accumulated to establish the just basic structure, the real saving rate can drop to zero:

> Real saving is required only for reasons of justice: that is, to make possible the conditions needed to establish and to preserve a just basic structure over time. Once these conditions are reached and just institutions established, net real saving may fall to zero.[38]

Hence Rawls makes a clear distinction between inter- and intragenerational justice, and expressly refuses to apply the difference principle to the question of justice between generations.

> The principle of just saving holds between generations, while the difference principle holds within generations.[39]

Therefore the just saving principle cannot be defined such that the worst off gain the greatest advantage. For as a consequence of such an approach, insufficient savings would be made, or indeed none at all.[40] If the difference principle were applied to the intergenerational relationship, it would actually prohibit the earlier generation from suppressing its own consumption in order to facilitate higher consumption by

---

[35] Koller, pp. 49 f., Rawls *TJ*, pp. 53 f.

[36] Koller, pp. 59 f., Rawls, *TJ*, p. 83.

[37] Rawls, *TJ*, p. 256.

[38] Rawls, *JF*, § 49.2, p. 159.

[39] Rawls, *JF*, § 49.2, p. 159.

[40] Hübner, p. 43.

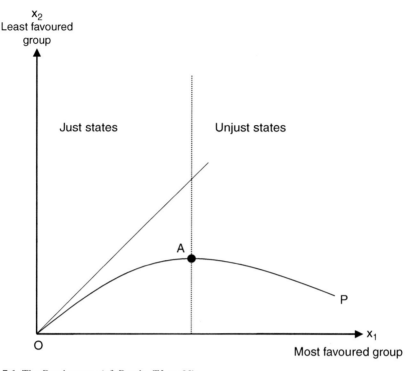

**Fig. 7.1** The Rawls curve (cf. Rawls, *TJ*, p. 66)

the next generation.[41] For Rawls, that outcome would be unacceptable since it would lead to the stagnation rather than the improvement of social conditions.[42]

Rawls attempted to represent the difference principle graphically (known as the 'Rawls curve').[43] In Fig. 7.1, $x_1$ represents the prospective income of an individual from the most advantaged social group and $x_2$ the prospective income of an individual from the least advantaged group. Point O is the starting point at which primary social goods, and particularly income, are distributed equally. Income could now, theoretically, be raised – e.g. progressing from the basic allocation along the bisector of the angle – on the egalitarian principle, to the equal advantage of both representative individuals.[44] Rawls, however, assumes a curve OP which passes below the bisector and climbs initially, but then reaches a maximum and begins to fall. The positive slope means a simultaneous increase in both incomes, $x_1$ and $x_2$, which

---

[41] Reuter, p. 186.

[42] On justice between the generations in Rawls, see Mathis: 'Future Generations in John Rawls's Theory of Justice'.

[43] Rawls, *TJ*, pp. 66 ff.

[44] Which would be unrealistic because of the incentive effects; see Sect. 9.4.3.

Rawls puts down to the advantages of social cooperation.[45] But social and economic cooperation is only advantageous to both individuals up to point A. Beyond that point, the worst-off individual loses income again. According to the difference principle, only movement along OA can be described as just, with A representing the 'perfectly just' situation. The states along AP are unjust because they are not consistent with the difference principle.

The first and second principles of justice are not coordinate; hence, from a formal point of view alone, a further principle is required, namely a criterion for resolving conflicts between the two principles. As mentioned before, Rawls ascribes absolute priority to the first principle of justice under the *first priority rule*. Since liberty is deemed the utmost human good, it may not be traded off against other goods. Restriction of basic rights in return for individual or collective economic benefits is unjust in every case.[46] Rights to liberty may only be restricted to satisfy other competing rights to liberty – the exception being where such a restriction is necessary in order to bring about a change in the overall level of civilization, so as to give everyone the benefit of such liberties within a foreseeable period of time.[47] Here a *utilitarian momentum* enters into the theory. Improving the level of civilization is actually a collective interest, for which individual interests may in this case be sacrificed.[48]

For the second principle of justice, the *second priority rule* applies (the priority of justice over productivity and standard of living). The rule states that productivity and utility maximization (principle 2a) are subordinate to fair equality of opportunity (principle 2b).[49]

## 7.4 Critique

Rawls's *Theory of Justice* is one of the most significant works of political philosophy of the twentieth century. According to Hart:

> No book of political philosophy since I read the great classics of the subject has stirred my thoughts as deeply as John Rawls's *A Theory of Justice*.[50]

John Chapman points out Rawls's success in combining simplicity and complexity:

> Rawls's theory has both the simplicity and the complexity of a gothic cathedral.[51]

---

[45] This is often referred to as the 'trickle down effect', which means that if the rich have plenty on their table, more scraps will drop down for the poor.

[46] Höffe, *Rawls*, p. 12.

[47] Rawls, *TJ*, pp. 474 ff.

[48] Höffe, *Rawls*, p. 12.

[49] Rawls, *TJ*, pp. 266 f.

[50] Hart, 'Liberty', p. 223.

[51] Chapman, p. 588.

Naturally, Rawls's theory has also encountered a good deal of criticism. Libertarian[52] critics such as Robert Nozick or James M. Buchanan find Rawls's concept of society too interventionist.[53] For communitarians[54] (Michael Sandel, Benjamin Barber, Michael Walzer and Alasdair MacIntyre among others), Rawls's theory is too liberal, on the one hand, because it puts too little emphasis on community, and too abstract on the other,[55] a point of criticism also voiced particularly by Seyla Benhabib. The most frequent points of criticism are set out briefly below.

## 7.4.1 Anthropological Premisses

Michael Sandel is offended at Rawls's tacit assumption of certain *anthropological premisses* in his argumentation. This refers to the fact that the subject only figures as a featureless, isolated being – an 'unencumbered self'.[56] Alasdair MacIntyre describes Rawls's original position as a meeting of castaways who have been shipwrecked on an uninhabited island and afflicted by collective amnesia.[57]

Criticism of the view of man which underlies liberal political theories is as old as liberal political theory itself. Forst makes the following pertinent comment:

> Since Hobbes conceived of people "as if they had just emerged from the earth like mushrooms and grown up without any obligation to each other", since he extricated humankind from the Aristotelian-scholastic ethical universe and thus prepared the way for liberalism, the latter has been confronted with the accusation of atomism. This criticism is directed particularly against liberal state contract theory. [. . .] As to whether man has to be presented as a "zoon politicon" within an ethically all-embracing "polis", or as a virtuous political "citoyen", as part of an "objective spirit" of the morality of a nation, or as a member of a social class in a particular historical situation, different tendencies in the criticism of liberalism differ – but what all these critiques have in common is that the "liberal self" is understood as an abstract, artificial product of a theory which is concerned with the defence of individual rights and which, to this end, elevates the independent individual to the normative focal point.[58]

---

[52] In America, 'libertarians' are liberals who support a night-watchman state with an emphasis of the classic rights of liberty, in the sense of defensive rights of the citizen vis à vis the state. Rawls is not a libertarian but a 'liberal', a social liberal.

[53] Kukathas and Pettit, pp. 74 ff.

[54] 'Communitarianism' is a collective term for various modern critics of liberalism. The communitarian movement grew up in America in the 1980s and emphasizes the value of an intact, solidarity-based and moral community. A distinction is made between progressive and conservative communitarians.

[55] Kukathas and Pettit, pp. 92 ff.

[56] Sandel, p. 24.

[57] MacIntyre, pp. 232 f. According to Rawls, the parties in the original position do not know who they are, but are privy to general knowledge about society. In reality, the situation would more likely be the other way round.

[58] Forst, p. 20.

Sandel argues precisely in this tradition, namely that a concept of the human individual must be mistaken if it envisions people as independent of all value convictions and free of any intersubjective attachment. Obviously, as subjects, we are always influenced by intersubjectively acquired value orientations, so it is implausible to assume ethically neutral, unsituated individuals.[59] This criticism can be countered, however, with the argument that the autonomous self is not meant ontologically but normatively. Forst elaborates:

> That the self is there "before" its goals is [. . .] to be understood *normatively* and not *ontologically* (as Sandel believes): there is no ethical value which would objectively and universally have priority over deontological norms, which is why these norms form a framework for possible conceptions of the good.[60]

Therefore Rawls's conception reflects an individualistic view of society, which is not neutral towards different political views and individual plans for life. Rawls relativizes this objection with the argument that the general realization of justice is, in itself, a community value as well.[61] He wants social cooperation to be understood as a system of mutual enrichment and realization. Since this takes place within the framework of justice, he claims, justice per se is a constitutive element of this common endeavour.[62]

By conceiving of the person in his later writings as *reasonable* rather than merely *rational*, Rawls definitively rebuts the charge that his human being is isolated from society. Since reasonable people always consider the impacts of their actions on others, on the very basis of this characteristic they are in a normative relationship with one another.

## 7.4.2  The Veil of Ignorance

Rawls uses the veil of ignorance to mask all traces of individuality, and arrives at a universal, moral, impartial subject. With this device he creates a new 'moral point of view'.[63] However, Seyla Benhabib doubts that Rawls's original position can form the starting point for a just society: in her opinion, the undelineated person behind the veil of ignorance cannot be a proper person at all. Most importantly, this being would not be capable of taking in the other person's point of view, she argues, because there is no distinction between the self and the other. Benhabib replaces the generalized other with the concrete other: to understand the other, one needs to know more – not less – about him. In her view, one cannot judge morally relevant situations without reference to knowledge about the history, character traits, desires and behaviours of the parties involved.[64] An element of artificiality thus

---

[59] Sandel, pp. 24 ff.

[60] Forst, p. 25.

[61] Rawls, *TJ*, p. 464.

[62] Forst, p. 27.

[63] Höffe, *Rawls*, pp. 21 f.

[64] Benhabib, pp. 180 ff.

attaches to Rawls's theory of justice: the parties are only apparently impartial, for they are simply incapable of thinking and acting morally, as real people. And they are certainly not conscious of any deontological obligation to be impartial.

### 7.4.3 The Maximin Choice Rule

In accordance with the maximin rule as a principle of choice under uncertainty, the parties in the original position are supposed to choose a social order in which they could still expect great advantages even if they had to live at the very bottom of the social and economic hierarchy. But the maximin rule is neither rationally derived nor really plausible. Although everyone might be expected to have an interest in a social existential minimum, the idea that this minimum could be maximized is only intuitive if the assumed attitude to life is pessimistic and risk-averse.[65] Benjamin Barber believes that the maximin rule cannot be explained by rational behaviour, but is rather the expression of Rawls's presupposition that individuals in the original position are psychologically predisposed towards certainty:

> Rawlsian man in the original position is [. . .] unwilling to enter a situation that promises success because it also promises failure, unwilling to risk winning because he feels doomed to losing, ready for the worst because he cannot imagine the best, content with security and the knowledge he will be no worse off than anyone else because he dares not risk freedom and the possibility that he will be better off – all under the guise of "rationality".[66]

Yet Barber does not consider risk-seeking people to be irrational. He believes that there are at least some individuals in the original position who would choose an unlikely chance of wealth and power, even if this meant risking hunger and death.[67] In summary, it can be said that it is not rational choice in itself which ensures that the parties in the original condition opt for the difference principle, but the assumption of risk aversion.

### 7.4.4 The Reflective Equilibrium

Rawls does not attempt to provide an ultimate justification for his theory. According to Hans Albert, everyone who endeavours to find an ultimate justification ends up in the *Münchausen trilemma*: one has the choice between an infinite regression – i.e. going back further and further in search of reasons, which is not practically feasible – or a deduction based on circular logic, which arises because the justification process relies on statements which appear to require justification themselves. A third possibility is that one decides to break off the process at a certain point (e.g. by determining axioms). An ultimate justification is thus excluded.[68]

---

[65] Höffe, *Rawls*, p. 21.

[66] Barber, p. 299.

[67] Barber, pp. 297 f.

[68] Albert, *Kritische Vernunft*, p. 13.

Rawls uses the reflective equilibrium in order to avoid the ultimate justification problem. Regardless of that, the question arises as to whether the concept of the reflective equilibrium permits positive decisions to be reached at all, or whether it only helps to eliminate inadequate proposals. According to Höffe, it is a negative method that is not suitable for distinguishing the positive merits of particular proposals.[69]

## 7.4.5 The Monological Model

An analysis which competes with Rawls's theory of justice is the discourse ethics of Jürgen Habermas and Karl-Otto Apel, according to which it is fundamentally possible to justify moral judgements rationally in practical discourse. The participants in discourse have no choice but to assume an ideal discourse situation in which everyone is allowed to participate equally and speak freely. The decisive difference between Rawls's theory of justice and Habermas's and Apel's discourse ethics is that the theory of justice is monological, as opposed to the discursive principle which applies in practical discourse. So it is not sufficient for one individual to reflect on whether everyone could agree to certain norms; for that matter, it is not even sufficient for every single person to reflect on these matters privately. Only when a real exchange of arguments takes place will practical discourse arise.[70] The risk with a monological discourse, according to Habermas, is that an individual will consider his own reflections to be generally applicable.[71]

## 7.4.6 Universalism

Value relativists, who regard different moral ideas as having equal value and equal merit, object to the ethnocentrism of universalistic theories: purportedly universal theories are usually based on the moral codex of a particular civilization. Rawls's theory of justice is indeed tailored to Western democracies. The problem, as Benbahib sees it, is that a justification of morality which defines itself solely as a method for testing and generating moral rules either has so few premises that its actual premises are trivial, or the said justification has to rely on substantial premises so that the methods are no longer purely formal but are already based on normative stipulations. Therefore Benhabib proposes that normative premises should be declared openly and, conversely, all-embracing claims to universality should be abandoned.[72]

---

[69] Höffe, *Rawls*, pp. 24 f.

[70] Ott and Mathis, p. 215.

[71] Habermas, pp. 77 f.

[72] Benhabib, pp. 42 ff.

In his later book, 'Political Liberalism', Rawls addresses this critique and emphasizes that his theory is to be viewed in the context of Western democratic societies:

> [I]t is a moral conception worked out for a specific kind of subject, namely, for political, social, and economic institutions. In particular, it applies to what I shall call the "basic structure" of society, which for our present purposes I take to be a modern constitutional democracy.[73]

With this pronouncement, Rawls definitively gives up any claim to universality for his theory of justice.

## 7.4.7 The Liberty Principle

Since the first principle of justice places the priority on basic liberties, an important preliminary decision has been made: basic liberties have priority over improving the material living situation. Accordingly, citizens can never 'trade in' certain freedoms in return for a higher standard of living. But this is not necessarily the case: whilst it is quite plausible that nobody will want to be enslaved, it can equally be assumed that some politically disengaged citizens would willingly relinquish their political rights in return for a more luxurious life. On this point, Hart says:

> It might be merely that some men, perhaps a majority, perhaps even all, in a society might wish to surrender certain political rights the exercise of which does not appear to them to bring great benefits, and would be willing to let government be carried on in some authoritarian form if there were good reasons for believing that this would bring a great advance in material prosperity.[74]

In the Kantian tradition, Rawls makes a preliminary decision to favour liberty. In fact, the priority of liberty is not a compelling outcome of the situation of choice in the original position but more of a normative premiss, tacitly assumed by Rawls.[75]

## 7.4.8 The Difference Principle

The difference principle demands that 'the least advantaged' group should be identified and that their prospects should be maximized. But how can this group be determined? No cardinal measure of utility can be theoretically defined in order to enable interpersonal comparisons.

The problem is that various socioeconomic primary goods, such as social opportunities and powers, economic prospects and the social conditions for self-respect, are decisive for the application of the difference principle. Rawls does not, however, develop an overall index for these primary goods because it presents him

---

[73] Rawls, *PL*, p. 11.

[74] Hart, 'Liberty', p. 244.

[75] Hart, 'Liberty', p. 247.

with difficult methodological problems. To get around the problem of weighing the different primary goods and that of cardinal comparisons of utility, he makes the simplifying assumption that the various primary goods correlate positively with one another, i.e. someone who has more income will automatically have more self-respect or better health than someone with less income. In effect, Rawls is using the income of the people concerned as a yardstick. However, this is a questionable standard since it neglects other important aspects.[76]

Moreover, Amartya Sen criticized the difference principle in relation to the definition of an objective index of primary goods.[77] Sen's point is that this objective view fails to do justice to people's needs.

> If people were basically very similar, then an index of primary goods might be quite a good way of judging advantage. But, in fact, people seem to have very different needs varying with health, longevity, climatic conditions, location, work conditions, temperament, and even body size (affecting food and clothing requirements).[78]

For example, one problem is that people do not all need an equal amount of medical care. Yet under the difference principle, a disabled person would not be entitled to more.[79] Given the objective nature of the index of primary goods, clearly individual preferences have no part to play. The original idea behind this was to exclude preferences for expensive luxuries, but by the same token, it also affects people who rely on special provision, e.g. for particular medical needs. Sen believes this justification to be questionable, arguing that this view leads to unacceptable cases of hardship.[80] In 'Justice as Fairness – A Restatement' (2001) Rawls engages with Sen's critique once more and indicates that in the original position, the primary goods would not yet have been specified in detail. Adjustments would be possible at the stage of legislation and adjudication, at which time due regard could be given to particular circumstances:

> The further specification of those rights and liberties is left to the constitutional, legislative, and judicial stages as more information is made available, and particular social conditions can be taken into account. In outlining the general form and content of basic rights and liberties, we must make their special role and central range of application sufficiently clear so that at each later stage the process of specification is guided in a suitable way.[81]

These relativizations are hardly convincing for Sen, who even finally accuses Rawls of a certain fetishism in his concept of primary goods, which fails to take account of the relationship between people and goods:

---

[76] Bausch, p. 111.

[77] Sen, 'Equality', pp. 213 ff.; Rawls, JF, § 51.1, p. 168.

[78] Sen, 'Equality', pp. 215 f.

[79] Sen, 'Equality', p. 215.

[80] Sen, 'Equality', p. 215.

[81] Rawls, JF, § 51.5, p. 172.

Indeed, it can be argued that there is, in fact, an element of "fetishism" in the Rawlsian framework. Rawls takes primary goods as the embodiment of advantage, rather than taking advantage to be a relationship between persons and goods.[82]

Sen offers his 'capabilities approach' as an alternative to the concept of primary goods. He does not simply ask what goods or resources a person possesses (in the manner of Rawls and, for example, Dworkin[83]) or how satisfied someone is (as is the case in utilitarianism). Sen is far more concerned with analysing the position and value of goods and resources for human life, by asking what capabilities a person possesses and what he or she can do with them.[84]

Furthermore, the difference principle only demands that the worst-off should be among those who benefit from any advantages. Beyond that, it does not regulate the criteria for just distribution of total income. Theoretically, the difference principle permits disparities in income on any conceivable scale.[85] Distribution effects which impact on any other than the least advantaged group are not taken into consideration, as is shown by the following example (Table 7.1) of income distribution in a society with three groups.[86]

According to the difference principle, state B is preferable to state A because the worst-off group, group 3, benefits from the growth in social income. However, group 3's small gain in income is outweighed by group 2's greater income loss. Equally, there is now a greater disparity between groups 1 and 3 and between groups 1 and 2. The problem of the difference principle, therefore, is that it focuses one-sidedly on the welfare of the worst-off group in society instead of considering income distribution as a whole.[87]

Here, too, Rawls makes an optimistic assumption: he assumes that the prospects of the various groups improve evenly in the course of economic development.[88] This assumption bears very little relation to empirical reality, however: experience shows that economic progress creates winners and losers, and is a sociopolitical bone of contention for that very reason. The difference principle only decrees that the worst off must gain from it, but does not prohibit losses from being incurred by other groups.

**Table 7.1** Three groups in society undergo a change in income distribution from state A to state B

|         | Group 1 | Group 2 | Group 3 | Total |
|---------|---------|---------|---------|-------|
| State A | 100     | 80      | 60      | 240   |
| State B | 127     | 62      | 61      | 250   |

---

[82] Sen, 'Equality', p. 216.

[83] See Ronald Dworkin: *Sovereign Virtue*.

[84] See Amartya Sen: *Inequality Reexamined*.

[85] Bausch, pp. 128 f.

[86] Cf. Schernikau, p. 133.

[87] Schernikau, pp. 133 f.

[88] Rawls, *TJ*, pp. 69 f.

# Part III
# Wealth, Efficiency and Justice

# Chapter 8
# Richard Posner's Theory of Wealth Maximization

*The idea that law should attempt to promote and facilitate competitive markets and to simulate their results in situations in which market-transaction costs are prohibitive – the idea that I call "wealth maximization" – has affinities with both Kantian and utilitarian ethics: with the former, because the approach protects the autonomy of people who are productive [. . .]; with the latter, because of the empirical relation between free markets and human welfare.*[1]

## 8.1 Introduction

Richard Allen Posner (*1939) is the figurehead of the economic analysis of law movement and one of its major pioneers. As Coase notes:

> In the development of the economic analysis of the law [. . .] Posner has clearly played the major role.[2]

Unlike most other representatives of this movement, who come from the discipline of economics, Posner is a lawyer. He has been a professor at the University of Chicago Law School since 1969, and was appointed a United States federal judge in 1981. He has published a multitude of books and over a hundred articles, mainly on the economic analysis of law.[3]

The extraordinary aspect of Posner's work, and its major claim to distinction, is his intensive scrutiny of the philosophical foundations of the economic analysis of law. He developed the concept of *wealth maximization* which was to form the value foundation for economic analysis. Although – as we shall see – the concept is not particularly persuasive, it yields many insights into the logic of the efficiency mindset – excruciating though this can be, at times! – whilst also demonstrating the limitations of economic analysis of law.

---

[1] Posner, *Overcoming Law*, pp. 403 f.

[2] Coase, 'Law and Economics', p. 251.

[3] Gray, p. 665.

K. Mathis, *Efficiency Instead of Justice?*, Law and Philosophy Library 84,
DOI 10.1007/978-1-4020-9798-0_8, © Springer Science+Business Media B.V. 2009

## 8.2 Overview

In his textbook, *Economic Analysis of Law* (1972), Posner devoted little thought to the philosophical foundations of economic analysis of law. He believed their normative foundations to be rooted in utilitarianism (first phase).

In his essay 'Utilitarianism, Economics, and Legal Theory' (1979), for the first time Posner outlines the concept of *wealth maximization* as an ethical principle, and in this way attempts to disassociate himself from utilitarianism. He cites efficiency as the sole legal principle (second phase).

At the beginning of the 1980s, Posner tries to bolster his ethic of wealth maximization by justifying it in terms of *consensus theory*. Invoking the concept of ex ante compensation, he constructs a hypothetical consensus to supplement the Kaldor-Hicks criterion (third phase).

By the mid-1980s Posner begins to relativize his positions, and thus paves the way for a transition towards the *pragmatism* that he has advocated since the 1990s. He now sees efficiency as an important legal principle, but not necessarily the only one (fourth phase).

## 8.3 Utilitarianism

In the first edition of *Economic Analysis of Law*, in the introductory chapter which only runs to eight pages, Posner does not explicitly comment on the normative foundations of economic analysis of law. He merely gives a summarized description of the method adopted for the economic approach. At the beginning of Chapter 25, 'Legal Sanctions and Crime Control', however, Posner does make a link between economic theory and Bentham's utilitarianism: he states that the usual justification for punishment of criminals by the state is the idea of deterrence, a rationale for punishment which was advanced by Jeremy Bentham as an application of his general theory of human behaviour. According to Bentham, humans were rational maximizers of their own satisfaction, and would therefore desist from actions which caused them more pain than pleasure. Crimes could thus be prevented by threatening perpetrators with a punishment, the pain of which would exceed the pleasure resulting from the perpetration of the crime.[4] Posner draws the following conclusion:

> Bentham's utilitarianism, in its aspect as a positive theory of human behaviour, is another name for economic theory. Pleasure is value and pain is cost.[5]

H. L. A. Hart inferred from this that the economic analysis of law was founded on utilitarian values:

---

[4] Posner, *EAL 1*, p. 357.

[5] Posner, *EAL 1*, p. 357.

> [U]tilitarianism is quite explicitly acknowledged as the inspiration of the contemporary Chicago-bred school of the economic analysis of law [. . .].[6]

Later Posner regretted that he had not clearly distinguished between his normative theory and utilitarianism.

> [U]ntil recently I have insufficiently distinguished between the two systems of thought [. . .].[7]

At the time of the first edition, Posner had not yet apparently formed the intention of disassociating himself from utilitarianism. He evidently believed that some form of utilitarianism was indeed the normative basis of economic theory. At that time, he had not yet developed his normative concept of wealth maximization.

## 8.4   Wealth Maximization as an Alternative to Utilitarianism

In 'Utilitarianism, Economics, and Legal Theory' (1979), Posner advocates the concept of 'wealth maximization' as an ethical counter-concept to utilitarianism. Critics, he asserted, were qualifying his theory as a version of utilitarianism, and thereupon attacking utilitarianism. They were probably doing so because they were more familiar with the terminology of philosophy than with that of the social sciences, or because they wanted to exploit the current wave of hostility to utilitarianism. Nevertheless, he claimed, wealth maximization was a better basis for a normative legal theory than utilitarianism:

> The important question is whether utilitarianism and economics are really the same thing. I believe they are not and, further, that the economic norm I shall call "wealth maximization" provides a firmer basis for a normative theory of law than does utilitarianism.[8]

Posner defends the conception developed in 'Utilitarianism, Economics, and Legal Theory' in various other publications during the 1980s.

### 8.4.1   Wealth Maximization

Wealth maximization means that a transaction, or some other change in the use or the ownership of resources, is advantageous if it increases social wealth. In relation to the law, Posner suggests that where transaction costs are prohibitive, i.e. where a voluntary bargaining solution cannot be reached because the costs associated with the exchange of services are too high, the market – the outcome of voluntary transactions – should be simulated *by means of state compulsion.*

---

[6] Hart, 'American Jurisprudence', p. 143.

[7] Posner, 'Utilitarianism', p. 104.

[8] Posner, 'Utilitarianism', p. 103.

This approach attempts to reconstruct the likely terms of a market transaction in circumstances where instead a forced exchange took place – to mimic or simulate the market, in
other words.[9]

The idea is curiously simple yet, at the same time, paradoxical: making use
of state compulsion, the model of voluntary transactions in competitive markets
should be imposed, by analogy, on legal decisions. Should private arrangements fail
to ensure efficiency because transaction costs are prohibitively high, the state will
dispense justice in line with the goal of efficiency and *mimic the market*.[10]

### 8.4.1.1 Wealth

The 'wealth' of a society, according to Posner, is the sum of all tangible and intangible goods, which are valued in monetary terms as follows: either according to
*willingness to pay*, i.e. the maximum price that a potential buyer is willing to pay
for a good, or – in the event that someone already owns the good – according to
the minimum price which would have to be offered to induce the potential seller
to sell.[11]

Wealth is the value in dollars or dollar equivalents [...] of everything in society. It is measured by what people are willing to pay for something, or if they already own it, what they
demand in money to give it up. The only kind of preference that counts in a system of wealth
maximization is thus one that is backed up by money – in other words, that is registered in
a market.[12]

Strictly speaking, the buyer's willingness to pay is actually a *marginal willingness to pay*. Willingness to pay needs to be determined separately for each unit of
a good, since it is not normally constant but declines, in keeping with the law of
*diminishing marginal utility* (Gossen's first law), as the number of units increases.
Marginal willingness to pay is represented by the demand curve on a price-quantity
graph. Conversely, the supply curve shows the prices at which sellers are willing to
sell goods. Normally the quantity offered increases as the price rises, which is why
supply curves normally rise.

### 8.4.1.2 Explicit and Implicit Markets

The market in which goods are valued need not be an explicit one, i.e. goods can also
be traded without making any explicit reference to a monetary price. Particularly in
the private sphere, many goods are exchanged in implicit markets:

Even today, much of economic life is organized on barter principles; the "marriage market",
child rearing, and a friendly game of bridge are some examples. These services have value

---

[9] Posner, *EAL 5*, p. 16.

[10] For the critique of this concept, see Sect. 4.3.4.2.

[11] Cf. Posner, 'Justice', p. 15.

[12] Posner, 'Utilitarianism', p. 119.

which could be monetized by reference to substitute services sold in explicit markets or in other ways.[13]

This also shows that the concept of wealth as defined by Posner bears no relation to concepts such as gross national product or gross domestic product, which are obtained by multiplying the prices of goods by quantities of goods. These units of measurement are only of use for capturing transactions in explicit markets and, what is more, at market prices, which does not tie in with Posner's conception. In his view, implicit markets or 'shadow markets' as well as corresponding 'shadow prices' have to be included in the analysis:

> [R]emember that wealth as used by economists is not an accounting concept; it is measured by what people would pay for things (or demand in exchange for giving up things they possess), not by what they do pay for them. Thus leisure has value and is a part of wealth, even though it is not bought and sold. We can speak of leisure having an implicit or shadow price.[14]

Assuming that one had the choice between working 40 hours a week for €2, 000 or 30 hours for €1, 500. If you choose the second option, it means that the ten extra hours of leisure time are worth more to you than €500; perhaps they are worth €600, for instance. This is still a wealth-maximizing choice, because you are choosing the option which is worth most to you. Or to put if another way: you are 'buying' 10 hours of leisure time for €500, for which you would be prepared to pay €600. Thus both personal and – ceteris paribus – social wealth is increased, and this holds true despite the fact that it reduces gross national product.[15]

A further point to consider is that gross national product and related figures measure monetary flows whereas wealth represents a stock variable.[16] In any case, wealth maximization is not, as a fundamental principle, a pecuniary concept – as is demonstrated, for instance, by implicit markets – even though money is used as the unit of measurement.[17]

### 8.4.1.3  Actual and Hypothetical Markets

In addition to these actual (explicit or implicit) markets, *hypothetical* markets are of central importance for the law. Actual markets are based on voluntary transactions, whereas hypothetical markets come into play in relation to *involuntary* transactions (e.g. when torts are committed). Posner explains this with reference to two situations:[18]

---

[13] Posner, 'Utilitarianism', p. 120.

[14] Posner, *EAL 5*, p. 17.

[15] Cf. Posner, 'Justice', pp. 17 f.

[16] Posner, 'Wealth', p. 93.

[17] Posner, 'Inquiry', p. 101.

[18] Posner, 'Utilitarianism', p. 120.

In the first case, person A offers person B €5 for a bag of oranges, and the latter accepts. It is clear that social wealth has increased as a result of this deal: before the transaction, B had a bag of oranges which were worth less than €5 to him, and A had €5. Afterwards, B has €5 whilst A has the bag of oranges which, to her, are worth more than €5. On Posner's analysis, both are consequently wealthier after the transaction than before it.

In the second case, A does not buy the oranges from B but accidentally destroys them. A court which applies the *Learned Hand formula*[19] of negligence liability would ask itself whether the costs of the accident are greater or less for A than her expected gain from the activity which incidentally gave rise to the accident. In order to answer this question, the court would have to assess how much the oranges were worth to B, and what was the value to A of rushing around carelessly.

Posner admits that the courts can only simulate the market inexactly. Nevertheless he reckons this procedure to be effectual:

> The purist would insist that the relevant values are unknowable since they have not been revealed in an actual market transaction, but I assume that (in many cases anyway) a court can make a reasonably accurate guess as to the allocation of resources that would maximize wealth. Since, however, the determination of value (that is, willingness to pay) made by a court is less accurate than that made by a market, the hypothetical-market approach should be reserved for cases, such as the typical accident case, where market-transaction costs preclude use of an actual market to allocate resources efficiently.[20]

Unlike voluntary transactions, which increase not only social wealth but also utility in the utilitarian sense – otherwise the transaction would never take place –, the model of the hypothetical market always increases social wealth but does not necessarily increase utility in the process. This may be explained by means of the following example:

Let us assume that a factory emitted pollutants which reduced the value of neighbouring properties in a residential area by €2 million in total. This damage could only be alleviated by moving the factory to another location, which would cost €3 million. On the principle of wealth maximization, we would conclude that the factory should not move elsewhere because this would wipe out €1 million of wealth. However, if we switched our attention to utility in the utilitarian sense, we might come to a different conclusion. It is quite conceivable that the neighbours' collective utility gain from the removal of the factory would be greater than the corresponding utility loss which – we assume – would be incurred by the owners of the factory.[21]

With involuntary transactions, one can equally conceive of instances in which the converse applies, and social utility increases but not social wealth. In that case, the model of the hypothetical market is not applicable, as the following example shows:

Let us assume that a poor man decides to steal a diamond necklace for a beautiful woman. Imagine that the necklace has a market value of €10, 000 and is worth

---

[19] See Sect. 4.4.1.7b.

[20] Posner, 'Utilitarianism', p. 120.

[21] Posner, 'Utilitarianism', pp. 120 f.

an equal amount to its present owner, i.e. she would only sell the necklace for a minimum of € 10, 000. Let us assume that the optimum fine for this theft (calculated from the value of the necklace, the probability of catching and sentencing the thief, the court and enforcement costs, etc.) is € 25, 000. Since the penniless thief cannot pay this amount, in utility terms it would correspond to an equivalent of three years' imprisonment. In these circumstances it seems a plausible assumption that the theft increases total social utility (including that of the thief), although the thief cannot pay the fine. For the latter must gain some level of utility from the theft which exceeds society's utility loss as a result of the theft, and which is reflected in the optimum fine. Otherwise the thief would not commit the theft. Social wealth is not increased, however, because the penniless thief could never pay for the necklace. Consequently no hypothetical market can be construed.[22]

It would be different, according to Posner, if someone who had adequate financial resources broke into a closed kiosk and stole food so as not to starve. In this case the model of the hypothetical market can be applied: it can be assumed that, analysed in terms of wealth maximization, the food was of greater value to the thief than to the owner. For the thief would have been able to buy and pay for the food if the kiosk had been open and staffed, i.e. if an actual market had existed.[23]

### 8.4.1.4 Protestant Virtues and the Invisible Hand

Posner believes that wealth maximization is in better concordance with 'our moral intuitions' than utilitarianism. What he means by these moral intuitions are the Protestant virtues:

> [T]he wealth-maximization principle encourages and rewards the traditional virtues ("Calvinist" or "Protestant") and capacities associated with economic process. The capacities (such as intelligence) promote the efficiency with which resources can be employed; the virtues (such as honesty, and altruism in its proper place) by reducing market transaction costs do the same.[24]

Most conventional virtues – expressed in such injunctions as 'promises must be kept' or 'you should always tell the truth' – can be derived from the principle of wealth maximization, according to Posner. His view is that following these rules makes transactions easier because it is a way of lowering transaction costs (e.g. the costs of detailed contract negotiations or court costs). This promotes trade, and consequently it also increases wealth.[25]

Posner proceeds to show why an honest buyer is morally superior to a thief, illustrating this with the example of the necklace:[26] someone who buys the necklace

---

[22] Posner, 'Utilitarianism', p. 121.

[23] Posner, 'Utilitarianism', p. 121.

[24] Posner, 'Utilitarianism', p. 124. This argumentation is similar to Max Weber's, who also sees a connection between the Reformation and economic development.

[25] Posner, 'Utilitarianism', p. 123.

[26] Posner, 'Utilitarianism', pp. 122 f.

for € 10, 000 is morally superior to someone who steals it, because he increases not only his own welfare but also the seller's.[27] Moreover, in all probability, the buyer has earned the € 10, 000 through productive work. This, too, will have benefited other people apart from himself, e.g. employers or customers. Thus, all productive people give more to society than they take from it:

> For, if we assume that a person's income is less than the total value of his production, [...] it follows that the productive individual puts into society more than he takes out of it. Hence not only does the buyer in our example confer a net benefit on the owner of the necklace (who wouldn't accept $10,000.— for it unless it was worth less to her), but at every stage in the accumulation of that money through productive activity net benefits were conferred on other people besides the producer. The thief, in contrast, provides no benefit to the owner of the necklace or to anyone else. He may never have done a productive act in his life.[28]

According to Posner, altruism can be interpreted in the same vein: other people always stand to benefit from a productive person who offers goods and services in markets.[29] Ultimately, then, the whole of society benefits from the diligent individual's profit motive. This argumentation is already familiar in the form of Adam Smith's 'invisible hand'.[30]

The fact that productive work and voluntary transactions in markets always benefit other people besides ourselves brings us to the concept of the 'surplus' as used in welfare economics.

### 8.4.1.5  Consumer and Producer Surplus

Let us assume that person A would be prepared to pay € 1, 000 for person B's stamp collection, which means that € 1, 000 is what it is worth to A. Person B would be prepared to sell the stamp collection for € 800. So, to him, it is worth € 800. If the sale takes place at € 1, 000, B's wealth will increase by € 200, A's will remain the same, and social wealth will rise by € 200.[31] An increase in wealth, in this sense, is equivalent in meaning to an *increase in efficiency*.[32]

Were A and B to agree on a price of € 900, social wealth would still grow by € 200, but this time A and B would each be € 100 richer. The difference between the price a potential buyer would be willing to pay for a unit of goods and the (lower) effective price to be paid is called the 'consumer surplus'. The difference between the minimum price that a potential seller will accept and the (higher) effective price achieved is called the 'producer surplus'. Gains in wealth are nothing other than the 'surpluses' that can be achieved by suppliers and buyers engaging in market transactions.

---

[27] It is not clear here whether utility or wealth is meant here. However, since voluntary Pareto-superior transactions will always increase both, it does not matter.

[28] Posner, 'Utilitarianism', p. 123.

[29] Posner, 'Utilitarianism', pp. 123 f.

[30] See Sect. 5.3.

[31] Cf. Posner, 'Justice', p. 15.

[32] A Pareto improvement if nobody is made worse off, and a Kaldor-Hicks improvement otherwise.

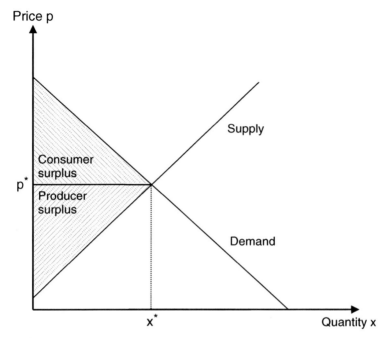

**Fig. 8.1** Consumer and producer surplus

In Fig. 8.1, in a market with multiple sellers and buyers, the aggregate consumer surplus generated by the purchase of quantity $x^*$ at market price $p^*$ corresponds to the triangle above the price line. The triangle below the price line represents the producer surplus generated under the same conditions. For unit quantities exceeding amount $x^*$, both the consumer surplus and the producer surplus would be negative, so such transactions would not be worthwhile for players on either side of the market; they would also tend to diminish social wealth.

Staying with our example, society would also be €200 wealthier if B were forced to make a gift of the stamp collection to A. Whilst this would make B €800 poorer, it would leave A €1,000 richer, which results in a positive balance of €200. If, on the other hand, A were forced to return the stamp collection to B – at whatever price – social wealth would once again fall by €200.

#### 8.4.1.6   Willingness to Pay Determines the Allocation of Resources

As we have seen, then, the transaction price is of no consequence from the point of view of society; *all that matters is that the good is transferred in the 'right' direction*, i.e. to whoever values it the most. Nevertheless, this is no mere appraisal of utility in the utilitarian sense, because of course one must also be in a position to pay for the good if one wishes to acquire it. *According to Posner, a society can only increase its wealth if every resource or every good finds its way to the owner who is, or at least would be, willing to pay the most for it.*[33]

In a market economy, it is voluntary transactions which ensure that goods reach the place where they are of most value, so as to maximize wealth. Such transactions are *Pareto superior* because no-one would voluntarily enter into a transaction which would leave one worse off. Likewise, at the time of the original allocation of resources, Posner believes resources should go to whoever values them most highly. In accordance with the *Coase theorem*, the original allocation of rights makes no difference to efficiency, provided that transaction costs are zero.[34] If one gives up this unrealistic assumption, however, the right to a resource should be allocated to whoever would 'be most likely – if there were no transaction costs – to acquire it anyway. Even rights in one's own person are justified according to this principle:

> It is true that if market transactions were costless, it would be a matter of indifference to the economist where an exclusive right was initially vested. The process of voluntary exchange would costlessly reallocate the right to whoever valued it the most. Once the unrealistic assumption of zero transaction costs is abandoned, however, the assignment of rights becomes determinate [. . .]. If transaction costs are positive, the wealth maximization principle requires the initial vesting of rights in those who are likely to value them the most. [. . .] This is the economic reason for giving a worker the right to sell his labor and a woman the right to determine her sexual partners.[35]

Rights in one's own person should thus be allocated to their 'natural owner', because that person is likely to value them most highly.[36]

### 8.4.1.7  Kaldor-Hicks Efficiency as the Definitive Criterion

The Pareto criterion is not normally applicable, because there will almost always be somebody who will be made worse off by any intervention. In most instances, therefore, economists would expect to use the Kaldor-Hicks criterion.[37] To satisfy the wealth maximization principle, a transaction need be *neither voluntary nor Pareto superior*. It may just as well be *involuntary* provided that it satisfies the *Kaldor-Hicks criterion*, i.e. if the benefit to society would be at least sufficient to enable *hypothetical compensation* of the losers (potential Pareto superiority).[38] Economic policy or the dispensation of justice are specific contexts in which interventions or decisions complying with this criterion are possible. And in such cases, the state is supposed to mimic the market.

---

[33] On Posner's proposal of an 'auction rule' to determine the greatest willingness to pay, see Sect. 3.3.3.2 above.

[34] See Sect. 4.3.

[35] Posner, 'Utilitarianism', p. 125.

[36] Posner, 'Utilitarianism', pp. 125 f.

[37] Posner, *EAL 5*, p. 15.

[38] See Sect. 3.3.

What matters is that the Kaldor-Hicks criterion of hypothetical compensation must always be applied with the intent of wealth maximization. The standard, then, is always wealth as defined by Posner rather than the utilitarianist definition of utility. *Hence, by Posner's definition, wealth maximization and the Kaldor-Hicks criterion are the same thing. Accordingly, a rise in Kaldor-Hicks efficiency always entails an increase in wealth.*[39]

The following example is cited as an illustration of hypothetical compensation in the case of an involuntary transaction:[40]

Let us assume that it would cost person A €1, 000 to prevent an accident which would cause person B to suffer expected damage of €900. For simplicity's sake, the probability of damage is assumed to equal 1, i.e. it is certain to occur.[41] The infliction of damage is not a voluntary transaction between A and B, and nor is it Pareto superior because B's wealth will be reduced as a result. The principle of wealth maximization is nevertheless satisfied, because if A had spent €1, 000 on preventing €900-worth of damage, society would be left €100 the poorer. In keeping with the Kaldor-Hicks criterion, injurer A could compensate victim B for the €900-worth of damage and still have €100 in hand. As we know, however, it is sufficient for A to be able to compensate B; actual compensation is not required.

### 8.4.1.8 Wealth Maximization is Already Anchored in Practice

As this example shows, the *Learned Hand formula* is another rule which corresponds to the Kaldor-Hicks concept. It stipulates that negligence and a concomitant obligation to pay damages will only be found when the expected value of damage exceeds the costs to the injurer of preventing such damage.[42] Thus Posner's principle of wealth maximization coincides with the standard used to determine negligence in the American common law tradition.

However, the principle of wealth maximization also accords with the justification for controlling monopolies under competition law:[43] in Fig. 8.2, under conditions of competition, quantity $x_c$ is sold at price $p_c$. As a result of this transaction, consumer wealth increases by the amount of the triangle above the price line (the consumer surplus) and the suppliers' wealth by the amount of the triangle below the price line (the producer surplus).

If the monopolist wants to maximize profit, he will restrict the amount supplied to $x_m$ so as to achieve the higher price $p_m$. The result is a shift of wealth from consumers to producers (shaded rectangle). This transfer represents a redistribution

---

[39] Naturally wealth can also be increased through Pareto-superior voluntary transactions.

[40] Cf. Posner, 'Justice', p. 16.

[41] This would be equivalent to damage of €9, 000 with a 0.1 probability of occurrence, which produces the same expected value of €900-worth of damage.

[42] On the Learned Hand rule, see Sect. 4.4.1.7b.

[43] Cf. Posner, 'Justice', p. 16.

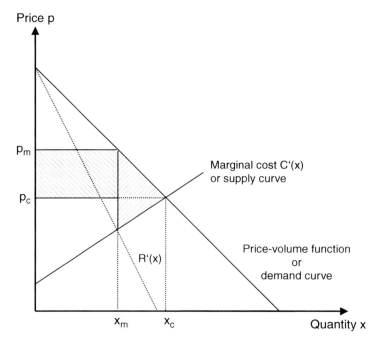

**Fig. 8.2** Comparison of competitive market and supply monopoly

from consumer surplus to producer surplus, and hence it does not – per se – reduce social wealth.[44] However, social wealth is reduced by the amount of the shaded triangle which is called the 'dead weight loss'.[45] This reduction in social wealth comes about because certain consumers are less inclined to buy the product or indeed stop buying it altogether at the higher price, which reduces the consumer surplus; and the monopolist, in turn, is unable to earn income or generate a producer surplus from these unrealized transactions.

If the monopolist is now forced to set competitive prices, or if the monopoly is broken by some other means, the social 'dead weight loss' is eliminated, and social wealth duly rises as shown by the shaded triangle. The monopolist could be compensated for the reduction in his surplus by returning to him the surplus represented by the rectangle, which would still leave a gain in social wealth of the amount shown by the triangle. However, the compensation is only hypothetical and does not actually have to be paid; this in turn satisfies the Kaldor-Hicks criterion.

---

[44] Even so, social wealth can still be diminished, because there is an incentive to deploy resources unproductively for the purpose of building monopolistic positions in order to siphon off profits (known as 'rent seeking').

[45] Another common term is 'welfare loss', but this could cause confusion here because 'welfare' often denotes social utility, and could thus also be a utilitarian category.

## 8.4.2 Comparison with Utilitarianism

What wealth maximization and utilitarianism have in common is that they maximize a certain social value, and do so without regard to its distribution among the individual members of society. However, the maximand is not always the same: utilitarianism maximizes the utility or the happiness of society, whereas wealth maximization maximizes social wealth.[46] It should be noted in this connection that economists often talk about 'utility' when they actually mean 'wealth'. Moreover, according to Posner the correlation between utility in the utilitarian sense and wealth is positive:[47] this would mean that a wealthy person must be a happier one.[48]

Posner takes the view that wealth maximization is based on the same type of consequentialist ethic as utilitarianism but does not exhibit the same weaknesses as utilitarianism. The main difference, he says, is that utilitarianism emphasizes *consumption* whereas wealth maximization emphasizes *production*. For in Posner's view, utilitarianism relies solely on the ability to enjoy utility, which gives no incentive for the kind of productive activity that furthers human civilization. Although leisure time represents a value even under wealth maximization, this has to be 'bought' by abstaining from the income one would otherwise gain from employment.[49] Overall, wealth maximization is geared towards the individual's productive activity:

> I stress the difference between capacity for pleasure and production for others as the key to distinguishing utilitarianism and wealth maximization as ethical systems.[50]

Because there is a more immediate relationship between work and remuneration in a market economy than in a planned economy, Posner asserts, under the conditions of a market system the economy grows more rapidly and prosperity is much greater. *Ultimately wealth maximization promotes the utility of a society far more powerfully than utilitarianism could directly*:

> It seems, then, that wealth maximization is the political principle that utilitarianism needs, if it is to work. For it is apparent that to try to maximize happiness directly – by switching around resources in accordance with varying individual capacities to enjoy them – would lead to poverty and misery in fairly short order, by destroying incentives to work and by setting up hedonism and self-indulgence over frugality and hard work as the qualities that society rewards.[51]

---

[46] Posner, 'Justice', p. 18.

[47] Posner, 'Inquiry', pp. 87 f.

[48] Inhabitants of rich countries do generally seem to be happier than inhabitants of poor countries (on this topic see e.g. Frey and Stutzer (eds.): *Happiness and Economics*; and Frey: *Happiness: A Revolution in Economics*). For individuals, however, it is not necessarily the case that greater wealth correlates with greater happiness. The poor generally become happier when their material situation improves. If they move into the middle class, though, they begin to compare themselves with the rich, which can once again engender dissatisfaction. The definitive factors are thus the *relative position* within society and the *change* in material situation over the course of a lifetime.

[49] Posner, 'Justice', p. 19.

[50] Posner, 'Utilitarianism', p. 104.

[51] Posner, 'Justice', p. 20.

Posner goes on to criticize utilitarianism on a number of other grounds, and underscores the advantages of his own theory:

### 8.4.2.1 The Boundary Problem

Utilitarianism, he asserts, has a boundary problem which is manifested in a variety of ways. The term 'happiness' describes a feeling. Many animals also have feelings, and so logically this fact ought be taken into account in the utilitarian calculus. But Posner finds this problematic:[52]

> Since utility in the broad sense used by contemporary utilitarians is possessed by (many) animals, the inclusion of sheep and pigs seems required by the theory. [...] However, there is something amiss in a philosophical system that cannot distinguish between people and sheep.[53]

Thus, according to Posner, under a utilitarian ethic one could not reproach, for example, a driver who swerved to avoid two sheep at the risk of killing one child, since his conduct potentially increases the sum of happiness in the world. Posner finds this result contradictory to our moral intuitions, however.[54]

Under wealth maximization, he points out, this problem does not arise because only humans participate in market transactions and are capable of demonstrating willingness to pay. In contrast, animals only count indirectly, to the extent that they serve the purpose of increasing wealth. The optimal size of a flock of sheep, for instance, is determined not by the sheep's ability to enjoy utility, argues Posner, but by the point of intersection between the marginal product[55] and marginal cost of keeping sheep.[56]

A boundary problem can arise even when only people are taken into account. For instance, it is not immediately clear whether foreigners or the unborn should be included in the utility calculus. An allied consideration for Posner is the old question of whether average or total utility should be maximized:

> If the poorer half of the population of Bangladesh were killed, the standard of living of the remaining half [...] would rise because of the higher ratio of people to land and other natural resources. However, the total happiness might well be less. Similarly, a high birth rate may cause a reduction in the standard of living of a crowded country and along with it, in the average happiness of the country, but this loss may be more than offset by the satisfactions, even if somewhat meager, of the added population.[57]

The unborn cannot be directly included in wealth maximization because they cannot take part in actual market transactions. It would, however, be conceivable to

---

[52] Posner, 'Justice', p. 19.

[53] Posner, 'Utilitarianism', p. 112.

[54] Posner, 'Utilitarianism', p. 112.

[55] Strictly speaking, this is actually marginal revenue.

[56] Posner, 'Utilitarianism', p. 128.

[57] Posner, 'Utilitarianism', p. 113.

take the unborn into account by invoking the concept of the hypothetical market. One could estimate whether additional population would be economically sustainable. On the one hand, a rise in population could deplete the wealth of a heavily populated region; on the other hand, in a sparsely inhabited country with plenty of resources it could bring about a gain in wealth:

> Productive people put more into society than they take out of it. [...] Hence so long as the additional population is productive, the existing population will benefit.[58]

The same applies to immigrants. Posner advocates free immigration, provided that there is *no entitlement to state support*. Consequently only productive, and hence wealth-enhancing, individuals would become immigrants, and that in turn would benefit the whole of society. As long as all negative externalities associated with the immigrants[59] were internalized, Posner believes, there would be no conflict between maximizing total wealth and average wealth either.[60]

### 8.4.2.2 The Measurement Problem

A further difficulty of utilitarianism, in Posner's view, is the lack of a method for measuring utility. Utility is a subjective matter, he points out, and thus difficult to quantify.[61]

In fact, the only possible measurement is an *intrapersonal, ordinal* comparison of utility by an individual. That is, on the basis of personal preferences, one person can place various states in a rank order of utility but without ascribing to them a precise utility value, which would be necessary in order to make a *cardinal* comparison of utility. An *interpersonal* comparison of utility, i.e. a comparison of different people's utility, must be considered almost impossible.[62] In contrast, Posner points out, wealth is easier to measure than happiness:

> Wealth is, however, much easier to measure than happiness even though hypothetical prices play so important a role in determining wealth. It is much easier to estimate a demand curve (and so consumer surplus) than to estimate any sort of aggregate happiness function.[63]

In real markets, every transaction – in the absence of externalities – is wealth-enhancing. Hypothetical markets, however, give rise to a measurement problem, but a less serious one than the measurement problem presented by utilitarianism. For example, if a doctor has treated an unconscious accident victim, the doctor's right to due payment can be logically derived from the rational assumption that, had the victim been capable of negotiating, he or she would have consented to medical treatment at the stated price. Aside from that, Posner points out that the concept of

---

[58] Posner, 'Utilitarianism', pp. 128 f.

[59] Similar arguments apply in respect of the unborn.

[60] Posner, 'Utilitarianism', p. 129.

[61] Posner, 'Justice', p. 19.

[62] See Sect. 6.3.3.

[63] Posner, 'Justice', p. 19.

the hypothetical market is only applicable if the costs of a market transaction are prohibitively high.[64]

### 8.4.2.3  The Problem of Moral Monstrousness

'Moral monstrousness', which Posner considers the greatest problem of utilitarianism, arises for two reasons: firstly, because utilitarianism will not distinguish between different kinds of pleasures,[65] and secondly, because utilitarianism is prepared to sacrifice an innocent individual on the altar of the common good.[66]

If, for example, someone were to derive very great utility from pulling the legs off flies, whilst another person liked to feed pigeons but only gained moderate enjoyment from it, the first person's deed would be considered a better one, even taking into account the animals' feelings. Moreover, such actions as killing off a grouchy old person who was getting on everyone's nerves would be morally acceptable. Equally, the extermination of an unpopular minority – e.g. the Jews in the Third Reich – could be justified in utilitarian terms, if it were a possible means of increasing the utility of society.[67]

*Wealth maximization avoids or mitigates these problems because it is geared towards people's work and production, which are finite, and not the capacity to enjoy utility, which is theoretically unlimited.*

> Merely having the capacity to enjoy something, or wanting because of envy or spite to make others miserable, has no status in an ethic of wealth maximization. To have something you like you must either be willing to pay for it (if you do not own it already), which means that you must work to get the money to pay for it, or you must already have paid for it and hence own it. More precisely, you must have something that other people value and hence that you can trade to them for the things you want, and ultimately that something is productive work.[68]

According to Posner, it is of no importance whether one has earned money oneself or inherited it. In the latter case, he argues, one is consuming by proxy for whoever made the productive effort. The only cases which must be ruled out are those in which someone obtained money illegally, by such means as theft or extortion. The definitive criterion is that money must be earned through productive effort.[69] The 'utility monster' has no place in a system of wealth maximization. The circumstance that one must be willing to pay for everything places a limit on wants:

> The fact that I might derive so much gusto from torturing people as to exceed their misery in a felicific weighing would not make me a good man or give me the right to torture people. I

---

[64] Posner, 'Utilitarianism', p. 130.

[65] Unlike John Stuart Mill; see Sect. 6.3.4.

[66] Posner, 'Utilitarianism', p. 116.

[67] Posner, 'Utilitarianism', pp. 116 f.

[68] Posner, 'Justice', pp. 19 f.

[69] Posner, 'Justice', p. 29.

would have to buy my victim's consent, and these purchases would soon deplete the wealth of all but the wealthiest sadists.[70]

In a wholly utilitarian system, the utility monster would not be restrained by any kind of budget restrictions. Under wealth maximization, however, the available wealth sets a limit for each individual, and protects other people's rights since they can demand compensation for infringements that take place on a consensual basis.[71]

In relation to the aforementioned example of the Jews, this brings Posner to the following conclusion:

> If Nazi Germany wanted to get rid of the Jews, in a system of wealth maximization it would have had to buy them out.[72]

Utilitarianism has to value all kinds of antisocial behaviour, because even feelings such as envy or sadism are a common source of pleasure. In contrast, wealth maximization is based on the mutual benefit of exchange transactions. The individual – however egoistic he may be – cannot increase his own advantage without benefiting others in the process. Even incredibly egoistic individuals cannot avoid generating more wealth for society that they obtain themselves, Posner claims, because productive work produces a consumer surplus for others, whereas idleness does not.[73]

To the Kantian reproach that wealth maximization does as little as utilitarianism to protect human life, Posner responds that only fanatics would refuse to weigh human life in the balance with property. Posner explains this with the example already mentioned of the driver who swerves to avoid sheep, and in doing so, puts a child's life at risk. This time, however, he assumes that 100,000 sheep were at issue:

> [L]et there be 100,000 sheep worth in the aggregate more than any money value that can reasonably be ascribed to the child; must not the economist regard the driver as a good man, or at least not a bad man, when he decides to sacrifice the child? My answer is yes – and the same answer is given all the time in our (and every other) society. Dangerous activities are regularly permitted on the basis of a judgement that the costs of avoiding the danger exceed the costs to the victims. Only the fanatic refuses to trade off lives for property, although the difficulty of valuing lives is a legitimate reason for weighing them heavily in the balance when only property values are in the other pan.[74]

Posner, then, sees nothing abnormal about weighing human life in the balance with other legal goods, and thus deems it wholly compatible with our moral intuitions.[75]

---

[70] Posner, 'Utilitarianism', p. 131.

[71] Posner, 'Utilitarianism', p. 132.

[72] Posner, 'Utilitarianism', p. 133.

[73] Posner, 'Utilitarianism', p. 132.

[74] Posner, 'Utilitarianism', p. 133.

[75] In this vein, one could even claim that in reality even aesthetic grounds could be given weight against human life: if for example trees are planted along a street, inevitably it is part of the equation that any accidents they cause may result in the occasional loss of human life.

### 8.4.2.4  Utilitarianism as Justification for State Interventionism

The use of utilitarianism to justify state intervention is something that Posner finds particularly abhorrent. If, in the absence of empirical findings, one assumes that all people have the same utility functions, and if one also works on the assumption of diminishing marginal utility, then the utility of society – leaving aside the issue of redistribution costs – would be maximized if income were distributed equally. Utilitarianism thus offers a basis for state redistribution, which Posner obviously finds questionable.[76] Posner essentially refuses to accept any justification for redistribution,[77] and believes that the only people who can assert claims are those who work productively for others:

> [T]hose who do not produce what others want have no claims [. . .].[78]

For in a system of wealth maximization, the mere fact that A can gain greater utility from a certain sum of money than B is no basis for taking money from B and giving it to A, Posner explains: such a transfer may increase society's happiness but not its wealth.[79]

## 8.4.3  Application of Wealth Maximization to Ethical Questions

In the annex to his article 'Utilitarianism, Economics, and Legal Theory', Posner discusses four ethical questions, which he attempts to answer with the help of his theory: the death penalty, the right to privacy, trade in babies and organs, and freedom as wealth.

### 8.4.3.1  The Death Penalty[80]

Posner believes that the acceptability or otherwise of the death penalty depends on the answer to the following question: are the social benefits of any reduction in crime achieved by means of the death penalty greater or less than the social costs of the death penalty? The relevant costs – always compared to a more lenient form of punishment – are the following:

(1) The reduction in social costs attributable to crime reduction resulting from deterrence
(2) The additional costs of the death penalty for the delinquent
(3) The additional costs of the death penalty for an innocent person condemned to death
(4) The additional costs of trial and execution

---

[76] Posner, 'Utilitarianism', p. 115.

[77] Unless they were wealth-enhancing; see Sect. 8.4.4 below.

[78] Posner, 'Justice', p. 24.

[79] Posner, 'Utilitarianism', p. 131.

[80] Posner, 'Utilitarianism', pp. 136 f.

On (1): Posner concedes that the deterrent effect of the death penalty is disputed. He believes, however, that empirical research should bring clarity to this area.[81]

On (2): Here one would have to measure the 'value of life'. Posner avoids this contentious problem by reserving the death penalty for deliberate killings only, i.e. murders. Then one life will have been lost on each side of the balance sheet, and the corresponding values – which are assumed to be equal – cancel each other out.

On (3): The expected value of these additional costs must be determined. Since Posner considers the probability of a miscarriage of justice to be low, he consequently puts a very low estimate on the expected value of these costs.

On (4): The costs of trial in death penalty cases are higher, but an execution is cheaper than imprisonment. On balance, he considers the additional costs to be very low and perhaps even negative.

Bearing in mind that the additional costs of the death penalty to the delinquent (2) are cancelled out by reserving the death penalty for murders alone, it is only necessary to weigh up the cost reduction resulting from deterrence (1) against the total additional costs of condemning an innocent person, and any additional trial and execution costs (3 + 4).

### 8.4.3.2  Right to Privacy[82]

People often like to keep certain personal information secret, for instance their medical history or criminal record. To what extent should the law protect this sort of confidentiality?

Posner explains his point of view by citing an example: a prostitute was brought to trial for a murder, but was acquitted. Subsequently she moved to a new town, changed her name, got married, and led a blameless life. Seven years after her acquittal, a newspaper published an article about this woman's life story. She sued the newspaper and the court awarded her damages.

According to Posner, a person conceals certain information in order not to deter other people from entering into social transactions which are to that person's benefit. This practice, he believes, can be compared with a vendor of products concealing material defects. Dishonest behaviour, however, is a cause of high transaction costs and a barrier to the effective functioning of markets. This applies not just to the market in traded goods or to the labour market, but also to implicit markets such as the marriage market.

In this example, admittedly, the objection can be raised that people are likely to react in excessive and irrational ways to revelations about a former prostitute's past. Posner, however, assumes that the average person knows how to handle such information and would not therefore attach too much value to it. He believes the court's verdict to be wrong because it is detrimental to efficiency, but does not believe that

---

[81] The thought experiment obviously makes the assumption that the death penalty has a deterrent effect.

[82] Posner, 'Utilitarianism', pp. 137 f.

it gives any grounds for the use of surveillance to intrude into the private sphere. This would simply waste a great deal of resources because, firstly, surveillance itself is costly, and secondly, people would have to take expensive steps to protect themselves from possible surveillance. Furthermore, the fear of surveillance would reduce people's quality of life.

This example clearly shows how Posner attempts to justify rights *derived from the wealth maximization principle*: on that view, a right exists if it increases wealth or efficiency. Thus, in the present case a right to privacy exists, but only in relation to active surveillance.

### 8.4.3.3  Markets in Babies and Human Organs[83]

According to Posner, wealth maximization demands a far-reaching guarantee of freedom to contract. Restrictions on the lawful conclusion of contracts would only be permissible in cases of fraud, duress and incapacity to act, and where monopolies and externalities are found. But Posner objects to more extensive provisions, e.g. anti-profiteering laws, and would find other restrictions on the content of contracts equally unacceptable, e.g. restrictive provisions on adopting children or trading in human organs.

In the United States, Posner notes, there is an acute lack of children offered for adoption. The classic features of a shortage can be noted: long waiting lists, i.e. couples are expected to wait up to seven years to adopt a baby, whilst a flourishing black market operates in parallel, where high prices are paid for child adoptions (up to $40,000). Posner attributes this to the artificial restriction of prices to a level far below that which would bring supply and demand into equilibrium (remuneration is limited to the mother's additional costs of maintenance and medical care during the pregnancy, which do not generally exceed $2,000).

If these restrictions were lifted, the price of babies would fall below that on the black market, but would be higher than the compensation that is currently allowed. Consequently the supply of babies would rise overall and society would become wealthier. According to Posner, this solution would be preferable to the current situation involving a combination of non-market allocation of babies on the one hand and a black market on the other. From the perspective of wealth maximization, therefore, there is nothing immoral about the idea of a market in babies.[84]

Posner also discusses the question of whether a market in kidneys should be allowed. Since people have two kidneys but can manage with just one, and since only minor risks attach to surgical removal of a kidney, he finds that there are no medical objections to the sale of a kidney. In spite of this, he thinks it probable that relatively few people would sell a kidney, so that the price of kidneys would be relatively high. Nevertheless, the supply of kidneys would rise noticeably from its

---

[83] Posner, 'Utilitarianism', pp. 138 f.

[84] Because morality, too, is derived from wealth maximization.

current level. From the viewpoint of wealth maximization, a free market in kidneys should be welcomed, not least because there would only be winners:[85]

> Kidney sales would be wealth maximizing since, being voluntary, they would not occur otherwise. Probably most sellers would be relatively poor people; but they would, of course, be richer after the sale.[86]

The only objection that could possibly be raised against a trade in kidneys, according to Posner, is that it would reduce the incidence of unremunerated kidney donation. However, since such donations almost always take place within families, a market in kidneys would barely impinge upon them.

### 8.4.3.4 Liberty as Wealth[87]

Posner takes the view that political rights have no priority over economic rights. Ultimately it makes no difference whether somebody is unable to travel abroad because the state prohibits it, or because the person concerned lacks the necessary financial resources. Liberty is equally restricted in both cases. Consequently, from the viewpoint of wealth maximization, there is no difference in principle between political and economic rights. It follows that it is permissible to weigh these against one another in the balance.

## 8.4.4 Critique

### 8.4.4.1 Rationality of Actors

One objection to wealth maximization is the assumption that actors engaging in voluntary transactions – which are the benchmark – will be rational. Cento Veljanovski also finds it problematic that Posner focuses on actual preferences, and derives an ethical benchmark from the resulting market outcome:

> [I]t is not self-evident why consumer preferences expressed through "dollar votes" in the marketplace should be authoritative standards of personal let alone societal welfare. Why should the preferences of the stupid, young or mentally ill be accepted merely because they are able and willing to pay to facilitate them. Posner, by using the market as the benchmark would take tastes as given and derive his ethics from them while remaining silent as to their relative worth.[88]

Posner concedes that wrong choices could indeed be made, and that this would arise for two types of reasons. One the one hand, choices may be made in a state of poor or impaired judgement, in which people are susceptible to deception,

---

[85] Because these are voluntary transactions which satisfy the Pareto criterion.

[86] Posner, 'Utilitarianism', p. 139.

[87] Posner, 'Utilitarianism', p. 140.

[88] Veljanovski, 'Limits', p. 11.

fraudulent trickery or duress. But he argues that such choices cannot be called voluntary, and nor are they wealth maximizing.[89]

On the other hand, he points out, choices must often be made under uncertainty. Hence it is normal for some of these choices to prove wrong *ex post*, even though *ex ante* they may have been rational. Posner demonstrates this with an example:

Let us assume that one had a choice between two jobs. In the first job, one would have a certainty of earning € 50, 000 per year; the second would pay € 500, 000 (with a probability of 0.9) or nothing (with a probability of 0.1). The expected value of income from the first job is € 50, 000 and from the second job € 450, 000 (0.9 × 500, 000 + 0.1 × 0). However, since some uncertainty attaches to the remuneration of the second job, the relevant expected value – if one is risk-averse, which is assumed to be the case – has to be reduced, perhaps to € 250, 000. Ex ante, then, under these conditions it is rational to choose the second job. Of course, in the unlikely eventuality that one really did earn nothing, Posner concedes, it would certainly be a great disappointment. However, this would not alter the fact that it was the right choice to have made.[90]

In reality, though, even ex ante, far from all choices made by market players are rational.[91] And even if they were – in which case the market could be viewed as a rational voting process, – one could still object to the very unequal distribution of voting rights. In a market, the standard is not 'one man one vote' but '*one dollar one vote*'. A market outcome is thus the result of a large number of choices, some more rational than others, with voting rights distributed *plutocratically*. Moreover, when it comes to moral questions, it is problematic simply to focus on 'raw' preferences. So, for a variety of reasons, it makes little sense to attribute a moral value to the market outcome. Instead, it is better to understand the market outcome as an ordinary fact which is *amoral*[92] in nature. By the same token, drawing moral conclusions from the market outcome is also impossible. Posner's approach involves the impermissible derivation of an 'ought' from an 'is', i.e. a naturalistic fallacy.[93]

### 8.4.4.2  Logical Inconsistencies

Ronald Dworkin objects that the criterion for determining the level of social wealth is not clear. For most people, he explains, there is a difference between the price they would pay for a good which they did not possess and the price they would demand from a buyer for a good which they already owned. Sometimes the price is higher in the first case, because often one covets one's neighbour's property more than one's own (the 'grass is greener phenomenon'). But more frequently, the price is higher

---

[89] Posner, 'Justice', p. 22.

[90] Posner, 'Justice', p. 22.

[91] On the question of rationality, also see Sect. 2.2.4.

[92] That is, morally neutral (not to be confused with 'immoral').

[93] See Sect. 3.1 above.

in the second case: somebody will generally ask more for an item that he already possesses than he would be prepared to pay to purchase it.[94]

The latter phenomenon is known as the *endowment effect*. In numerous experiments it has been proven that subjects' asking prices were, on average, around *double* the prices that they were willing to pay as buyers. Originally this effect was thought to be the result of *habituation* to certain goods. People are never keen to part with treasured possessions that they have become attached to over time. However, since the endowment effect can observably occur immediately after taking possession of the purchased good (the 'instant endowment effect'), today the primary explanation is assumed to be *loss aversion*.[95]

The 'grass is greener phenomenon' theoretically leads to an unstable outcome because a good is always valued more highly by non-owners than by its owner. Hence it might be expected to change hands constantly, although in practice this is highly unlikely because of the associated transaction costs. In fact, the endowment effect tends to motivate owners to retain their goods. To that extent, it becomes relevant to consider who owns which goods to begin with. Nevertheless, Posner's concept of wealth is not fundamentally shaken by these effects.

The criticism of Posner's concept of wealth raised by Veljanovski is that it is geared towards willingness to pay alone, and does not take account of the cost of production. It would be more appropriate to maximize the difference between what people are willing to pay and the cost of production, because this would equate to the total of the producer and consumer surplus.[96] For Veljanovski, Posner's definition is as spectacularly wrong as the comparable claim that firms should maximize turnover rather than profit.[97]

The logical inconsistency of the Kaldor-Hicks criterion is a particularly serious problem. In some circumstances, the Kaldor-Hicks criterion may be satisfied by a transition from one state A to another state B, yet may also be satisfied by reversing the transition from state B back to state A (the Scitovsky paradox). Even if this case should seldom arise, it is still a serious flaw that afflicts the Kaldor-Hicks criterion.[98]

### 8.4.4.3 Wealth Maximization as an End in Itself or an Instrument?

Dworkin raises the fundamental question of whether wealth maximization or efficiency can be a desirable goal for society at all. This is expressed in the very titles of his two critical articles on Posner's theory of wealth maximization: 'Is Wealth

---

[94] Dworkin, 'Value', p. 192.

[95] Eidenmüller, pp. 126 ff.

[96] This is only correct if the fixed costs amount to zero, which is the case in the long run. Otherwise Veljanovski is right; moreover his view could very well coincide with Posner's intentions, although the latter expresses himself less precisely.

[97] Veljanovski, 'Limits', p. 6.

[98] See Sect. 3.3.3.1.

a Value?' (1980) and 'Why Efficiency?' (1980).[99] Dworkin initially criticizes the
personification of society which underlies the wealth maximization concept:

> [I]t is unclear why social wealth is a worthy goal. Who would think that a society that
> has more wealth [...] is either better or better off than a society that has less, except
> someone who made the mistake of personifying society, and therefore thought that a
> society is better off with more wealth in just the way any individual is. Why should
> anyone who has not made this mistake think that social wealth maximizing is a worthy
> goal?[100]

Dworkin proposes several possible ways of answering this question:

(1) Social wealth is a *component* of social value. Two variant forms of this analysis
    can be distinguished:

    (a) Wealth is the *only component* of social value.
    (b) Wealth is *just one of a number of components*, all of which contribute to
        social value.

(2) Social wealth is not a component of social value and therefore not a value in its
    own right but merely an instrument for increasing social value. Here, again, a
    number of different views are possible:

    (a) An increase in wealth is the cause of improvements in other social values;
        e.g. it reduces poverty.
    (b) Social wealth is an ingredient of social value, i.e. it creates the prerequisites
        for increasing social value. The wealthier a society, for example, the more
        easily it can combat poverty.
    (c) Wealth is neither a cause nor an ingredient of social value, but a surrogate
        for it. If, for instance, one wishes to increase social utility in the utilitarian
        sense, one will achieve this better by maximizing wealth rather than social
        utility directly. This is somewhat like aiming for a false target in order to
        achieve the desired objective more successfully. This 'second best solution'
        works as long as there is a high correlation between the two goals.[101]

Not the least of Dworkin's reasons for rejecting wealth as a social value is
that an increase in social wealth can be accompanied by a reduction in social
utility:

> Once social wealth is divorced from utility, at least, it loses all plausibility as a component
> of value.[102]

Not even for an individual is wealth a value as such. It is just an instrument for
achieving other goals:

---

[99] Posner refers to Dworkin as his best critic.

[100] Dworkin, 'Value', p. 194.

[101] Dworkin, 'Value', pp. 194 f.

[102] Dworkin, 'Value', p. 200. See also Sect. 8.4.1.3 above.

> Money or its equivalent is useful so far as it enables someone to lead a more valuable, successful, happier, or more moral life. Anyone who counts it for more than that is a fetishist of little green paper.[103]

Jules Coleman similarly denies that wealth – in contrast to the utilitarian concept of utility – has an intrinsic value:

> Unlike happiness or well-being, wealth is not something of intrinsic value. If the pursuit of wealth is a good, it must be because pursuing wealth promotes other things of value.[104]

Veljanovski is another who shares that view, stating that for homo economicus (economic man), wealth is a means, not an end:

> Economic man does not have a preference for wealth but for some end captured by the term "maximizing utility". Wealth is a means not an end.[105]

He finds the distinction between the concept of wealth maximization and the economic concept of utility maximization[106] purely semantic. What Posner denotes as 'wealth' is merely *an enumerator for the bundle of goods* available to a household in order to maximize utility. From this, Veljanovski infers that both concepts belong to a form of 'constrained utilitarianism':

> Not only is there no difference between wealth and economic maximization but both are a species of utilitarianism – what can be called constrained utilitarianism, the constraint being imposed by the scarcity of society's resources or, to use Posner's language, preferences backed up by willingness-to-pay.[107]

Veljanovski appears to be mixing up two things here, however: although economic man's possible courses of action are constrained by the budget restriction, his behaviour is motivated by *individual utility*, i.e., *personal utility* is maximized. But this does not correspond to the usual definition of the utility principle, which is implicitly geared towards *social utilitarianism*; in other words, the *utility of society* should be maximized, regardless of how that utility is distributed among the members of society.[108] Wealth maximization, which invokes the Kaldor-Hicks principle, would be a form of social utilitarianism, if it is a form of utilitarianism at all. The name '*constrained utilitarianism*' would then be appropriate indeed. In determining aggregate social utility, the utility of individuals only matters to the extent that it is backed by a corresponding willingness to pay.

Posner has variously emphasized the instrumental character of wealth maximization.[109] Dworkin considers an instrumentalist view more defensible, but points out that in these circumstances, one first needs to define with precision the goal or goals

---

[103] Dworkin, 'Value', pp. 200 f.

[104] Coleman, 'Efficiency', p. 527.

[105] Veljanovski, 'Limits', p. 8.

[106] See Sect. 2.4.1.

[107] Veljanovski, 'Limits', p. 8.

[108] See Sect. 6.3.7.

[109] For example Posner, 'Justice', p. 20.

that one wishes to achieve by means of wealth maximization. In this case, neither the rights nor the associated initial endowment with resources could be derived from the principle of wealth maximization, says Dworkin. Otherwise Posner is in a danger of advancing a *circular* argument:

> But if wealth maximization is only to be an instrumental value [...] then there must be some independent moral claim for the rights that wealth maximization recommends. [...] We cannot specify an initial assignment of rights unless we answer questions that cannot be answered unless an initial assignment of rights is specified.[110]

Coleman also believes that wealth maximization cannot explain the initial endowment with rights or, indeed, resources. But he justifies this with more circular logic: according to Posner, resources should be allocated to whoever demonstrates the greatest willingness to pay. That depends on individual wealth, however, which in turn is dependent upon the allocation of resources – the very factor one is attempting to derive.[111]

Veljanovski's argumentation is similar: markets are not defined before the assignment of property rights has been settled. But as the assignment of property rights is a legal question, the market outcome will also depend on these legal institutions. Hence the market outcome cannot be referred to as a standard for justifying the initial endowment with property rights.[112]

According to Coleman, any instrumentalist justification of wealth maximization is doomed to failure: firstly, it is not plausible that a society can achieve its goals better by striving for only one goal, namely the maximization of its wealth, rather than pursuing a combination of goals directly. Secondly, wealth maximization cannot offer a comprehensive moral theory since it is not in a position to justify the underlying rights and obligations.[113]

### 8.4.4.4  Income Distribution

Another important objection to wealth maximization is that demand in markets is limited by income. A rich person can afford to buy more than a poor one, and can therefore exert a higher level of demand. According to Veljanovski:

> [...] Kaldor-Hicks efficiency is not income distribution neutral, which is to say that it gives greater priority to those with income and market power. To the extent that the existing distribution of wealth is deemed "unjust" in society the ethical appeal of the Kaldor-Hicks test must corresponding diminish.[114]

It is even possible to be so poor that one's only choices are either to become a rich person's slave or else to starve. Posner considers such enslavement compatible

---

110 Dworkin, 'Value', pp. 207 f.

111 Coleman, 'Efficiency', p. 524.

112 Veljanovski, 'Limits', p. 6.

113 Coleman, 'Efficiency', p. 530.

114 Veljanovski, 'Limits', p. 12.

with wealth maximization, because it is still better than starvation. Consequently slavery, if it is 'voluntary', should be legally permissible:

> In the case of restricted choice made by the poor person, we may well want to allow the transaction to be enforced, because it provides a method by which the poor person can improve his welfare, however slightly. It may be a very bad thing to allow a person to become another's slave but it may be a better thing than making him starve. Even choices within an extremely restricted feasible set may make the chooser better off and thereby make society wealthier.[115]

It is obvious, however, that the original distribution of income or the initial endowment with resources plays an important role. An egalitarian society has a different structure of demand from a society with marked income disparities. In the latter, there is more demand for luxury goods; in the former, more demand for everyday necessities. Moreover, in the absence of redistribution measures, income disparities tend to widen in the longer term because the rich have more resources at their disposal with which they can generate more income. As Veljanovski puts it:

> [T]he wealth maximization principle [...] gives greater weight to those who are already favoured by the distribution of rights in society and will therefore tend systematically to favour those individuals that already have wealth.[116]

Nonetheless, Posner is not completely averse to taking the problem of initial endowment seriously, and attempts *to make use of the wealth maximization principle* to find grounds for disapproving of a very inequitable initial endowment. If all resources belonged to one individual to begin with, then very high *transaction costs* would arise if this person wanted to give the other members of society incentives to work productively. In the long term, Posner believes, a society with a more egalitarian initial endowment of resources is wealthier because it incurs fewer transaction costs.[117] A further objection he raises to a very inequitable initial allocation of all resources is the risk of creating monopolies, which are not efficient:

> A further consideration relevant to the initial distribution of rights is the inefficiency of monopolies [...], which argues for parcelling out rights in small units to many different people in order to make the costs of assembling the rights into a single bloc large enough to confer monopoly power prohibitive.[118]

On the other hand, Anthony Kronman is equally fearful that a system of wealth maximization could amplify income disparities still further. As new rights are assigned on the basis of willingness and ability to pay, this works to the advantage of those already in possession of money and resources, which Kronman finds unfair:

> An individual's wealth is defined by his ability and willingness to pay, so the principle of wealth maximization necessarily favors those who already have money, or the resources with which to earn it, and are therefore able to pay more than others to have a new legal rule

---

[115] Posner, 'Justice', p. 23.

[116] Veljanovski, 'Limits', p. 21.

[117] Posner, 'Justice', p. 24.

[118] Posner, 'Utilitarianism', p. 126.

defined in the way that is favorable to them. The principle of wealth maximization gives an additional advantage to those who are already advantaged, and this quite rightly strikes us as unfair.[119]

The distribution of talents and handicaps can largely be put down to chance. Wealth maximization accentuates natural disparities, whether these confer individual advantages or disadvantages. Those who have already been fortunate in the 'natural lottery' are favoured even more. However, unlike Posner, Kronman believes that social institutions should mitigate the effects of the 'natural lottery'. He finds it virtually 'perverse' if the law actually amplifies natural disparities.[120]

Posner not only believes that wealth maximization has no amplifying effect whatever on income disparities, but fundamentally objects to any redistributive measures in the course of the political process. Firstly, high costs are attached to such programmes, and secondly, there is no persuasive justification for the state to take something away from a productive person in order to give it to someone who is unproductive:

> The second [reason] is the difficulty of finding a principled basis for the state's forcing a person who is productive to support a person who [...] is unproductive. I am not convinced that there is.[121]

Posner does admit that in a system of wealth maximization, regrettably, people without means only count insofar as they function as an argument in the utility function of somebody with wealth. In this system, individuals each possess their own set of abilities, and society has no duty to support the poor, even if a needy person is not to blame for being poor:

> If he happens to be born feeble-minded and his net social product is negative, he would have no right to the means of support though there was nothing blameworthy in his inability to support himself. This result grates on modern sensibilities yet I see no escape from it that is consistent with any of the major ethical systems.[122]

According to Posner, state transfers are only justified if they add to the wealth of society. So, firstly, transfers could reduce crime because they counteract the incentives for committing criminal acts. Secondly, the alleviation of poverty by means of voluntary donations would benefit not only the donors but also third parties, since poverty arouses uncomfortable feelings even in those who are not directly affected. Hence the reduction of poverty would be a public good which would justify state intervention.[123]

Posner would also see redistribution as justifiable in order to ensure political stability or to support education, particularly the education of the poor, because that would be a means of raising their productive potential and thus enhancing social

---

[119] Kronman, p. 240.

[120] Kronman, p. 242.

[121] Posner, 'Justice', p. 24.

[122] Posner, 'Utilitarianism', p. 128.

[123] Posner, 'Utilitarianism', p. 131.

wealth. However, these transfers would be tightly limited and only take place within the state system of taxation and expenditure, not under civil law for instance.[124] It would be equally compatible with wealth maximization for productive people to set up a social insurance scheme, to insure themselves against the uncertainties of life which might pose a risk to their own productivity.[125]

According to Veljanovski, Posner's refusal to address the question of distributive justice amounts, in practice, to the implicit assumption that the existing distribution of rights and income is just. But because this is not necessarily the case, according to Veljanovski, wealth maximization has little ethical appeal. One would first have to ensure that any initial endowment with rights was arranged justly.[126] Yet even this, by itself, would be nowhere near a sufficient condition to make wealth maximization an attractive ethical basis.

### 8.4.4.5  The Problem of Inalienable Rights

Probably the gravest objection to wealth maximization – and indeed to utilitarianism – is that it does not guarantee the inalienable rights of the individual as a matter of principle. Posner also concedes that under a system of wealth maximization, slavery and torture would be entirely possible:

> If a person wants to sell himself into slavery or participate in a sadomasochistic (but thoroughly voluntary) orgy or submit voluntarily to a legal system in which torture and lynching are used to increase the efficacy of crime prevention, nothing in a system of wealth maximization seems to forbid the transaction, whether the transaction is explicit or implicit.[127]

Apart from that, Posner points out that certain forms of slavery already exist which are accepted by society; forced labour in a prison, for instance. Moreover, slavery represented progress from a historical point of view insofar as victorious tribes began to enslave the males from a conquered people as an alternative to killing them. On that basis, a blanket condemnation of any form of forced labour is unjustified. On the other hand, Posner still considers slavery to be inefficient, because overseeing slave labour is too costly compared with the costs of supervising workers employed under contract:

> They would, in short, reject slavery, an inefficient institution under modern conditions. With unimportant exceptions, the costs of monitoring the output of a slave today would be much higher than the costs of monitoring a free man's output through contract.[128]

In a modern society, then, slavery is ruled out de facto where wealth maximization is applied as an ethical principle. But this is not the same as an absolute prohibition on slavery. Posner nonetheless thinks it unlikely that wealth maximization

---

[124] Posner, 'Wealth', p. 95.

[125] Posner, 'Justice', p. 24.

[126] Veljanovski, 'Limits', pp. 19 f.

[127] Posner, 'Justice', p. 25.

[128] Posner, 'Wealth', p. 94.

would bring slavery and other monstrous institutions in its wake; he rather believes that the demand for efficiency is in keeping with our moral intuitions:

> Thus, while the theoretical possibility exists that efficiency might dictate slavery or some other monstrous rights assignments, it is difficult to give examples where this would actually happen. I conclude that it is possible to deduce a structure of rights congruent with our ethical intuitions from the wealth-maximization premise.[129]

The example of slavery demonstrates that wealth maximization does not protect the basic rights of the individual on principle. Consequently, wealth maximization is no more commendable than utilitarianism in this respect. Economic evaluation of all spheres of life reduces all questions to a scarcity problem. This makes everything exchangeable – in both senses: tradeable and replaceable. The principle is applied inexorably, even to human beings: they are exchangeable too, as long as a replacement of the same economic value can be found. But this view may pose a *threat to human dignity*. Kant expresses himself unequivocally on the matter:

> In the kingdom of ends everything has either value or dignity. Whatever has a value can be replaced by something else which is equivalent; whatever, on the other hand, is above all value, and therefore admits of no equivalent, has a dignity.[130]

## 8.5  Consensus Theoretical Justification of Wealth Maximization

In a third phase, Posner attempted to underpin the principle of wealth maximization with consensus theoretical arguments. In his article, 'The Ethical and Political Basis of the Efficiency Norm in Common Law Adjudication' (1980) he developed a consensus theoretical approach following on from Rawls. In the third chapter of his book *The Economics of Justice* (1981), he repeats the arguments in favour of wealth maximization from 'Utilitarianism, Economics, and Legal Theory' (1979), and in the fourth chapter of the same work he adds the consensus theoretical justification of his theory. The Kaldor-Hicks principle, he states, is not consensual as such because there are always losers who would withhold their consent. In order to solve this problem, Posner introduces the argumentational device of *ex ante compensation*.[131]

### 8.5.1  The Squaring of the Circle

The advantage of the Kaldor-Hicks criterion over the Pareto criterion is that its application is not limited to cases which make nobody worse off. The Pareto criterion can claim not only to be compatible with utilitarianism – because a Pareto-superior change always increases social utility – but also to respect the autonomy of

---

[129] Posner, 'Efficiency Norm', pp. 538 f.

[130] Kant, *Fundamental Principles*, p. 274.

[131] Posner, *Economics*, pp. 92 ff.

individuals (a 'Kantian' or 'libertarian' requirement, according to Posner) since it relies on their voluntary consent.[132]

To satisfy the Kaldor-Hicks criterion, in contrast, a measure need not necessarily increase social utility nor respect the autonomy of the individual because, as we know, the consent of the losers is not required. Posner attempts to respond to these objections, or at least temper them, with the help of ex ante compensation:

> I want to defend the Kaldor-Hicks or wealth-maximization approach, not by reference to Pareto superiority as such or its utilitarian premise, but by reference to the idea of consent that [...] provides an alternative basis to utilitarianism for the Pareto criterion. The notion of consent used here is what economists call ex ante compensation.[133]

Posner subsequently forms a view of wealth maximization as a theory which is compatible with both utilitarianism and with Kantian positions:

> Wealth maximization as an ethical norm gives weight both to utility, though less heavily than utilitarianism does, and to consent, though perhaps less heavily than Kant himself would have done.[134]

Via the consensus argument, Posner seeks to make a connection with Kantian, or libertarian, theories. He acknowledges that such theories emphasize individual rights somewhat more prominently than wealth maximization does, and endeavour to grant the individual as much freedom – including, especially, freedom of contract – as possible. But, he points out, guaranteeing freedom of contract is also in the interest of wealth maximization. The coercive character of the Kaldor-Hicks rule could pose a problem, however. Yet Posner believes that principle to be consensual once ex ante compensation is taken into account, and so finds his concept entirely compatible with these theories.[135]

## 8.5.2  The Concept of Ex Ante Compensation

Ex ante compensation works on the principle that the 'price is paid' for the consent of the potential losers, so that they, too, can benefit from an advantage that accrues to all under the wealth maximization system. Thus, on balance they, too, end up better off *ex ante* (but not necessarily *ex post*, depending on the specific circumstances).

Posner explains the principle with reference to various examples. Firstly he compares consent to wealth maximization with the purchase of a lottery ticket. Anyone who buys a ticket implicitly agrees to the eventuality of a loss. Posner understands ex ante compensation in the following terms: if, for example, an entrepreneur loses money due to tough competition, he has been compensated for it ex ante, because the expected value of the entrepreneur's income must have contained a premium

---

[132] Posner, 'Efficiency Norm', p. 532.

[133] Posner, 'Efficiency Norm', pp. 533 f.

[134] Posner, *Economics*, p. 98.

[135] Posner, 'Justice', p. 21.

for risk to cover the risk of losses resulting from competition. Another example: imagine that property prices in a district fell because a large firm moved away. The owners of neighbouring properties – who had to anticipate this relocation – had received compensation ex ante by paying a lower purchase price for their properties; the probability of the firm's move away was already accounted for in this reduced price.[136]

Posner's favourite example of ex ante compensation, however, is liability for road accidents. Here he works on the assumption that negligence is more efficient than strict liability, i.e. the total of insurance premiums paid by potential injurers and victims would be lower under a negligence system than a strict liability system.[137] Posner concludes that a negligence system is advantageous for all, because all would benefit from an overall reduction in insurance premiums. The benefit of lower premiums would be ex ante compensation which would, on average, outweigh any disadvantages of basing liability on negligence. This does not imply that a negligence system would make everyone better off *ex post* in any given case; but that issue is irrelevant under the concept of ex ante compensation.[138]

## 8.5.3 Differences from Rawls's Theory

Posner sees his own consensus approach and Rawls's as sharing common liberal roots. But he dislikes the thrust of Rawls's theory towards the social state, particularly the difference principle. And because the abilities one will eventually have are unknown in the original position, the all-important distinction between productive and unproductive members of society is blurred:

> But any theory of consent based on choice in the original position is unsatisfactory [...] because [it] opens the door to the claims of the nonproductive. In the original position, no one knows whether he has productive capabilities, so choices made in that position will reflect some probability that the individual making the choice will turn out to be an unproductive member of society [...]. The original-position approach thus obscures the important moral distinction between capacity to enjoy and capacity to produce for others.[139]

Hence Posner prefers the *natural ignorance* of actual people to artificial ignorance in an original position:

> I prefer therefore to imagine actual people, deploying actual endowments of skill and energy and character, making choices under uncertainty. This is choice under conditions of natural ignorance rather than under artificial ignorance in the original position.[140]

---

[136] Posner, *Economics*, p. 94.

[137] Whether this is actually so is an empirical question. Here it is merely assumed to be so.

[138] Posner, *Economics*, p. 95.

[139] Posner, *Economics*, p. 100.

[140] Posner, *Economics*, pp. 100 f.

Posner propounds *implicit consent* as the basis for a consensus, because the problem in many cases is that there is no practicable method of obtaining explicit consent. This, for Posner, is no reason at all to give up the consensus principle. What needs to be asked, as for a judge's supplementary interpretation of a contract, is what the parties would have agreed if they had explicitly made provisions:

> If there is no reliable mechanism for eliciting express consent, it follows, not that we must abandon the principle of consent, but rather that we should look for implied consent, as by trying to answer the hypothetical question whether, if transaction costs were zero, the affected parties would have agreed to the institution. This procedure resembles a judge's imputing the intent of parties to contract that fails to provide expressly for some contingency.[141]

Moreover, Posner is not completely rigid on the matter of consent. Unanimity is not an absolute requirement:

> [O]nly a fanatic would insist that unanimity be required to legitimize a social institution such as the negligence system.[142]

Posner has to concede that not all rules which maximize wealth are consensual. For example, if A's labour were worth more to B than to A, then it would be efficient for A to become B's slave. Similarly, forced labour could certainly be more efficient in some circumstances than the hiring of employees. Arrangements of that kind would hardly be compatible with the consensus principle, though:

> [I]n such situations slavery might be wealth maximizing, but it presumably would not be consented to.[143]

Posner concludes that although efficiency conflicts at times with the concepts of autonomy and consensus, it still deserves to be given strong moral weight.[144]

## 8.5.4 Critique

Anthony Kronman finds Posner's attempt to make the Kaldor-Hicks principle consensual fundamentally questionable, because it then becomes indistinguishable from the Pareto principle. The key characteristic of the Kaldor-Hicks criterion is, after all, that in contrast to the Pareto principle it only requires potential compensation. If we now bring actual compensation into the equation – and even an ex ante form of compensation is deemed actual – then, according to Kronman, it means that we are giving up the Kaldor-Hicks principle.[145]

---

[141] Posner, 'Efficiency Norm', p. 535.

[142] Posner, *Economics*, p. 97.

[143] Posner, *Economics*, p. 102.

[144] Posner, *Economics*, pp. 102 f.

[145] Kronman, p. 238.

Ronald Dworkin is another who criticizes Posner's consensus theoretical approach. He points out that the consensus as Posner conceived of it is a counterfactual one – in which certain qualities such as self-interest are ascribed to the actors – and not an actual consensus.[146] There is most certainly *no* implicit consent on the part of the actors, as Posner assumes. On the contrary, the consent imputed to them is a counterfactual or *fictive consent*. A counterfactual consensus, Dworkin contends, is not even a watered-down form of consensus; it is *no consensus at all*.[147]

Since there is no actual consent, just a counterfactual assumption of consent, the 'natural ignorance' imputed to the actors is itself arbitrary and even more artificial than the radical ignorance of Rawls's original position. Thus, Posner's approach is not an enhanced version of Rawls's, but a utilitarian type of argumentation.[148] Further evidence of this, according to Dworkin, is that Posner waters down the consensus principle by not regarding unanimous consent as absolutely necessary. However, this is a basic breach of the consensus criterion, which is an all-or-nothing principle. If it is diluted, Dworkin argues, it collapses and becomes a utilitarian principle.[149]

All in all, Dworkin deems Posner's attempt to underpin wealth maximization with consensus theory a failure. It strikes him as a mere façade, erected with the intention of giving the theory a veneer of Kantianism. Yet instead, he asserts, Posner's argumentation falls back on utilitarianism:

> Posner is pleased to claim that wealth maximization combines the most appealing features of both the Kantian concern with autonomy and the utilitarian concern with individual preferences, while avoiding the excesses of either of these traditional theories. His argument from counterfactual consent is meant to supply the Kantian features. But this is spurious: In fact the idea of consent does not work at all in the theory and the appeal to autonomy is therefore a facade. [...] His relaxed version of Paretianism is simply utilitarianism with all the warts.[150]

On this point, Kronman's opinion is similar: Posner claims to offer an ideal combination of utilitarianism and Paretianism – understood by Posner as an expression of Kantian autonomy of the individual. The approach was supposed to avoid the dangers of both extremes (fanaticism and 'moral self-pity' on the Kantian side and moral atrocities such as the utility monster, slavery, etc. found in uncompromising utilitarianism).[151] But Kronman dismisses that as an illusion. In no way is wealth maximization a happy compromise between these two extremes, retaining the good elements and eliminating their worst features; in fact, the contrary is nearer to the mark:

---

[146] Dworkin, 'Efficiency', p. 542.

[147] Dworkin, 'Efficiency', p. 544.

[148] Dworkin, 'Efficiency', p. 545.

[149] Dworkin, 'Efficiency', pp. 547 f.

[150] Dworkin, 'Efficiency', pp. 548 f.

[151] Kronman, p. 228.

If anything, just the opposite is true: wealth maximization exhibits the vices of both and the virtues of neither.[152]

Even if a utilitarian formed the opinion that human beings had rights which should limit the maximization of social utility, this line of reasoning would not lead him to wealth maximization. And conversely, if somebody who believed in the importance of autonomy and basic rights nevertheless formed a view that it was permissible to restrict the rights of individuals in extreme cases as a means of significantly increasing social utility, they would be just as unlikely to arrive at the principle of wealth maximization. For wealth maximization is an absurd, irrational and incoherent principle which cannot be justified from any starting position:

> I happen to believe that a combination of utilitarian and voluntarist principles best expresses our moral judgements and best equips us to deal with the dilemmas of moral life. But whichever of these two elements one takes primary, wealth maximization is an absurd principle to adopt. Wealth maximization is not only an unsound ideal, it is an incoherent one which cannot be defended from any point of view.[153]

According to Kronman, wealth maximization does in fact constrain utilitarianism, in that it is geared towards willingness and ability to pay. This constraint militates against utilitarian objectives on the one hand, without being founded on a Kantian attitude of respect for the individual on the other. Wealth maximization is – if anything – a kind of utilitarianism which is constrained by something vague and of doubtful value:

> Wealth maximization is not utilitarianism limited by a respect for rights: if it is a species of utilitarianism at all, wealth maximization is utilitarianism constrained by a respect for something which is neither rights nor utility, something of uncertain and [...] dubious value.[154]

## 8.6 Pragmatic Justification of Wealth Maximization

From as early as the mid-1980s, Posner began to relativize his theory. In the essay 'Wealth Maximization Revisited' (1985) he explicitly stops short of claiming wealth maximization as a universal ethic:

> My goal is therefore quite modest. I do not seek to "convert" anyone to wealth maximization. I merely want to persuade you that it is a reasonable, though not a demonstrably or a universally correct, ethic [...].[155]

In his more recent writings, the consensus argument plays only a subordinate role, if any. Now moral intuitions are held up as the ultimate test of the validity of

---

[152] Kronman, p. 228.

[153] Kronman, pp. 228 f.

[154] Kronman, p. 234.

[155] Posner, 'Wealth', p. 90.

moral theories; indeed, of theories in general. Posner commends his theory as compatible with most moral views and refers to its similarity with utilitarianism. In the book, *The Problems of Jurisprudence* (1990), Posner completes the definitive retreat into *pragmatism*, as he calls his new position. Yet he holds firm to the fundamental concept of wealth maximization, although he has to admit that economic success depends not only on individual effort but also, to a great extent, on luck.

### 8.6.1 Exclusivity Claim Abandoned

While Posner persists in treating efficiency or wealth maximization as an important criterion, it is no longer necessarily the only one:

> Although no effort will be made in this book to defend efficiency as the only worthwhile criterion of social choice, the book does assume, and most people probably would agree, that it is an important criterion.[156]

Making value judgements is not part of the economists' remit; what they can do is advise politicians as to how particular objectives can be achieved:

> But one thing that should be clearly understood from the outset is that economists do not claim the competence to make ultimate value judgements. They can illuminate the effects of public policies, actual or proposed, on efficiency in its economic sense or senses, but they cannot tell the policy maker how much weight to assign efficiency as a policy goal, though they may be able to advise him concerning the feasibility of achieving other goals, such as a more equal distribution of income.[157]

Posner expressly admits that wealth maximization is dependent upon the initial assignment of property rights; in other words, the distribution of wealth. Furthermore Posner concedes to his critics that:

(1)  His normative theory is not suitable for solving all problems.
(2)  It is not founded on any all-embracing moral theory (as, for instance, utilitarianism is).
(3)  Wealth has no intrinsic, non-instrumental value as, for instance, 'goodness' or 'happiness' do in other philosophical theories.[158]

Yet Posner does not accept that these concessions weaken his position. He states that he has become very sceptical about attempts to construct coherent moral theories. To a great extent, moral convictions are a foregone conclusion and remain largely impervious to the reasons put forward to defend or refute them. Often people are quite clear about something being morally wrong, but do not exactly know why:

> It would for example be extraordinarily odd for someone to say, "I know and believe that torturing children is bad, but I would like to know why it is bad." One might or

---

[156] Posner, *EAL 5*, p. 13.

[157] Posner, *EAL 5*, p. 16.

[158] Posner, 'Inquiry', p. 101.

might not be able to give him a reason; but it is quite unlikely that one could affect his belief.[159]

It is therefore rather unrealistic to assume that one could change people's beliefs with arguments, when they have not formed these beliefs on the basis of arguments in the first place. And it would be irrational to give up a deeply held moral conviction simply because one could not think of a retort to some recondite argument. This does not mean that moral convictions cannot be changed. But they are more likely to change as a result of *experience* – and seldom based on arguments. Posner contends that not even philosophers acquired their moral convictions on the basis of arguments, and this is all the more true of the rest of the population.[160]

## 8.6.2 Division of Labour Between the Judiciary and the Legislature

Posner believes that the courts should be committed to wealth maximization, whereas the legislature should be responsible for distributive justice:

> The judge whose business is enforcing tort, contract, and property law lacks effective tools for bringing about an equitable distribution of wealth, even if he thinks he knows what such a distribution would be. [...] A sensible division of labor has the judge making rules and deciding cases in the areas regulated by the common law in such a way as to maximize the size of the social pie, and the legislature attending to the sizes of the slices.[161]

When Posner refers to the 'legislature', essentially he means only the legislation on taxation and transfer law. Applied to the Swiss legal system, for instance, Posner's demand would be akin to calling for private law to be guided by the efficiency principle, whereas – to balance things out, as it were – public law should be guided by aspects of distributive justice.[162]

## 8.6.3 Moral Intuitions as the Ultimate Test

He agrees that, like utilitarianism, wealth maximization suffers from the problem that in some cases it clashes with the prevailing moral intuitions. However, moral intuitions are the *ultimate test* of moral theories:

> This [...] points to a deeper criticism of wealth maximization as a norm or value: like utilitarianism, which it closely resembles, [...] it treats people as if they were the cells of a single organism; the welfare of the cell is important only insofar as it promotes the welfare of the organism. Wealth maximization implies that if the prosperity of the society can be promoted by enslaving its least productive citizens, the sacrifice of their freedom is worthwhile. But

---

[159] Posner, 'Inquiry', pp. 101 f.

[160] Posner, 'Inquiry', p. 102.

[161] Posner, *Jurisprudence*, p. 388.

[162] Cf. Schäfer and Ott, p. 31.

this implication is contrary to the unshakable moral intuitions of Americans, and [...] conformity to intuition is the ultimate test of a moral (indeed of any) theory.[163]

Modern society no longer has any consistent moral convictions, he believes, and even an individual person may hold views which are not internally consistent. Overall, however, wealth maximization – leaving certain exceptions aside – is in harmony with a large number of different moral convictions. Thus, to a certain extent, it is a common denominator.[164]

## 8.6.4 Rapprochement Towards Utilitarianism

Since Posner wishes to present his normative theory as compatible with as many other moral theories as possible, he places stronger emphasis than in the third phase on what it has in common with utilitarianism. He continues to reject state interventionism, which can be justified on utilitarian grounds, yet simultaneously admits that his concept has great similarity with utilitarianism. Thus Posner emphasizes the instrumental character of wealth maximization even more:

> What, in short, is the ethical basis of the Kaldor-Hicks concept [...]? One answer is that the things that wealth makes possible – not only or mainly luxury goods, but leisure, comfort, modern medicine, and opportunities for self-expression and self-realization – are major ingredients of most people's happiness, so that wealth maximization is instrumental to utility maximization. This answer ties efficiency to utilitarianism.[165]

Posner also suggests that wealth maximization could be invoked as a decision-making rule for rule utilitarianism. For, he contends, the goals of utilitarianism can be better achieved by means of wealth maximization than by utilitarianism itself:

> It is curious, but true that to aim directly at maximizing happiness, by distributing and redistributing wealth to those who would get the most pleasure from it, is self-defeating because it results in a poor und unhappy society. Wealth maximization is a more effective instrument for attaining the goals of utilitarianism than utilitarianism itself. Stated otherwise, wealth maximization is the correct rule of decision in a system of rule utilitarianism.[166]

With this instrumentalist view of wealth maximization, Posner once again moves much closer to the utilitarianism which was his original departure point, but with which he preferred not to be associated for some time. In doing so, he also builds a bridge to welfare economics positions founded on the basis of classical utilitarianism. Louis Kaplow and Steven Shavell, for example, see wealth as a proxy for utilitarian social welfare.[167] In 'Law, Pragmatism, and Democracy' (2003), Posner

---

[163] Posner, *Jurisprudence*, pp. 376 f.

[164] Posner, 'Inquiry', p. 103.

[165] Posner, *EAL 5*, p. 16.

[166] Posner, 'Wealth', p. 98.

[167] Kaplow and Shavell, *Fairness*, pp. 36 f.

explicitly refers to wealth maximization as a consequentialist ethic, which is related to utilitarianism yet at the same time distinct from it.[168]

## 8.6.5 The Constitution as a Safety Net

Posner points out that even the best judges cannot rule on difficult cases without drawing on their own discretion. So the question that arises is what this discretion should be based upon. Posner believes that judges should be guided by the principle of wealth maximization since it combines utilitarian with individualistic elements, suggesting that it may provide a consensual basis. This is already largely the case in America, where even concepts such as fairness or justice are used as proxies for wealth maximization:

> Wealth maximization combines [...] elements of utilitarianism and individualism, and in so doing comes closer to being a consensus political philosophy [...]. It would be easy to show [...] that many invocations of fairness and justice, [...] and other familiar principles or methods of judicial decision-making are proxies for wealth maximization.[169]

He concedes that wealth maximization does indeed contradict moral intuitions in certain areas. This is demonstrated by the example of slavery, but the same is true of torture and lynch-mob justice. But, he points out, the American constitution offers a remedy by forbidding such practices.[170]

## 8.6.6 Retreat Into Pragmatism

In invoking the constitution, Posner definitively gives up the attempt to postulate wealth maximization as a comprehensive normative principle from which all rights can be derived. For, first and foremost, a comprehensive moral theory would have to be capable of justifying the elementary principles which are usually laid down in the constitution. Thus the reference to the constitution is akin to a declaration of bankruptcy.

Posner also admits that there is no sound philosophical justification of wealth maximization but, as ever, sees this as no reason to abandon it:

> It may be impossible to lay solid philosophical foundations under wealth maximization, [...] but this would be a poor reason for abandoning wealth maximization, just as the existence of intractable problems in the philosophy of science would be a poor reason for abandoning science.[171]

---

[168] Posner, *Pragmatism*, p. 65.

[169] Posner, 'Wealth', p. 104.

[170] Posner, 'Wealth', pp. 104 f.

[171] Posner, *Jurisprudence*, p. 384.

He claims that the strongest argument for wealth maximization is not moral but pragmatic in nature, based on the benefits of living in countries where markets operate more or less freely:

> The strongest argument for wealth maximization is not moral, but pragmatic. [...] We look around the world and see that in general people who live in societies in which markets are allowed to function more or less freely not only are wealthier than people in other societies but have more political rights, more liberty and dignity, and are more content [...] – so that wealth maximization may be the most direct route to a variety of moral ends.[172]

Posner understands 'pragmatic' in the colloquial sense and disassociates himself from American pragmatism – from Richard Rorty, for one, whose political and economic naivety he mocks.[173] When he calls for jurisprudence to become more pragmatic, he means that it should deal less with semantic and metaphysical issues and more with the factual and the empirical:

> The object of pragmatic analysis is to lead discussion away from issues semantic and metaphysical and toward issues factual and empirical. Jurisprudence is greatly in need of such a shift in direction. Jurisprudence needs to become more pragmatic.'[174]

Posner's main argument in favour of a system of wealth maximization up to this point was always that under this system, the productive were rewarded for their efforts, which is morally desirable. With regard to this argument, too, Posner has become sceptical. Whether someone can generate high income in the market is heavily dependent upon good luck:

> Unfortunately, wealth maximization is not a pure ethic of productivity and cooperation, not only because even lawful efforts at maximizing wealth often make some other people worse off, but more fundamentally because luck plays a big role in the returns to market activities. What is worse, it is always possible to argue that the distribution of productivity among a population is itself the luck of the genetic draw, or of upbringing, or of where one happens to have been born, and these forms of luck have no ethical charge.[175]

Thinking about the aleatory elements in a person's life further undermines the ethical appeal of wealth maximization. For Posner this is one more reason to retreat into pragmatism:

> So, once again, the foundations of an overarching principle for resolving legal disputes are rotten, and one is driven back to the pragmatic ramparts.[176]

Lastly, Posner admits that the economic approach and the concept of wealth maximization are not equally well suited to all areas of law. Most particularly where matters hinge on aspects of distribution policy, and in relation to a number of other

---

[172] Posner, *Jurisprudence*, p. 382.

[173] Posner, *Jurisprudence*, p. 384.

[174] Posner, *Jurisprudence*, p. 387.

[175] Posner, *Jurisprudence*, pp. 391 f.

[176] Posner, *Jurisprudence*, p. 392.

controversial issues – e.g. the legalization of abortion – the economic analysis of law reaches its limits.[177]

## 8.7 Summary

The retreat into pragmatism makes it evident that Posner finally had no choice but to realize that his position – which he has revised several times in any case – was ultimately unpersuasive:

(1) The attempt to conceive of wealth maximization as an alternative to utilitarianism, which preserves its good elements and eliminates its worse characteristics, must be considered a failure. In fact, Posner has achieved rather the opposite of what he set out to do: *wealth maximization eliminates the good characteristics of utilitarianism and preserves its weaknesses.* Although wealth maximization restrains the 'utility monster' by imposing the constraint of willingness to pay, this does not solve the problem of inalienable rights. In the end, the 'utility monster' is just replaced by the 'wealth monster'. Wealth maximization is thus a blighted version of classical utilitarianism, and not the fundamentally new ethical concept that Posner originally took it for.
(2) The consensus theoretical underpinning of wealth maximization is even less persuasive. *The Kaldor-Hicks criterion is not consensual, because there are always losers, and they will not consent.* Not all members of a society can count on benefiting from a system of wealth maximization in the long run. By relativizing the consensus principle – not requiring everyone's consent, just most people's – Posner parts company with consensus theory. By definition, consensus means unanimity: anything less is not a consensus at all.
(3) With regard to his pragmatic argumentation, admittedly Posner is less open to attack, but neither does his position have the same force. *On the other hand, the suggestion of striving for the efficiency goal instrumentally, as a means of pursuing other social goals, sounds highly plausible.* With more resources, more goals can be achieved. It is a truism that a larger cake can be cut into larger slices. But that is far from guaranteeing that distribution will be just, by whatever definition one chooses. Therefore there is still a need to clarify with greater precision the relationship between efficiency and justice.

---

[177] Posner, *Overcoming Law*, p. 404.

# Chapter 9
# Justice and Efficiency

*[The] tradeoff [...] between equality and efficiency [...] is, in
my view, our biggest socioeconomic tradeoff, and it plagues us
in dozens of dimensions of social policy. We can't have our
cake of market efficiency and share it equally.*[1]

## 9.1 Introduction

Two different goals – such as justice and efficiency – can essentially stand in three
possible relations to one another:

(1) Goal harmony,
(2) Goal neutrality,
(3) Goal conflict.

Where the relation is one of goal harmony, the pursuit of one goal would be
beneficial for the other goal, too. For example, pursuing the efficiency goal would
simultaneously bring about a just outcome; or vice versa, having just institutions
would encourage efficiency at the same time. In a situation of goal neutrality, the
pursuit of one goal has no effect on the achievement of the other.[2] The majority of
economists would tend to assume that the relation between efficiency and justice is
one of goal conflict. Here the assumption is that justice and efficiency are substitutable, up to a certain point. This relationship of interchangeability is known as a
trade-off. To quote Brian Barry:

> The fundamental idea [...] is that although two principles need not to be reducible to a sin-
> gle one, they may normally be expected to be to some extent substitutable for one another.[3]

Julian Le Grand distinguishes two types of trade-off: a trade-off on the values
level – Barry's understanding of the term – and a trade-off on the production level.[4]
The values trade-off expresses how much justice a person or a society is *prepared*

---

[1] Okun, p. 2. Okun uses the term 'equality' which is geared towards distributive justice. Other
authors more commonly use the term 'equity', and less frequently 'fairness' or 'justice'.

[2] Lukes, pp. 36 f.

[3] Barry, p. 6.

[4] Le Grand, p. 555.

K. Mathis, *Efficiency Instead of Justice?*, Law and Philosophy Library 84,
DOI 10.1007/978-1-4020-9798-0_9, © Springer Science+Business Media B.V. 2009

*to sacrifice* in order to achieve more efficiency (or vice versa). With a production trade-off, on the other hand, the question is: how much justice *must be sacrificed* in order to achieve a certain level of efficiency (or vice versa)?[5] And whereas the values trade-off is dependent upon individual values, the production trade-off is determined by empirical facts.

## 9.2 Justice

### 9.2.1 Types of Justice

A classic distinction between types of justice goes back to the fifth book of Aristotle's *Nicomachean Ethics*. Aristotle begins by assuming a universal justice which is the most perfect virtue and contains all the other virtues within it. Thereafter he distinguishes two particular types of justice: distributive and commutative justice:

> (A) one kind is that which is manifested in distributions of honour or money or the other things that fall to be divided among those who have a share in the constitution (for in these it is possible for one man to have a share either unequal or equal to that of another), and (B) one is that which plays a rectifying part in transactions between man and man. Of this there are two divisions; of transactions (1) some are voluntary and (2) others involuntary – voluntary such transactions as sale, purchase, loan for consumption, pledging, loan for use, depositing, letting (they are called voluntary because the origin of these transactions is voluntary), while of the involuntary (a) some are clandestine, such as theft, adultery, poisoning, procuring, enticement of slaves, assassination, false witness, and (b) others are violent, such as assault, imprisonment, murder, robbery with violence, mutilation, abuse, insult.[6]

*Distributive justice* is applied in the allocation of benefits by the state. On this principle, rights are distributed to the people in accordance with their honour, i.e. according to their social status and their merit to the community. Although allocations may be meted out unequally, it must be done according to the same standard.

The first application of commutative justice is in private transactions (in bilateral contracts). It requires the equalization of goods with other goods, without distinction of person. For example, in a contract of sale, the goods tendered should correspond in value to the consideration paid. In addition to voluntary transactions, it also applies to involuntary transactions (torts or crimes): the compensation should be proportionate to the loss and the punishment proportionate to the wrong. The first type of commutative justice is also known as *justice in exchange*, and the second can also be called *corrective justice*.[7]

---

[5] Schefczyk and Priddat, p. 428.

[6] Aristotle, *NE V 6, 1130b–1131a*.

[7] Höffe, *Gerechtigkeit*, p. 23.

When discussion turns on a possible conflict between justice and efficiency, usually the type of justice in question is *distributive justice*, with specific reference to the just distribution of income. When economists talk about justice, this is usually the type of distributive justice they mean. For economic analysis of law, however, this perspective is too narrow. After all, the efficiency criterion is applied primarily to non-contractual liability law, contract law and criminal law. Thus it is no less interesting to examine how *commutative justice* and *corrective justice* relate to efficiency.

## 9.2.2 Distribution Criteria

While the principle of equality applies without limitation in the case of justice in exchange and corrective justice, under distributive justice inequality is possible as long as all distribution is governed by the same standard. Hagel follows Perelman in distinguishing the following six distribution criteria:

### 9.2.2.1 To All in Equal Measure

According to this criterion, all people must be treated in the same way, i.e. without regard to any special characteristic which may distinguish them from one another. Such aspects as age, gender, skin colour, wealth, social status etc. must be disregarded. In this sense, death is undoubtedly just: it comes to all people without regard to any privileges they may have.[8]

In relation to income distribution, this criterion is generally associated with *equality of outcome*: that is, for every member of society to receive the same income. However, this interpretation is not compelling, given that a case can also be made for a concept of *equality of opportunity*,[9] meaning that while everybody may not necessarily receive the same income, they should at least all receive the same initial endowment with production factors.

### 9.2.2.2 To All According to Their Convictions

This criterion focuses on people's inner attitudes and values. Because we can only observe people's conduct, which may stem from worthy convictions, but we cannot observe convictions themselves, this is not an operational criterion. Nevertheless, from a theological perspective it can be a comfort to a morally decent person because it holds out the hope that, despite the many injustices of this life, there will be one final possibility of justice in the hereafter.[10]

---

[8] Perelman, p. 16.

[9] Hagel, p. 253.

[10] Hagel, p. 257.

### 9.2.2.3 To All According to Their Rank

This is an aristocratic conception of justice which consists in treating people according to their social status. *Quod licet Jovi, non licet bovi*[11] as the Latin proverb says. In antiquity, native citizens and free men were accorded a privileged status compared to foreigners and slaves. In medieval times there were various classes, from the nobility and the clergy to the serfs who toiled on the land.[12] Other examples are the caste system in India – which still exerts a strong influence to this day, although officially abolished – and the former policy of apartheid in South Africa.

This aristocratic distribution principle is regularly extolled and vehemently defended by its beneficiaries. In reality, however, it is a strategy verging on the morally indefensible for upholding and defending privileges which, for their part, have mostly proceeded from dubious circumstances.

### 9.2.2.4 To All According to Their Legal Entitlement

This conception corresponds to the famed *suum cuique*[13] of the Romans, whereby justice means rendering to all people what the law says is their rightful due. Thus, there is no more to being just than requiring the judge to follow the law.[14] The drawback of this criterion is that it can only be applied at a secondary level, which is once the legal due has itself been normatively justified.[15]

### 9.2.2.5 To All According to Their Needs

Need-based distribution means that income is allocated in accordance with people's inner motivation to alleviate certain states of deprivation. But it is far from easy to determine what people's needs are. Clearly, dire need of the kind which stems from hunger or illness can be recognized directly. In contrast, needs which go beyond the provision of basic necessities are difficult to ascertain because they are not directly apparent. On the other hand, perhaps it is not even desirable to pander to people's every fancy, and the decision to meet only essential needs is a deliberate one. But the problem of defining a 'minimum subsistence income' illustrates how difficult it is to circumscribe which needs are essential.[16]

---

[11] What is permitted to Jupiter is not permitted to the ox.

[12] Perelman, pp. 18 f.

[13] To every man his due.

[14] Perelman, pp. 19 f.

[15] Hagel, p. 258.

[16] Perelman, pp. 35 ff.

### 9.2.2.6 To All According to Their Merit

If an action is directed towards achieving specific results, then it is appropriate to apply the principle of merit. An actor's endeavour is rewarded with corresponding remuneration or some other form of recognition. Classic examples of the application of this criterion are sporting or artistic contests, or the grading of school work.[17]

The principle of merit creates incentives for certain forms of work, although the rewards often depend on the circumstances. Work for which there is little or no demand or willingness to pay in the market will be poorly rewarded or even unrewarded, even if it is of high quality or great artistic value. So it was that the painter Vincent van Gogh spent his lifetime in abject poverty, even though the works of art he created are of inestimable value today.[18]

## 9.2.3 Static Versus Dynamic Concept of Distributive Justice

The classical distribution criteria just discussed are based on a *static* concept of distributive justice. Most contemporary theories of distributive justice are *dynamic*, however; that is to say, they advocate neither a specific just distribution nor an ideal distribution. They advocate institutional structures which enable individuals to do certain things or to realize life plans regardless of the exact result of the ultimate income distribution.

Rawls's understanding of distributive justice belongs firmly in this category. His approach is not primarily about defining a particular share of social resources. Endowments of material primary goods may indeed differ, as long as the difference principle is observed. Primary goods are necessary because they facilitate a certain freedom of choice, and hence the realization of individual life plans.[19] If the appropriate just institutions are in place, distributive justice is satisfied even if the outcome is an unequal distribution of income:

> [This] enables us to regard distributive justice as a case of *pure background procedural justice*: when everyone follows the publicly recognized rules of cooperation, the particular distribution that results is acceptable as just whatever that distribution turns out to be [. . .].[20]

According to Rawls, static theories of distributive justice are based on a 'historical process view' whereas dynamic theories consist of a 'social process view'. His approach has the advantage of requiring only the establishment of '*background justice*', which marks out the framework for social cooperation without the constant need to make comparisons between the relative positions of individuals.[21]

---

[17] Hagel, pp. 258 f.

[18] HAGEL, p. 261.

[19] See Sect. 7.3 above

[20] Rawls, *JF*, § 15.3, p. 54 (author's emphasis).

[21] Rawls, *JF*, § 15.3, pp. 54 f.

With regard to the goal conflict between distributive justice and efficiency, to be discussed below, the *assumption* will be made that a more equitable distribution of income is fundamentally preferable to a less equitable distribution. The same thing will apply *a fortiori* to starting opportunities. The efficiency goal, in contrast, gives due recognition to the merit principle.

## 9.3 Efficiency

### 9.3.1 The Concept

When people talk about efficiency – during a political discussion, for instance – what they usually mean is productivity or the performance of the economy. This is reported in terms of domestic product or, for a comparative figure over time, the rate of economic growth.[22] With this in mind, Polinsky's definition of efficiency is straightforward enough to be understood by anyone:

> [E]fficiency corresponds to the "size of the pie", while equity has to do with how it is sliced.[23]

But does this account of efficiency lend itself to a more technical interpretation of efficiency, i.e. as Pareto efficiency or Kaldor-Hicks efficiency? – Depending on whether or not it is acceptable for some people to lose out from an increase in efficiency, one efficiency criterion or the other will be applicable. Polinsky leaves this question open. Let us therefore look at the following example, quoted by von Weizsäcker in order to justify the benefits of rationalization measures:

> Let us consider, for example, a rationalization project. Its negative impact is heavily concentrated on a small group of affected employees, who will perhaps lose their jobs, and competitors, who will fall behind the rationalizing competitor. The beneficial impacts of rationalization – apart from increased profits for the firm undertaking rationalization – are distributed among many people who profit from the lower price of the product. [...] Each individual may be negatively affected by one such project, but will be positively affected by all the others at the same time. Since every single rationalization project generates more benefit than harm, it can be expected that the individual citizen will typically derive more benefit than harm from rationalization on aggregate. This may be valid typically; but perhaps not in every individual case.[24]

According to von Weizsäcker, rationalization programmes always give rise to winners and losers. Although on average everyone reaps the benefits in the long-term, such benefits cannot be guaranteed in any given instance. Hence it is evident that von Weizsäcker can only mean the Kaldor-Hicks type of efficiency, as one

---

[22] Sometimes efficiency is confused with 'effectiveness'. Effectiveness is the extent to which a defined goal is attained using specific means (also known as a 'target-actual comparison'). Cf. von Arnim, p. 51.

[23] Polinsky, p. 7.

[24] von Weizsäcker, p. 130.

would almost always expect in the context of such discussions. This permits the following conclusion:

*An increase in efficiency normally means an increase in economic output without regard for income distribution.* If we now replace the somewhat vague concept of 'economic output' with Posner's term 'wealth', then we arrive at Kaldor-Hicks efficiency in the technical sense. For ultimately, according to Posner, wealth maximization and Kaldor-Hicks efficiency mean the same thing.

### 9.3.2  Is Efficiency a Goal At All?

Before the relationship between justice and efficiency can be discussed, it is necessary to resolve the question of whether efficiency can be viewed as a goal at all. As we know, Posner abandoned his earlier position that wealth in itself, and hence efficiency, represented the goal of society. Efficiency is far rather an *instrument* for achieving other social goals. According to Dworkin, a trade-off between means and ends makes no sense – unless efficiency is thought of as a 'false target' for other goals:

> It makes no sense to speak of trading off means against ends [. . .]. Someone who speaks this way must have in mind an entirely different point. He might mean, for example, that sometimes we achieve more of the desired end if we aim only at what is (in this sense) a means. That is the "false target" instrumental theory [. . .].[25]

Likewise, Le Grand does not view efficiency as an actual goal in itself, but as a means of striving towards another possible goal, such as increasing social utility.[26] As we know, however, only an increase in Pareto efficiency – and not Kaldor-Hicks efficiency – will always bring about an increase in social utility. Therefore efficiency is only of limited use as a 'false target' for increasing social utility in the utilitarian sense.

## 9.4  Specific Goal Relations

### 9.4.1  Justice In Exchange and Efficiency

Let us imagine that in a society, goods were distributed more or less equally, but the members of that society only had certain tradeable goods at their disposal. Some people would have sugar, others tobacco. Soon these people would probably realize that they had different goods, and would start wanting to exchange certain goods. Then somebody might trade, say, two kilograms of sugar for a kilogram of tobacco. The trade would go ahead by voluntary consensus, the parties involved being fully

---

[25] Dworkin, 'Wealth', p. 204.

[26] Le Grand, 561 f.

informed about the alternative trades they could otherwise make. What would be the effect of this trade on the utility of the parties involved? Would they simply have exchanged goods of equal value, and now be as well off as they were before? Or would the transaction leave them better off?[27]

According to Aristotle, the exchange of goods is a question of price justice. The just price (*iustum pretium*) should be determined in such a way that the payment and what is rendered in return are in equilibrium. If the traded goods are equal in value in this sense, then based on the Aristotelean view, nobody is better or worse off after the trade. Now economic theory questions the validity of this equality principle: the person who wants the tobacco does in fact value a kilogram of tobacco more highly than two kilograms of sugar. By the same token, two kilograms of sugar are worth more to the other person than one kilogram of tobacco. Consequently, those involved benefit from the trade and are better off than they were before. In other words they experience a utility gain. For if both parties to the trade were not to benefit, they would not have any incentive to trade.[28]

The different valuations of goods are based on people's differing preferences. Some prefer apples, others prefer pears: *de gustibus non est disputandum*.[29] People will trade goods as long as both parties involved can benefit – or if at least one stands to benefit without making the other worse off. Thus society's utility increases for as long as somebody can be made better off without putting someone else in a worse position. This fits the definition of a Pareto-superior change. The lesson is that social utility can be increased through trade until efficient consumption has been achieved.[30]

This line of argument does, however, presuppose the model of perfect competition.[31] In reality, business firms try to stifle competition through monopolies or cartels – and there is sufficient incentive for them to do so.[32] A state *cartel control authority* can intervene correctively here. This has the desired effect not only upon efficiency but also, as a rule, on distribution because consumers benefit from lower prices. A further possibility is to institute *direct price controls* – in the form of price monitoring, for instance – or *statutory price regulation*, examples of which can still be found in Swiss rent law and in some aspects of the regulation of agriculture. However, interventions in the price mechanism on the grounds of efficiency are not without their problems. It is true that a price control system – in a similar way to a cartel control authority – can tackle inflated monopoly prices, which encourages efficiency. But it becomes problematic when price control or any other form of state regulation is used to try to keep prices artificially above or below the competitive price. This was how price support in agriculture led to excessive production, for example.

---

[27] Cf. Fletcher, p. 156.

[28] Cf. Fletcher, p. 157.

[29] There is no disputing about taste.

[30] Cf. Fletcher, p. 157; see Sect. 3.2.1.2.

[31] See Sect. 3.2.2.

[32] See end of Sect. 5.4.3.

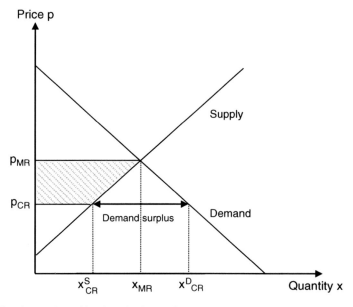

**Fig. 9.1** Housing market with price-elastic supply

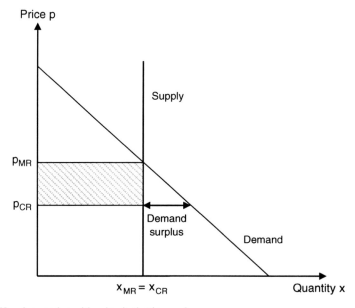

**Fig. 9.2** Housing market with price-inelastic supply

The same problem can arise in private Fair Trade initiatives, such as the Max Havelaar Foundation, for example. Its approach, once again, attempts to impose prices which are higher than the market norm. If plunging prices in world markets are caused by oversupply, then any artificial price stabilization gets in the way of the necessary adjustment processes. Thus, in the long term, the effects are counterproductive. If, on the other hand, Fair Trade campaigns engage with this problem and foster sustainable development, they are entirely worthwhile.

Another example of price regulation is found in Swiss rent law, where cost-covering rent is given priority over market rent (i.e. a maximum price limit is set for rent). The extent to which this has a negative influence on efficiency depends mainly on the price-elasticity of the supply of housing, i.e. the responsiveness of the quantity of homes on offer to a change in rent.

Two contrasting cases will be analysed below. In the first case, the supply-side response is price-elastic, which is reflected here in a rising supply curve (Fig. 9.1). In the second case, the supply is completely price-inelastic, i.e. it remains constant, represented by the vertical supply curve (Fig. 9.2). In the case of a price-elastic supply curve, at the cost-covering rent ($p_{CR}$) the supply of housing declines to $x_{CR}^S$ as compared with the supply at the market rent ($p_{MR}$), and a market disequilibrium occurs (demand surplus).

Where the supply curve is price-inelastic, a market disequilibrium also arises, but the supply of housing at the cost-covering rent remains the same as at the market rent ($x_{CR} = x_{MR}$).

In respect of distribution, in both cases it is the tenants who benefit to the detriment of the landlords (shaded trapezium, shaded rectangle). Because the supply of housing declines in the first case, the efficiency losses are substantial. In the second case, on the other hand, no such efficiency losses occur because there is no reduction in the supply of housing.[33]

The patent method favoured by economists is to give the market free rein and conduct social policy via the national budget. In our example, however, price regulation has a decisive advantage over this solution, namely that no social transfer or administration costs are incurred; in other words, there is no burden on the public purse. And since the supply of living accommodation in Switzerland is determined primarily by spatial planning, the introduction of market rents would hardly increase the supply of housing. But the distributive effects of a market rent might well be very significant, considering that the costs of rent generally constitute a substantial proportion of household expenditure. Which solution is preferable here must be determined in the course of the political process. The decision ultimately depends upon how the impacts on efficiency and distribution are assessed and evaluated.[34]

---

[33] However, the market is still in disequilibrium, which is itself somewhat problematic. As a result, other allocation criteria beside price are bound come into play, which cannot always be designated as 'just'.

[34] See also Sect. 9.4.3 below.

### 9.4.2 Corrective Justice and Efficiency

According to the traditional view, the fundamental role of tort law is to provide the injured party with *compensation for the damage sustained* (principle of redress), whilst its *preventative function*, that of reducing damage, is a desirable by-product that is of secondary importance at best.[35] It does not systematically pursue the goal of efficiency. Nevertheless, efficiency is certainly desirable as long as it does not clash with corrective justice.

Guido Calabresi shares the opinion that legal rules in tort law should primarily be just, and need only be efficient as a secondary concern.[36] He nevertheless maintains that when it comes to the analysis of legal rules, the question of efficiency should be examined before the question of justice. The efficiency of legal norms can be determined on the basis of clearly comprehensible rules. In contrast, whether a legal rule is just is usually a thorny question. According to Calabresi, it is always easier to say what is *unjust*. Hence he suggests examining the question of whether liability rules are efficient first, and eliminating those rules which are deemed unjust as the next step:

> The fact that what is unfair is easier to define than what is fair, like the fact that what is fair in one system may be unfair in another, indicates that it would be better to examine the requirements of accident cost reduction first and then see how various untried methods and systems suggested by that goal compare in terms of fairness we use today [...].[37]

Following this procedure, attention could be given to both goals – compensation and efficiency –, whilst wholly inefficient legal rules would be excluded from the outset. Whether any of the efficient legal rules would also satisfy society's conceptions of justice remains an unanswered question.

For Coleman or Weinrib it is the concept of corrective justice that best explains the relationship between the injurer and the injured party. This view merits acceptance. But it does not necessarily rule out taking social costs into consideration when liability rules are being defined.[38]

### 9.4.3 Distributive Justice and Efficiency

In his book, *Equality and Efficiency: The Big Tradeoff* (1975), Arthur M. Okun describes the antagonism between efficiency and distributive justice as the greatest socioeconomic goal conflict of all, because the concept of efficiency follows the principle of the insatiability of needs:

> This concept of efficiency implies that more is better, insofar as the "more" consists of items that people want to buy.[39]

---

[35] Schäfer and Ott, p. 113.

[36] Calabresi, *Accidents*, p. 24.

[37] Calabresi, *Accidents*, p. 26.

[38] See more extensive discussion in Sect. 4.4.1.8 above.

[39] Okun, p. 2.

The goal conflict arises, he says, because redistribution is often bound up with efficiency losses. To illustrate this problem, Okun uses the image of the 'leaky bucket': a bucket is used to scoop water from a full container and pour it into another container which is empty. But because this bucket leaks, some water is lost on the way from one container to the other.[40] Okun goes on to list various factors which cause such leakage losses:

(1)  Redistribution entails *administrative costs*. The state must employ officials to collect taxes and hand out the money to claimants. Private individuals also face administrative costs, from form-filling to lawyers' fees in the event of legal disputes. These aspects absorb resources which could otherwise be deployed productively.[41]
(2)  Redistribution can have a negative effect on *work incentives*, both for taxpayers and for recipients.[42] For recipients of social transfers, there is little incentive to work if earnings from employment are penalized by deducting the full amount from the social transfer. In any case, higher income taxes lower the effective rate of post-tax pay for all working people. This presumably reduces the incentive to work. However, the opposite effect can also occur: households may increase their working hours to make up for higher taxes, in order to maintain their household income at a constant level (tax recovery). This second effect occurs primarily among high earners and in families in which both parents are not working full-time.
(3)  It is also possible for redistribution to have a negative effect on *saving and investment*.[43] Since poorer people normally have a higher rate of consumption than the wealthy, the fear is that less will be saved or invested, which holds back growth in the national economy. The counter-argument is that as consumer expenditure rises, the self-financing of business firms improves thanks to higher profits. The reserves built up by firms can thus compensate for the decline in savings by households.
(4)  Okun also fears that people's *values* could be negatively affected by redistribution, and anti-productive tendencies could detract from their attitude to work. Furthermore the population's sense of self-reliance could be weakened.[44] The counter-argument is that major income disparities in a society can foster far more destructive tendencies. Both poverty and extreme wealth lead to decadence and decay. Moreover, large income disparities weaken a society's cohesion.

The trade-off between justice and efficiency is often represented by means of a *transformation curve* (Fig. 9.3).[45]

---

[40] Okun, pp. 91 ff.

[41] Okun, p. 96.

[42] Okun, pp. 96 ff.

[43] Okun, p. 98.

[44] Okun, p. 100.

[45] See e.g. Stiglitz, p. 60.

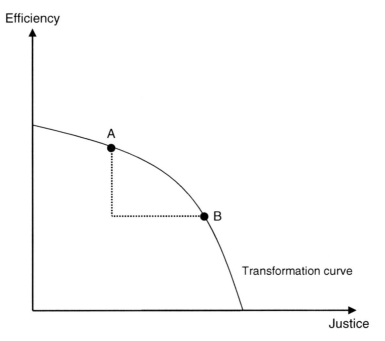

**Fig. 9.3** Trade-off between justice and efficiency (cf. Stiglitz, p. 60)

This transformation curve represents all the possible combinations of justice and efficiency. The negative slope means that more justice is associated with less efficiency, and vice versa. The concave line of the curve expresses that with growing concentration on one of the two goals, sacrifices increasingly have to be made in respect of the other goal. In order to establish the limits of redistribution according to this concept, there are two aspects to consider:[46]

(1)  On the one hand, there is an empirical question to clarify: what *actual trade-off* can be observed in a society between just income distribution and the efficiency of the economy (cf. the line of the transformation curve).
(2)  On the other hand, it is necessary to resolve the problem of *value competition* between efficiency and distributive justice. That is, society has to decide what mixture of justice and efficiency it wants (i.e. the choice of the optimal point on the curve).

Okun leaves open the empirical question of what line the transformation curve takes in individual countries; it has not been answered conclusively to this day. It is undeniable that redistribution entails administrative costs. Meanwhile the other arguments raised by Okun are very speculative, and the relevant research findings are contradictory and do not yield consistent results.[47]

---

[46] Hagel, p. 266.

[47] See e.g. Alesina and Rodrik: 'Distributive Politics and Economic Growth' or Persson and Tabellini: 'Is Inequality Harmful for Growth?'.

In a democracy, the second question is answered in the course of the democratic process. The taxation system, the social security system, the education sector and the public services all play a central role in redistribution. One particular approach to equalizing income distribution is to manipulate the initial endowment with resources, i.e. to equalize people's starting opportunities. An individual's initial endowment is heavily dependent on the parents' incomes and assets. Here corrective interventions could be made by means of *inheritance taxes*. On the other hand, starting opportunities can also be equalized by means of an *education system* which is accessible to all, either free of charge or at least on an affordable basis.[48]

It must also be borne in mind that the relation between efficiency and distributive justice need not always be a trade-off; on the contrary, in many areas there is a *positive correlation*:

(1)  An education system geared towards equalizing starting opportunities increases the number of *highly skilled workers*, and these can make a major contribution to value creation.
(2)  Sociopolitically motivated integration programmes for the unemployed foster their *reintegration* into the labour market.
(3)  Sociopolitical measures are fundamentally integrative in their effects and are thus a *means of counteracting crime*. This not only gives the population more security, but also reduces the costs of prosecution and law enforcement.
(4)  Societies with less inequality of income distribution generally have greater social and political stability. This makes such countries more attractive to investors.

These considerations show that the trade-off concept only highlights one aspect and is thus *one-dimensional*. There is no monocausal connection between efficiency and justice. In point of fact, there are *multiple interdependencies* between the two goals, and while they conflict in some respects, in many other ways they actually stand in a harmonious or at least a neutral relationship to one another.[49]

## 9.5  Separating Justice and Efficiency?

Posner proposed that the civil courts should be committed to the efficiency principle, whilst the public sector could concern itself with distributive justice.[50] So a modern legal system would have to be subdivided into two sections: the first, which would regulate the private exchange of goods and services, should be guided by the efficiency goal. The second, dealing with tax and social law, should counterbalance this

---

[48] From this perspective, both the raising of university tuition fees and the abolition of inheritance taxes are to be decisively rejected.

[49] Cf. Lukes, p. 37.

[50] Posner, *Jurisprudence*, p. 388.

by pursuing the goal of distributive justice.[51] In simplified terms: private law would have to prioritize the efficiency criterion, and public law would have to prioritize the principle of justice. Kaplow and Shavell share Posner's view:

> [R]edistribution through legal rules offers no advantage over redistribution through the income tax system and typically is less efficient.[52]

In their book *Fairness versus Welfare* (2002), Kaplow and Shavell even assert that giving independent consideration to principles of justice (especially corrective justice) in assessing legal rules – specifically within liability and contract law[53] – reduces welfare, and in certain instances actually makes everyone worse off:

> Under welfare economics [...] the analyst would not take into account factors that do not bear on individuals' well-being, notably, whether liability under the negligence rule is required by corrective justice or other notions of fairness that some would accord independent significance.[54]

They go on to try and prove this point using various constructed examples, and with apparent success. But there is a problem with this approach: in the context of their utilitarian analytical framework[55] the assertion that, compared to a policy which is exclusively social-welfare-oriented, separate consideration of non-utilitarian principles of justice diminishes welfare cannot be anything other than true. However, it would be necessary to give a rationale for preferring a utilitarian over a deontological ethic. That would require adopting a meta-ethical position. The idea that from a (preference-) utilitarian perspective of utilitarianism, deontological or mixed conceptions must be superior, should come as no surprise.[56] It is an utter *tautology* as Kaplow and Shavell frankly admit:

> [I]t is true that it is virtually a tautology to assert that fairness-based evaluation entails some sort of reduction in individuals' well-being, for notions of fairness are principles of evaluation that give weight to factors unrelated to individuals' well-being.[57]

The two authors emphasize that they are only averse to the independent consideration of principles of justice; whereas if these were integrated into the utility function of individuals as matters of preference ('tastes for fairness') and thus made a contribution to the welfare of society, it would be unproblematic:

---

[51] Schäfer and Ott, p. 31.

[52] Kaplow and Shavell, 'Income Tax', p. 667.

[53] See Kaplow and Shavell, *Fairness*, pp. 85 ff. and pp. 155 ff.

[54] Kaplow and Shavell, *Fairness*, p. 17.

[55] They themselves talk about 'welfare economics' and the consideration of 'well-being', explicitly distancing their utilitarian viewpoint from wealth maximization. Kaplow and Shavell, *Fairness*, pp. 5 and 35 ff. Even so, they continue to treat wealth as a proxy variable for social welfare. Kaplow and Shavell, *Fairness*, p. 37.

[56] For discussion of the advantages and disadvantages of such conceptions, see Chapters 6 and 7 above on utilitarianism and on John Rawls's theory of justice.

[57] Kaplow and Shavell, *Fairness*, p. 58; a similar statement is also found on p. 7.

We further note a particular source of well-being [. . .], namely, the possibility that individuals have a taste for notions of fairness, just as they may have a taste for art, nature, or fine wine.[58]

This would overcome the conflict between a utilitarian conception and principles of justice. Nevertheless, as a solution to the problem, it is dubious: it is dangerous to leave principles of justice to the taste, and hence the discretionary whim, of individuals, for it is uncertain whether these principles will be sufficiently weighted in a utilitarian calculus to warrant observance. Principles of justice are in danger of sinking in the morass of the social 'good' unless they are accorded some weight in their own right, as a corrective.

Although the concept put forward by Kaplow and Shavell fails to convince, their analysis does bring to light one or two useful insights. They conclude, for example, that any welfare loss that might arise as a consequence of taking principles of justice into account should be made transparent:

[B]ecause notions of fairness sometimes result in a reduction of individuals' well-being – and in certain cases lead to a reduction in every-one's well-being – when they are given weight as independent evaluative principles, the manner in which a notion of fairness sacrifices welfare should be identified clearly so that it will be possible to appreciate what is at stake in adopting the principle.[59]

This demand certainly merits approval: what it calls for is a legislative impact assessment regime (ex ante or prospective analysis) that determines what effects future laws will have,[60] as well as an evaluation of the effects of existing laws (ex post or retrospective analysis). However, Kaplow and Shavell provide no criteria for weighing up fairness and welfare – and their concept has no need of them, because fairness enters the equation only, at best, as a subjective preference in the utility function. Yet it remains equally unclear how these individual utility functions should be aggregated into a societal utility function. Nor do they resolve the known methodological problems of utilitarianism regarding the intrapersonal and interpersonal comparison of utility.[61]

Polinsky considers redistribution measures in contract law – e.g. via stricter seller's liability – to be ineffective, because the expected costs of liability would be shifted onto the consumer via the product price.[62] Conversely, according to Polinsky, redistribution via non-contractual liability law would be a fundamental possibility, since involuntary transactions do not normally offer cost-shifting opportunities.[63] In spite of this, he too prefers redistribution via the tax and transfer system, because it is not only cheaper but can also be effected with much greater precision:

---

[58] Kaplow and Shavell, *Fairness*, p. 21.

[59] Kaplow and Shavell, *Fairness*, p. 471.

[60] See for example the relevant arguments on regulatory impact analysis in Switzerland in Chapter 10.

[61] On these problems see Sect. 6.3.3 above. More generally, see also Coleman, 'Grounds', esp. pp. 1514 ff. and 1538 ff.

[62] Polinsky, p. 123.

[63] Polinsky, p. 124.

[R]edistribution through the government's tax and transfer system may be cheaper and is likely to be more precise. In other words, the potential conflict between efficiency and equity when income redistribution is costly should be considered in the design of the government's tax and transfer system, but not generally in the choice of legal rules.[64]

The proposition that social policy goals can be realized more effectively via the tax and transfer system than via private law is probably more accurate than not. Nevertheless, the idea of dividing the sectors to pursue the two goals of justice and efficiency separately remains unconvincing, for the following reasons:

(1) Allocation and distribution are indivisibly linked to one another. It is not possible to have efficient production on the one hand and just distribution on the other. *Taxes and transfers also have an influence on work incentives and the use of production factors.* Hence, redistribution via the state administrative apparatus is not necessarily always more efficient than redistribution through regulation of the private sector.

(2) On the contrary, it is more than likely that low-cost and effective redistribution can be carried out *equally well, specifically by means of private law.* As the example of rent law shows, redistribution by fine-tuning legislation under private law can indeed work well. In principle, there is absolutely no reason not to use private law – as a complement to tax law and social law – as an instrument of redistribution in certain cases.[65]

(3) *In specific instances it could lead to very absurd outcomes* if private law were focused solely on efficiency. Particularly in civil litigation, the parties are intent upon a ruling which is in tune with their conceptions of justice. They are unlikely to be satisfied with the reasoning that, although the ruling is not just, it encourages economic efficiency instead.

## 9.6 Summary

The demand that private law should exclusively pursue the goal of efficiency and public law the goal of justice must be rejected. *It is rather the role of the legislator, and the courts in their turn, to strike a subtle balance between conflicting rights in all areas of the law.* In doing so, the multiple interdependencies between efficiency and justice must be borne in mind. Moreover, the discussion should not be confined merely to the two goals of justice and efficiency, but should also be extended to other goals such as legal certainty or human dignity.[66] In every case a multitude of legal policy goals exist which could step forward to compete with the efficiency goal in instances where, perhaps, it is not so worthwhile to use private law for the pursuit of distribution policy goals.[67]

---

[64] Polinsky, p. 10.

[65] Eidenmüller, p. 321.

[66] Cf. Eidenmüller, p. 273.

[67] Eidenmüller, p. 316.

# Chapter 10
# Conclusions

> *When inefficiency reduces general productivity, worsens the structures of distribution and destroys the economic and political flexibility of the system as a whole, then one of the foremost victims is justice.*[1]

Jeremy Bentham's utilitarianism can be commended for its orientation to human needs and its equal treatment of every person, rich or poor. Under a system of wealth maximization, this is different: *the utility of the rich is privileged.* Moreover, the same objection must be raised to wealth maximization as to utilitarianism: the individual as such is not taken seriously, a flaw which is brought into particular focus by the *question of basic rights* and the *problem of distributive justice.* This impelled John Rawls to develop his two principles of justice. According to the first, the liberty principle, every individual must be endowed with basic rights. In the second, the difference principle, he offers a distribution criterion which is intended to prevent unduly large income disparities. As we have seen, however, the difference principle is not particularly effectual. In the Swiss system of law, basic rights are guaranteed by the constitution and the bulk of redistribution is negotiated through the ongoing political process.

Yet the critique of wealth maximization does not necessarily mean that the demand for efficiency is fundamentally unjustified. Efficiency and justice are by no means mutually exclusive; in fact, they stand in a complex interrelationship. Although this relationship is not without its strains, it is reasonable to conclude that the endeavour to realize both goals need not always be a competitive trade-off, and can in fact be undertaken cooperatively to large extent.[2]

The material crux of the positive correlation between efficiency and justice is the trivial point that it is only possible to distribute what is earned. If inefficiency reduces the domestic product, this also has repercussions for justice. This issue is particularly topical in relation to the state budget: higher economic growth would generate more tax revenues for the public purse. These in turn would enable the state to perform its functions better, thinking particularly of the promotion of education and training (equality of opportunity) and the financing of social security (social

---

[1] Kersting, *Soziale Gerechtigkeit*, p. 108.

[2] Kersting, *Soziale Gerechtigkeit*, p. 106.

K. Mathis, *Efficiency Instead of Justice?*, Law and Philosophy Library 84, DOI 10.1007/978-1-4020-9798-0_10, © Springer Science+Business Media B.V. 2009

justice). *Thus, efficiency is always one of the precepts of justice.* It is the irony of history that the accomplishments of the social state can only be secured through economic growth – that is, more market activity and greater economic efficiency.

Turning the table, however, it is equally possible to assert the demand for justice on the grounds of efficiency. If injustice diminishes people's productivity and will to work and undermines the legitimacy of the social system, then justice is proven to be a basic prerequisite of efficiency.[3] Besides justice and efficiency, however, legal certainty is another important principle of law. Moreover, in the long run, legal certainty is often conducive to efficiency. For it would hardly be worthwhile to engage in economic activity if one lived in fear of being deprived of one's duly-acquired rights at any moment for short-term reasons of efficiency.[4]

As these considerations show, the goal relations between the different legal principles are more intricate than they may appear at first glance. *Therefore the economic efficiency arguments need to be incorporated into a method for resolving value conflicts. In a democracy, this has to happen as part of the political decision-making process.*[5] Hence, in the Swiss legal system with codified law, the efficiency goal should be given due attention at the level of legislation and not delegated to the judicial process.[6]

According to Gustav Radbruch, the law should be guided by the following three principles: justice, expediency and legal certainty.[7] *Efficiency should be added to that list as a fourth principle of law.* This entails arranging the legal system so as to foster economic efficiency. Laws should thus be subjected to an 'efficiency test', which means that any given draft bill should be analysed, in the course of the legislative process, to establish its likely impacts on economic efficiency. *This should be done as part of a legislative impact assessment regime whereby the economic consequences of legal regulations are systematically examined.* For if the legislative process has regard for the economic consequences of laws, this is bound to have an effect on the judicial process as well.

In the United States, cost-benefit analyses have long been standard practice in relation to major new regulations. Since 1995, the OECD has recommended that its member countries should carry out Regulatory Impact Analysis (RIA) as part of the legislative process. Also, in the wake of the Mandelkern Report (2001), the European Union passed a plan to simplify and improve the regulatory framework. This imposes impact analysis for the most important legislative proposals.[8]

Since the year 2000, Switzerland has had its own instrument of regulatory impact analysis at the Confederation level which is geared towards the recommendations

---

[3] Kersting, *Soziale Gerechtigkeit*, pp. 106 ff.

[4] von der Pfordten, p. 352.

[5] von der Crone, pp. 46 f.

[6] Taupitz, p. 166.

[7] Radbruch, pp. 73 ff.

[8] On impact orientation in law, see e.g. Weigel, pp. 194 ff., and van Aaken, pp. 146 ff.

of the OECD.[9] Its constitutional basis is given in Art. 170 of the Swiss Federal Constitution, according to which the Federal Assembly has to ensure scrutiny of the effectiveness of Federal Government measures.[10] The specific statutory hook for prospective analysis of draft legislation is found in Art. 141 (2g) of the Parliament Act. Under this provision, the notices to draft bills proposed by the Swiss Federal Council[11] must include statements on the legislation's anticipated impacts on the economy, society and the environment, insofar as substantial comments on these aspects can be made. According to the decree and guidelines of the Swiss Federal Council of September 15, 1999, all legislation must now be subjected to an economic impact analysis before it is enacted. The analysis should include scrutiny of the following five points:

(1) Necessity and possibility of state action
(2) Impacts on individual social groups
(3) Impacts on the whole economy
(4) Alternative regulations
(5) Expediency in enforcement

So far, regulatory impact analysis in Switzerland has been utilized prospectively in the context of finalizing the details of legislation at Confederation level. Supplementary use is made of another instrument, the small and medium-sized enterprise (SME) compatibility test. For major regulations, a cost-benefit analysis is also required.

The strength of *cost-benefit analysis* is that it attempts a comprehensive evaluation of the economic impacts of a measure or a project. But attention should also be given to this method's weaknesses: the insistence on monetarization means that a financial value must be attached to all impacts, even those for which no market prices are available. Whilst it is relatively easy to evaluate costs in monetary terms, benefits must often be assessed using ad hoc reference data and rough approximations. These uncertainties produce valuations with rather broad scope for interpretation, which can cast doubt on the meaningfulness of the results. Moreover, future costs and benefits must be discounted to a reference point in time. Here the choice of the discount rate has significant implications for the result.[12]

A further point to bear in mind is that in a cost-benefit analysis, essentially it makes no difference which social groups are the beneficiaries of a legal regulation and who will have to bear the likely costs. As long as society's balance sheet is positive after all costs and benefits have been accounted for, that is sufficient. In the terminology of welfare economics, it is sufficient if the Kaldor-Hicks compensation criterion is satisfied. It would therefore be a desirable objective for all legal

---

[9] See OECD, *Regulatory Impact Analysis*.

[10] On the general situation in Switzerland, also see Mader, pp. 100 ff.

[11] The Swiss government.

[12] On the problems of cost-benefit analyses, see Lave, 'Benefit-Cost Analysis'.

regulations to be analysed with regard to their *impact on income distribution*, to enable political decision-makers to form a rounded overall judgement.

Less problematic than the normatively-laden efficiency criteria of welfare economics are the *analysis methods of positive economics*. In particular, it is helpful, to begin with, if analysis of the impacts of laws takes account of the *incentives* they exert on economic subjects. Even purely qualitative consideration can prove very useful in this regard. Such a review should be made the minimum standard for absolutely all legislation – not just at central government level, but also at subordinate levels of the state.

Under common law, it is principally the role of the courts to bring economic rationality into judgements. Under a codified law system, however, this is only possible within very narrow confines due to considerations of legitimization, given the principle of separation of powers and the legality principle. *Unless legitimized by the legislature, any recognition of economics-based argumentation strategies within the judicial process should be viewed with caution.*[13] Nevertheless, in certain legal circumstances, it is already possible for the legislator to instruct the administration and the courts explicitly to give due regard to efficiency as a legal principle.[14] In doing so, however, care must be taken not to overload the relevant enforcement authorities with the associated information procurement and processing work.

Either way, it is very important for lawyers to be sensitized during their training to the economic aspects of the law. Therefore, another desirable objective is to include economic analysis methods on the curriculum of law faculties – although this should come under a broader heading, like 'Law and Economics'. Such a subject is undoubtedly an enriching element of a legal education. Economic legal theory cannot and should not take the place of traditional methods of jurisprudence, but is an important complementary facet.

When asked what he found most interesting about the economic analysis of law, one of Posner's teachers is said to have replied, 'Its limits'.[15] In any critical reflection on the potential and the limits of economic analysis of law, the philosophical foundations play a key role. With that in mind, the author hopes this work will prove useful as a contribution to the interdisciplinary discourse.

---

[13] See esp. Eidenmüller, pp. 414 ff.; for criticism, also Janson, p. 152. On the economic analysis of court rulings, nevertheless, see Kötz and Schäfer, *Judex oeconomicus*.

[14] Swiss federal judge Hansjörg Seiler and Laurent Bieri take the view that in Switzerland, application of the 'Hand rule' in liability law would already be a fundamental possibility *de lege lata*. See Seiler: 'Wie viel Sicherheit wollen wir? Sicherheitsmassnahmen zwischen Kostenwirksamkeit und Recht'; also Bieri: 'La faute au sens de l'article 41 CO – Plaidoyer pour une reconnaissance explicite de la "règle de hand" '.

[15] Posner, 'Economic Approach', p. 772.

# Bibliography

Adams, Michael, *Ökonomische Theorie des Rechts: Konzepte und Anwendungen* (Frankfurt am Main et al., 2002)

Albert, Hans, *Traktat über rationale Praxis* (Tübingen, 1978; cited as: *Rationale Praxis*)

Albert, Hans, *Traktat über kritische Vernunft*, (4th edn., Tübingen, 1989; cited as: *Kritische Vernunft*)

Alesina, Alberto and Rodrik, Dani, 'Distributive Politics and Economic Growth', in *Quarterly Journal of Economics*, Vol. 109 (1994), pp. 465 ff.

Aristotle, *The Nichomachean Ethics*, trans. William David Ross (Oxford, 1908; cited as: *NE, book, chapter, section*)

Arrow, Kenneth J., *Social Choices and Individual Values* (2nd edn., New York, 1963)

Assmann, Heinz-Dieter, Kirchner, Christian and Schanze, Erich (eds.), *Ökonomische Analyse des Rechts* (Tübingen, 1993)

Axelrod, Robert, *Die Evolution der Kooperation*, trans. and with afterword by Werner Raub and Thomas Voss (5th edn., Munich, 2000); published in English as *The Evolution of Cooperation* (New York, 1984)

Barber, Benjamin, 'Justifying Justice: Problems of Psychology, Politics and Measurement in Rawls', in Norman Daniels (ed.), *Reading Rawls, Critical Studies on Rawls' 'A Theory of Justice'* (Oxford, 1975), pp. 292 ff.

Barry, Brian, *Political Argument* (2nd edn., London, 1990)

Baumol, William J., *Economic Theory and Operations Analysis* (3rd edn., London, 1972)

Bausch, Thomas, *Ungleichheit und Gerechtigkeit: eine kritische Reflexion des Rawlsschen Unterschiedsprinzips in diskursethischer Perspektive* (Berlin, 1993)

Beccaria, Cesare, *dei delitti e delle pene* (Milan, 1987)

Becker, Gary S., 'Crime and Punishment: An Economic Approach', in *Journal of Political Economy*, Vol. 76 (1968), pp. 169 ff.

Behrens, Peter, *Die ökonomischen Grundlagen des Rechts: politische Ökonomie als rationale Jurisprudenz* (Tübingen, 1986)

Benhabib, Seyla, *Selbst im Kontext: Kommunikative Ethik im Spannungsfeld von Feminismus, Kommunitarismus und Postmoderne* (Frankfurt am Main, 1995)

Bentham, Jeremy, *An Introduction to the Principles of Morals and Legislation*, ed. J. H. Burns and H. L. A. Hart (Oxford, 1996; cited as: *IPML, chapter, paragraph*)

Bentham, Jeremy, *A Fragment on Government*, ed. J. H. Burns and H. L. A. Hart (Cambridge et al., 1977; cited as: *FG, section*)

Bentham, Jeremy, 'Anarchical Fallacies: An Examination of the Declarations of Rights issued during the French Revolution', in John Bowring (ed.), *The Works of Jeremy Bentham*, Vol. 2 (New York, 1962), pp. 489 ff. (cited as: 'AF, article, paragraph')

Bieri, Laurent, 'La faute au sens de l'article 41 CO – Plaidoyer pour une reconnaissance explicite de la "règle de hand" ', *Schweizerische Juristen-Zeitung*, Vol. 103 (2007), pp. 289 ff.

Binswanger, Christoph, *Die Glaubensgemeinschaft der Ökonomen, Essays zur Kultur der Wirtschaft* (Munich, 1998)

Birnbacher, Dieter, 'Neue Entwicklungen des Utilitarismus', in Bernd Biervert and Martin Held (eds.), *Ethische Grundlagen der ökonomischen Theorie* (Frankfurt am Main and New York, 1989), pp. 15 ff. (cited as: 'Utilitarismus')

Birnbacher, Dieter, 'Sind wir für die Natur verantwortlich?', in id. (ed.), *Ökologie und Ethik* (Stuttgart, 1980), pp. 103 ff. (cited as: 'Natur')

Birnbacher, Dieter, 'Der Utilitarismus und die Ökonomie', in Bernd Biervert/Klaus Held/Josef Wieland (eds.), *Sozialphilosophische Grundlagen des ökonomischen Handelns* (Frankfurt am Main, 1990), pp. 65 ff. (cited as: 'Ökonomie')

Blaug, Mark, *The Methodology of Economics* (2nd edn., Cambridge, 1992)

Bohnen, Alfred, *Die utilitaristische Ethik als Grundlage der modernen Wohlfahrtsökonomik* (Monographien zur Politik, Heft 6; Göttingen, 1964)

Boie, Wiebe-Katrin, *Ökonomische Steuerungsinstrumente im europäischen Umweltrecht* (Berlin, 2006)

Brink, David O., *Moral Realism and the Foundations of Ethics* (Cambridge, 1989)

Buchanan, James M., 'An Economic Theory of Clubs', in *Economica*, Vol. 32 (1965), pp. 1 ff.

Calabresi, Guido, 'Some Thoughts on Risk Distribution and the Law of Torts' in *Yale Law Journal*, Vol. 70 (1961), pp. 499 ff.

Calabresi, Guido, *The Costs of Accidents: A Legal and Economic Analysis* (New Haven, 1970; cited as: *Accidents*)

Calabresi, Guido and Melamed, A. Douglas, 'Property Rules, Liability Rules, and Inalienability: One View of the Cathedral', in *Harvard Law Review*, Vol. 85 (1972), pp. 1089 ff.

Camerer, Colin F., Loewenstein, George and Rabin, Matthew (eds.), *Advances in Behavioral Economics* (Princeton, 2003)

Cansier, Dieter, 'Ausgestaltungsformen handelbarer Emissionsrechte und ihre politische Durchsetzbarkeit', in Holger Bonus (ed.), 'Umweltzertifikate: Der steinige Weg zur Marktwirtschaft', *Zeitschrift für angewandte Umweltforschung*, Sonderheft 9, (Berlin, 1998), pp. 97 ff.

Chapman, John W., 'Rawls' Theory of Justice', in *The American Political Science Review*, Vol. 69 (1975), pp. 588 ff.

Chaudhuri, Arun, *Ein neuer Ansatz zur ökonomischen Analyse des Deliktsrechts: am Beispiel BRD und USA* (Berlin, 1996)

Coase, Ronald H., 'The Nature of the Firm', in *Economica*, Vol. 4 (1937), pp. 386 ff.

Coase, Ronald H., 'The Federal Communications Commission', in *Journal of Law and Economics*, Vol. 2 (1959), pp. 1 ff. (cited as: 'Communications')

Coase, Ronald H., 'The Problem of Social Cost', in *Journal of Law and Economics*, Vol. 3 (1960), pp. 1 ff. (cited as: 'Social Cost')

Coase, Ronald H., 'Law and Economics at Chicago', in *Journal of Law and Economics*, Vol. 36 (1993), pp. 239 ff. (cited as: 'Law and Economics')

Coleman, Jules L., 'Efficiency, Utility, and Wealth Maximization', in *Hofstra Law Review*, Vol. 8 (1980), pp. 509 ff. (cited as: 'Efficiency')

Coleman, Jules L., 'The Economic Analysis of Law', in Roland J. Pennock and John W. Chapman (eds.), *Ethics, Economics, and the Law* (New York and London, 1982), pp. 83 ff. (cited as: 'Analysis')

Coleman, Jules L., *Markets, Morals and the Law* (Cambridge et al., 1988; cited as: *Markets*)

Coleman, Jules L., 'Tort Law and the Demands of Corrective Justice', in *Indiana Law Journal*, Vol. 67 (1991/92), pp. 349 ff.

Coleman, Jules L., *The Practice of Principles: In Defence of a Pragmatist Approach to Legal Theory* (Oxford et al., 2001) (cited as: 'Practice')

Coleman, Jules L., 'The Grounds of Welfare', in: *The Yale Law Journal*, Vol. 112 (2003), pp. 1511 ff. (cited as: 'Grounds')

Coleman, Jules L., 'The Costs of The Costs of Accidents', in *Maryland Law Review*, Vol. 64 (2005), pp. 337 ff. (cited as: 'Costs')

Cooter, Robert, 'Coase Theorem', in John Eatwell et al. (eds.), *The New Palgrave: A Dictionary of Economics* Vol. 1 (London, 1998), pp. 457 ff.

Cooter, Robert and Ulen, Thomas, *Law and Economics*, (2nd edn., Reading et al., 1997)

Diehr, Matthias, *Rechtsschutz im Emissionszertifikate-Handelssystem: Eine Betrachtung des Treibhausgas-Emissionshandelssystems unter besonderer Berücksichtigung rechtsschutzrelevanter Fragen der Emissionsgenehmigung und der Zuteilung von Emissionsberechtigungen* (Berlin, 2006)

Düppen, Bettina, *Der Utilitarismus: Eine theoriegeschichtliche Darstellung von der griechischen Antike bis zur Gegenwart* (Cologne, 1996)

Dworkin, Ronald, 'Why Efficiency?' in *Hofstra Law Review*, Vol. 8 (1980), pp. 563 ff.; page numbers cited from extract reprinted in Kenneth G. Dau-Schmidt and Thomas S. Ulen (eds.), *Law and Economics Anthology* (Cincinnati, 1998), pp. 541 ff. (cited as: 'Efficiency')

Dworkin, Ronald, 'Is Wealth a Value?', in *The Journal of Legal Studies*, Vol. 9 (1980), pp. 191 ff. (cited as: 'Value')

Dworkin, Ronald, *Sovereign Virtue: The Theory and Practice of Equality* (Cambridge, 2000)

Eckstein, Walther, 'Zur wissenschaftlichen Bewertung der "Theorie der ethischen Gefühle" ', in Horst Claus Recktenwald (ed.), *Ethik, Wirtschaft und Staat: Adam Smiths politische Ökonomie heute* (Darmstadt, 1985), pp. 123 ff.

Eidenmüller, Horst, *Effizienz als Rechtsprinzip: Möglichkeiten und Grenzen der ökonomischen Analyse des Rechts* (2nd edn., Tübingen, 1998)

Endres, Alfred, *Umweltökonomie. Lehrbuch* (3rd edn., Stuttgart, 2007)

Engel, Christoph et al., *Recht und Verhalten: Beiträge zu Law and Economics* (Tübingen, 2007)

Feess, Eberhard, *Umweltökonomie und Umweltpolitik* (3rd edn., Munich, 2007)

Fehr, Ernst and Fischbacher, Urs, 'Why Social Preferences Matter – The Impact of Non-selfish Motives on Competition, Cooperation and Incentives', in *The Economic Journal*, Vol. 112 (2002), pp. C1 ff.

Fezer, Karl-Heinz, 'Aspekte einer Rechtskritik an der economic analysis of law und am property rights approach', *Juristenzeitung*, Vol. 41 (1986), pp. 817 ff.

Fischermann, Thomas, 'Die Bibel der Liberalen', in Wilfried Herz (ed.), *ZEIT-Bibiliothek der Ökonomie* (Stuttgart, 2000)

Fletcher, George P., *The Basic Concepts of Legal Thoughts* (New York et al., 1996)

Forst, Rainer, *Kontexte der Gerechtigkeit: Politische Philosophie jenseits von Liberalismus und Kommunitarismus* (Frankfurt am Main, 1994)

Frank, Jürgen, *Kritische Ökonomie, Einführung in Grundsätze und Kontroversen wirtschaftlicher Theoriebildung* (Reinbek bei Hamburg, 1976)

Frey, Bruno S., *Moderne politische Ökonomie: Die Beziehungen zwischen Wirtschaft und Politik* (Munich and Zurich, 1977) (cited as: 'Politische Ökonomie')

Frey, Bruno S., *Umweltökonomie* (3rd edn., Göttingen, 1992; cited as: *Umweltökonomie*)

Frey, Bruno S., *Happiness: A Revolution in Economics* (Cambridge, 2008)

Frey, Bruno S. and Kirchgässner, Gebhard, *Demokratische Wirtschaftspolitik* (2nd edn., Munich, 1994)

Frey, Bruno S. and Stutzer, Alois, *Happiness and Economics: How the Economy and Institutions Affect Human Well-Being* (Princeton, 2002)

Frey, Bruno S. and Stutzer, Alois, (eds.), *Economics and Psychology: A Promising New Cross-Disciplinary Field* (Cambridge, 2007)

Friedman, Milton, *Essays in Positive Economics*, containing introd. Chapter 'The Methodology of Positive Economics' (Chicago, 1953)

Gäfgen, Gérard, *Theorie der wirtschaftlichen Entscheidung: Untersuchungen zur Logik und Bedeutung des rationalen Handelns* (3rd edn., Tübingen, 1974)

Gauch, Peter, 'Zum Stand der Lehre und Rechtsprechung. Geschichten und Einsichten eines privaten Schuldrechtlers', in *Zeitschrift für Schweizerisches Recht*, NF Vol. 119 (2000); Half Vol. I, pp. 1 ff.

Geigant, Friedrich et al., *Lexikon der Volkswirtschaft* (6th edn., Landsberg am Lech, 1994)

Gesang, Bernward, 'Gerechtigkeitsutilitarismus', in id. (ed.), *Gerechtigkeitsutilitarismus* (Paderborn et al., 1998), pp. 13 ff. (cited as: 'Gerechtigkeitsutilitarismus')

Gesang, Bernward, *Eine Verteidigung des Utilitarismus* (Stuttgart, 2003; cited as: *Verteidigung*)

Gintis, Herbert et al. (eds.), *Moral Sentiments and Material Interests: The Foundation of Cooperation in Economic Life* (Cambridge, 2005)

Goethe, Johann Wolfgang, *Faust, Part One*, ed. and trans. David Luke (Oxford, 1987; cited as: *Faust I, verse*)

Gray, Christopher B., *The Philosophy of Law: an Encyclopedia* (2 vols., New York, 1999)

Griffin, James, *Well-Being: Its Meaning, Measurement and Moral Importance* (New York, 1986)

Habermas, Jürgen, *Moralbewusstsein und kommunikatives Handeln* (Frankfurt am Main, 1983)

Hagel, Joachim, *Effizienz und Gerechtigkeit: Ein Beitrag zur Diskussion der ethischen Aspekte in der neoklassischen Wohlfahrtstheorie* (Baden-Baden, 1993)

Hardin, Garrett, 'The Tragedy of the Commons', in *Science*, Vol. 162 (1968), pp. 1243 ff.

Hart, Herbert L. A., 'Rawls on Liberty and its Priority', in id. (ed.), *Essays in Jurisprudence and Philosophy* (Oxford, 1983), pp. 223 ff. (cited as: 'Liberty')

Hart, Herbert L. A., 'Between Utility and Rights', in, id. (ed.), *Essays in Jurisprudence and Philosophy* (Oxford, 1983), pp. 198 ff. (cited as: 'Utility')

Hart, Herbert L. A., 'American Jurisprudence through English Eyes: The Nightmare and the Noble Dream', in id. (ed.), *Essays in Jurisprudence and Philosophy* (Oxford, 1983), pp. 123 ff. (cited as: 'American Jurisprudence')

Helvétius, Claude-Adrien, *De l'homme, de ses facultés intellectuelles, et de son éducation* (2 vols., Paris, 1989; cited as: *De l'homme, part, chapter*)

Hevia, Martin, 'Kronman on Contract Law and Distributive Justice', in *Journal of Contract Law*, Vol. 23 (2007), pp. 105 ff.

Hicks, John R., 'The Rehabilitation of Consumer's Surplus', in *Review of Economic Studies*, Vol. 8 (1941), pp. 108 ff.

Hoerster, Norbert, *Utilitaristische Ethik und Verallgemeinerung* (Freiburg and Munich, 1971)

Höffe, Otfried, *Politische Gerechtigkeit: Grundlegung einer kritischen Philosophie von Recht und Staat* (Frankfurt am Main, 1987; cited as: *Politische Gerechtigkeit*)

Höffe, Otfried, 'Einleitung', in id. (ed.), *Einführung in die utilitaristische Ethik: klassische und zeitgenössische Texte* (2nd edn., Tübingen, 1992), pp. 7 ff. (cited as: 'Ethik')

Höffe, Otfried, 'Einführung in Rawls' Theorie der Gerechtigkeit', in id. (ed.), *John Rawls, Eine Theorie der Gerechtigkeit* (Berlin, 1998), pp. 3 ff. (cited as: 'Rawls')

Höffe, Otfried, *Gerechtigkeit: eine philosophische Einführung* (Munich, 2001; cited as: *Gerechtigkeit*)

Hoffmann, Andreas, 'Der Preis des Marktes', in Nikolaus Piper (ed.), *Die grossen Ökonomen* (2nd edn., Stuttgart, 1996), pp. 293 ff.

Homann, Karl, 'Marktwirtschaftliche Ordnung und Unternehmensethik', in *Zeitschrift für Betriebswirtschaft*, Vol. 62 (1992), Suppl. 1, pp. 75 ff.

Homann, Karl and Suchanek, Andreas, *Ökonomik: eine Einführung* (Tübingen, 2000)

Hottinger, Olaf, *Eigeninteresse und individuelles Nutzenkalkül in der Theorie der Gesellschaft und Ökonomie von Adam Smith, Jeremy Bentham und John Stuart Mill* (Marburg, 1998)

Hotz, Beat, 'Ökonomische Analyse des Rechts – eine skeptische Betrachtung', in *Wirtschaft und Recht*, Vol. 34 (1982), pp. 293 ff.

Hübner, Dietmar, 'Justice over Time. Zum Problem der Gerechtigkeit zwischen den Generationen', in *Jahrbuch für Wissenschaft und Ethik*, Vol. 6 (2001), pp. 39 ff.

Hutcheson, Francis, *An Inquiry into the Original of our Ideas of Beauty and Virtue* (facs. edn., Hildesheim, 1991)

Jacobs, Reto, *Marktwirtschaftlicher Umweltschutz aus rechtlicher Sicht: Zertifikatlösungen im Luftreinhalterecht der USA und der Schweiz* (Zurich, 1997)

Janson, Gunnar, *Ökonomische Theorie im Recht: Anwendbarkeit und Erkenntniswert im allgemeinen und am Beispiel des Arbeitsrechts* (Berlin, 2004)

Johansen, Leif, 'The Bargaining Society and the Inefficiency of Bargaining', in *Kyklos*, Vol. 32 (1979), pp. 497 ff.

Kahneman, Daniel and Tversky, Amos, 'Prospect Theory: An Analysis of Decision under Risk', in *Econometrica*, Vol. XVLII (1979), pp. 263 ff.

Kaldor, Nicholas, 'Welfare Propositions of Economic and Interpersonal Comparisons of Utility', in *Economic Journal*, Vol. 49 (1939), pp. 549 ff.

Kant, Immanuel, *Fundamental Principles of the Metaphysic of Morals*, trans. Thomas Kingsmill Abbot, in Robert Maynard Hutchins (ed.), *The Critique of Pure Reason: The Critique of Practical Reason and Other Ethical Treatises: the Critique of Judgment* (Chicago, 1952; cited as: *Fundamental Principles*)

Kant, Immanuel, *The Science of Right*, trans. W. Hastie, ibid. (Chicago, 1952; cited as: *Science of Right*)

Kaplow, Louis and Shavell, Steven, 'Why the Legal System is less efficient than the Income Tax in Redistributing Income', in *The Journal of Legal Studies*, Vol. 23 (1994), pp. 667 ff. (cited as: 'Income Tax')

Kaplow, Louis and Shavell, Steven, *Fairness versus Welfare* (Cambridge et al., 2002; cited as: *Fairness*)

Kersting, Wolfgang, *Theorien der sozialen Gerechtigkeit* (Stuttgart and Weimar, 2000; cited as: *soziale Gerechtigkeit*)

Kersting, Wolfgang, *John Rawls zur Einführung* (Hamburg, 2001; cited as: *Einführung*)

Kirchgässner, Gebhard, 'Die neue Welt der Ökonomie', in *Analyse und Kritik*, Vol. 10 (1988), pp. 107 ff. (cited as: 'Ökonomie')

Kirchgässner, Gebhard, *Homo oeconomicus: das ökonomische Modell individuellen Verhaltens und seine Anwendung in den Wirtschafts- und Sozialwissenschaften* (2nd edn., Tübingen, 2000; cited as: *Homo oeconomicus*)

Kirchner, Christian, 'Ökonomische Theorie des Rechts', in *Schriftenreihe der Juristischen Gesellschaft zu Berlin*, Heft 151 (Berlin and New York, 1997)

Kittsteiner, Heinz-Dieter, 'Ethik und Teleologie: Das Problem der "unsichtbaren Hand" bei Adam Smith', in Franz-Xaver Kaufmann and Hans-Günter Krüsselberg (eds.), *Markt, Staat und Solidarität bei Adam Smith* (Frankfurt am Main, 1984), pp. 41 ff.

Kleinewefers, Henner, 'Ökonomische Theorie des Rechts. Über Unterschiede zwischen dem ökonomischen und dem juristischen Denken', in Detlev-Christian Dicke and Thomas Fleiner-Gerster (eds.), *Staat und Gesellschaft, Festschrift für Leo Schürmann* (Fribourg, 1987), pp. 83 ff.

Kliemt, Hartmut, 'Rawls' Kritik am Utilitarismus', in Otfried Höffe (ed.), *John Rawls, Eine Theorie der Gerechtigkeit* (Berlin, 1998), pp. 97 ff.

Koboldt, Christian, Leder, Matthias and Schmidtchen, Dieter, 'Ökonomische Analyse des Rechts', in Norbert *Berthold* (ed.) *Allgemeine Wirtschaftstheorie: neuere Entwicklungen* (Munich, 1995), pp. 355 ff.

Koller, Peter, 'Die Grundsätze der Gerechtigkeit', in Otfried Höffe (ed.), *Eine Theorie der Gerechtigkeit* (Berlin, 1998), pp. 45 ff.

Kötz, Hein and Schäfer, Hans-Bernd, *Judex oeconomicus: 12 höchstrichterliche Entscheidungen kommentiert aus ökonomischer Sicht* (Tübingen, 2003)

Kronman, Anthony T., 'Wealth Maximization as a Normative Principle', in *The Journal of Legal Studies*, Vol. 9 (1980), pp. 227 ff.

Kukathas, Chandran and Pettit, Philipp, *Rawls – A Theory of Justice* (California, 1990)

Külp, Bernhard, 'Wohlfahrtsökonomik I: Grundlagen', in Willi Albers et al. (ed.), *Handwörterbuch der Wirtschaftswissenschaft (HdWW)*, Vol. 9 (Stuttgart and New York, 1977–1983), pp. 469 ff.

Kunz, Harald, 'Kriminalität', in Bernd-Thomas Ramb and Manfred Tietzel (eds.), *Ökonomische Verhaltenstheorie* (Munich, 1993), pp. 181 ff.

Lave, Lester B., 'Benefit-Cost Analysis – Do the Benefits Exceed the Costs?', in Robert W. Hahn (ed.), *Risks, Costs and Lives Saved – Getting Better Results from Regulation* (New York and Oxford, 1996), pp. 104 ff.

Le Grand, Julian, *Equity and Choice. An Essay in Economics and Applied Philosophy* (London, 1991)

Locher, Klaus, 'Auswege aus Gefangenen-Dilemma-Situationen', in *Wirtschaftswissenschaftliches Studium* (WiSt), Vol. 20 (1991), pp. 60 ff.

Loewenstein, George, 'Willpower: A Decision Theorist's Perspective', in *Law and Philosophy*, Vol. 19 (2000), pp. 51 ff.

Lukes, Steven, 'On Trade-Offs between Values', in Francesco Farina et al. (eds.), *Ethics, Rationality and Economic Behaviour* (Oxford, 1996), pp. 36 ff.

MacIntyre, Alasdair, *After Virtue: A Study in Moral Theory* (London, 1981)

Mack, Elke, *Ökonomische Rationalität: Grundlage einer interdisziplinären Wirtschaftsethik?* (Berlin, 1994)

Mackie, John L., *Ethik: Auf der Suche nach dem Richtigen und Falschen*, trans. Rudolf Ginters (Ditzingen, 1981); published in English as, *Ethics: Inventing Right and Wrong* (Harmondsworth, 1977)

Mader, Luzius, 'Zum aktuellen Stand der Gesetzesfolgenabschätzung in der Schweiz', in Ulrich Karpen and Hagen Hof (eds.), *Wirkungsforschung zum Recht IV: Möglichkeiten einer Institutionalisierung der Wirkungskontrolle von Gesetzen* (Baden-Baden, 2003), pp. 96 ff.

Malloy, Robin Paul, *Law and Market Economy: Reinterpreting the Values of Law and Economics* (Cambridge, 2000)

Manstetten, Reiner, *Das Menschenbild der Ökonomie: Der homo oeconomicus und die Anthropologie von Adam Smith* (Munich, 2000)

Mathis, Klaus, 'Behavioral Economics', in: David S. Clark (ed.), *Encyclopedia of Law and Society – American and Global Perspectives*, Vol. 1 (Thousand Oaks/London/New Delhi, 2007), pp. 118 ff.

Mathis, Klaus, 'Future Generations in John Rawls's Theory of Justice', in: *Archiv für Rechts- und Sozialphilosophie* (ARSP), Vol. 95 (2009); first published in German as: 'Zukünftige Generationen in der Theorie der Gerechtigkeit von John Rawls', in: Sandra Hotz/Klaus Mathis (eds.), *Recht, Moral und Faktizität. Festschrift für Walter Ott* (Zurich and St. Gallen, 2008), pp. 181 ff.

Medick, Hans, *Naturzustand und Naturgeschichte der bürgerlichen Gesellschaft: Die Ursprünge der bürgerlichen Sozialtheorie als Geschichtsphilosophie und Sozialwissenschaft bei Samuel Pufendorf, John Locke und Adam Smith* (Göttingen, 1973)

Meyer, Willi, 'Die Methodologie der positiven Ökonomie und ihre Folgen', in Ernst Helmstädter (ed.), *Neuere Entwicklungen in den Wirtschaftswissenschaften* (Schriften des Vereins für Sozialpolitik, NF Vol. 98, Berlin 1978), pp. 19 ff.

Mill, John Stuart, 'Utilitarianism', in Alan Ryan (ed.), *Utilitarianism and other Essays* (London, 1987), pp. 272 ff. (cited as: 'Utilitarianism', chapter, paragraph)

Mishan, Edward J., *Cost-Benefit Analysis: an informal introduction* (4th edn., London et al., 1988)

Moore, George Edward, *Principia Ethica* (Cambridge, 1966; cited as: *PE*, chapter, section, paragraph)

Mühlbauer, Bernhard, *Emissionshandel – System und öffentlich-rechtlicher Rechtsschutz* (Baden-Baden, 2008)

Musgrave, Richard A., 'A Multiple Theory of Budget Determination', in *Finanzarchiv*; Vol. 17 (1956/57), pp. 333 ff.

Neumann, Manfred, 'Neoklassik', in Otmar Issing (ed.), *Geschichte der Nationalökonomie* (3rd edn., Munich, 1994), pp. 255 ff.

OECD, *Regulatory Impact Analysis: Best Practices in OECD Countries* (Paris, 1997)

Okun, Arthur M., *Equality and Efficiency – The Big Tradeoff* (Washington, 1975)

Olson, Mancur, *The Logic of Collective Action: Public Goods and the Theory of Groups* (21st edn., Cambridge, 2003)

Osterloh, Margit and Tiemann, Regine, 'Konzepte der Wirtschafts- und Unternehmensethik. Das Beispiel der Brent Spar', in *Die Unternehmung*, Vol. 49 (1995), pp. 321 ff.

Ott, Walter, *Der Rechtspositivismus: kritische Würdigung auf der Grundlage eines juristischen Pragmatismus* (2nd edn., Berlin, 1992)

Ott, Walter and Mathis, Klaus, 'Die Rechtstheorie von Jürgen Habermas: Eine kritische Würdigung', in *Zeitschrift für Schweizerisches Recht*, NF Vol. 121 (2002), Half Vol. I, pp. 203 ff.

Parfit, Derek, *Reasons and Persons* (Oxford, 1984)

Patzen, Martin, 'Zur Diskussion des Adam-Smith-Problems – ein Überblick', in Arnold Meyer-Faje and Peter Ulrich (eds.), *Der andere Adam Smith: Beiträge zur Neubestimmung von Ökonomie als Politischer Ökonomie* (Berne and Stuttgart, 1991), pp. 21 ff.

Perelman, Chaïm, *Über die Gerechtigkeit* (Munich, 1967)

Perman, Roger et al., *Natural Resource and Environmental Economics* (3rd edn., Harlow, 2003)

Perry, Stephen R., 'Comment on Coleman: Corrective Justice', in *Indiana Law Journal*, Vol. 67 (1991/92), pp. 381 ff.

Persson, Torsten and Tabellini, Guido, 'Is Inequality Harmful for Growth?' in *American Economic Review*, Vol. 84 (1994), pp. 600 ff.

Pheby, John, *Methodology and Economics: A Critical Introduction* (Houndmills et al., 1988)

Pies, Ingo, *Normative Institutionenökonomik: zur Rationalisierung des politischen Liberalismus* (Tübingen, 1993)

Pies, Ingo and Leschke, Martin, (eds.), *Gary Becker's Economic Imperialism* (Tübingen, 1998)

Pigou, Arthur C., *The Economics of Welfare* (reprint of 4th edn., London, 1932)

Polinsky, A. Mitchell, *An Introduction to Law and Economics* (2nd edn., Boston et al., 1989)

Posner, Richard A., *Economic Analysis of Law* (1st edn., Boston et al., 1972; cited as: *EAL 1*)

Posner, Richard A., 'The Economic Approach to Law', in *Texas Law Review*, Vol. 53 (1975), pp. 757 ff. (cited as: 'Economic Approach')

Posner, Richard A., 'Utilitarianism, Economics, and Legal Theory', in *The Journal of Legal Studies*, Vol. 8 (1979), pp. 103 ff. (cited as: 'Utilitarianism')

Posner, Richard A., 'The Ethical and Political Basis of the Efficiency Norm in Common Law Adjudication', in *Hofstra Law Review*, Vol. 8 (1980), pp. 487 ff.; cited page numbers refer to extract reprinted in Kenneth G. Dau-Schmidt and Thomas S. Ulen (eds.), *Law and Economics Anthology* (Cincinnati, 1998), pp. 531 ff. (cited as: 'Efficiency Norm')

Posner, Richard A., 'The Value of Wealth: A Comment on Dworkin and Kronman', in *The Journal of Legal Studies*, Vol. 9 (1980), pp. 243 ff. (cited as: 'Value')

Posner, Richard A., *The Economics of Justice* (Harvard 1981; cited as: *Economics*)

Posner, Richard A., 'Wealth Maximization Revisited', in *Notre Dame Journal of Law, Ethics and Public Policy*, Vol. 2 (1985), pp. 85 ff. (cited as: 'Wealth')

Posner, Richard A., 'The Justice of Economics', in *Economia delle scelte pubbliche*, Vol. 1 (1987), pp. 15 ff. (cited as: 'Justice')

Posner, Richard A., *The Problems of Jurisprudence* (Cambridge et al., 1990; cited as: *Jurisprudence*)

Posner, Richard A., *Overcoming Law* (Cambridge et al., 1995; cited as: *Overcoming Law*)

Posner, Richard A., 'Wealth Maximization and Tort Law: A Philosophical Inquiry', in David G. Owen (ed.), *Philosophical Foundations of Tort Law* (Oxford, 1995), pp. 99 ff. (cited as: 'Inquiry')

Posner, Richard A., *Economic Analysis of Law* (5th edn., New York, 1998; cited as: *EAL 5*)

Posner, Richard A., *Frontiers of Legal Theory* (Cambridge and London, 2001; cited as: *Legal Theory*)

Posner, Richard A., *Law, Pragmatism, and Democracy* (Cambridge and London, 2003; cited as: *Pragmatism*)

Radbruch, Gustav, *Rechtsphilosophie*, ed., Ralf Dreier and Stanley L. Paulson (Heidelberg, 1999)

Raphael, David D., *Adam Smith*, trans. Udo Rennert (Frankfurt am Main and New York, 1991); published in English as, *Adam Smith* (Oxford, 1985)

Rawls, John, *A Theory of Justice* (2nd edn., Cambridge, 1999; cited as: *TJ*)

Rawls, John, 'Social Unity and Primary Goods', in: Amartya Sen/Bernard Williams (eds.), *Utilitarianism and Beyond* (Cambridge UK, 1982), pp. 159 ff. (cited as: 'Primary Goods')

Rawls, John, *Political Liberalism* (New York, 1993; cited as: *PL*)

Rawls, John, *Justice as Fairness. A Restatement*, (ed.), Erin Kelly (Cambridge and London, 2001; cited as: *JF*)

Reuter, Hans-Richard, 'Der "Generationenvertrag". Zur ethischen Problematik einer sozialpolitischen Leitvorstellung', in Karl Gabriel/Hermann-Josef Grosse Kracht (eds.), *Brauchen wir einen neuen Gesellschaftsvertrag?* (Wiesbaden, 2005), pp. 171 ff.

Richter, Rudolf and Furubotn, Eirik G., *Neue Institutionenökonomik: eine Einführung und kritische Würdigung* (2nd edn., Tübingen, 1999)

Recktenwald, Horst Claus, *Über Adam Smiths 'The Theory of Moral Sentiments', Vademecum zu einem frühen Klassiker* (Düsseldorf, 1986)

Robbins, Lionel, *An Essay on the Nature and Significance of Economic Science* (London, 1937)

Sandel, Michael, 'Die verfahrensrechtliche Republik und das ungebundene Selbst', in Axel Honneth (ed.), *Kommunitarismus: Eine Debatte über die moralischen Grundlagen moderner Gesellschaften* (2nd edn., Frankfurt am Main, 1994), pp. 18 ff.

Schäfer, Hans-Bernd and Ott, Claus, *Lehrbuch der ökonomischen Analyse des Zivilrechts* (3rd edn., Berlin et al., 2000)

Schefczyk, Michael and Priddat, Birger P., 'Effizienz und Gerechtigkeit – Eine Verhältnisbestimmung in sozialpolitischer Absicht', in Wolfgang Kersting (ed.), *Politische Philosophie des Sozialstaats* (Weilerwist, 2000), pp. 428 ff.

Schefold, Bertram and Carstensen, Kristian, 'Die klassische Politische Ökonomie', in Otmar Issing (ed.), *Geschichte der Nationalökonomie* (3rd edn., Munich, 1994), pp. 63 ff.

Schernikau, Frank, *Zur Verbindung von Ethik und Ökonomie am Beispiel der Wohlfahrtstheorie: Ein dogmenhistorischer Abriss von Adam Smith bis in die Gegenwart unter besonderer Berücksichtigung von kardinaler Messbarkeit und interpersoneller Vergleichbarkeit* (Frankfurt am Main, 1992)

Schmidtchen, Dieter, 'Die ökonomische Analyse des Rechts', in Dieter Schmidtchen and Stephan Weth (eds.), *Der Effizienz auf der Spur: die Funktionsfähigkeit der Justiz im Lichte der ökonomischen Analyse des Rechts* (Baden-Baden,1999), pp. 9 ff.

Schumann, Jochen, 'Wohlfahrtsökonomik', in Otmar Issing (ed.), *Geschichte der Nationalökonomie* (3rd edn., 1994, Munich), pp. 215 ff. (cited as: 'Wohlfahrtsökonomik')

Schumann, Jochen, *Grundzüge der Mikroökonomischen Theorie* (7th edn., Berlin, 1999; cited as: *Mikroökonomie*)

Scitovsky, Tibor, 'A Note on Welfare Propositions in Economics', in *Review of Economic Studies*, Vol. 9 (1941), pp. 77 ff.

Scriven, Michael, 'Explanations, Predictions and Law', in Herbert Feigl and Grover Maxwell (eds.), *Minnesota Studies in the Philosophy of Science*, Vol. 3 (1962), pp. 170 ff.

Seelmann, Kurt, *Rechtsphilosophie* (2nd edn., Munich, 2001)

Seiler, Hansjörg, 'Wie viel Sicherheit wollen wir? Sicherheitsmassnahmen zwischen Kostenwirksamkeit und Recht', in *Zeitschrift des Bernischen Juristenvereins* (2007), pp. 140 ff.

Sen, Amartya K., *Collective Choice and Social Welfare* (San Francisco, 1979; cited as: *Collective Choice*)

Sen, Amartya K., 'Equality of What', in S. McMurrin (ed.), *The Tanner Lecture on Human Values*, Vol. 1 (Cambridge, 1980), pp. 195 ff. (cited as: 'Equality')

Sen, Amartya K., *Resources, Values and Development* (Oxford, 1984; cited as: *Resources*)

Sen, Amartya K., *Inequality Reexamined* (Cambridge, 1992)

Sibley, W. M., 'The Rational versus the Reasonable', in *Philosophical Review*, Vol. 62 (1953), pp. 554 ff.

Sidgwick, Henry, *The Methods of Ethics* (7th edn., Indianapolis and Cambridge, 1907)

Siemer, John Philipp, *Das Coase-Theorem: Inhalt, Aussagewert und Bedeutung für die ökonomische Analyse des Rechts* (Münster, 1999)

Simon, Herbert A., 'Rational Decision Making in Business Organizations', in *American Economic Review*, Vol. 69 (1979), pp. 493 ff.

Smart, John J. C., 'An Outline of a System of Utilitarian Ethics', in id. and Bernard Williams (eds.), *Utilitarianism For and Against* (Cambridge et al., 1973), pp. 3 ff.

Smith, Adam, *The Theory of Moral Sentiments*, (ed.), Knud Haakonssen (Cambridge, 2002; cited as: *TMS*, part, section, chapter, paragraph)

Smith, Adam, *An Inquiry into the Nature and Causes of the Wealth of Nations*, 2 vols., (ed.), R. H. Campbell et al. (Oxford, 1979; cited as: *WN*, book, chapter, section)

Sohmen, Egon, *Allokationstheorie und Wirtschaftspolitik* (Tübingen, 1976)

Stigler, George J., *The Theory of Price* (3rd edn., New York, 1966)
Stiglitz, Joseph E., *Finanzwissenschaft* (Munich and Vienna, 1989)
Stone, Martin, 'On the Idea of Private Law', in *Canadian Journal of Law and Jurisprudence*, Vol. 9 (1996), pp. 235 ff.
Sunstein, Cass R. (ed.), *Behavioral Law and Economics* (Cambridge, 2000)
Taupitz, Jochen, 'Ökonomische Analyse und Haftungsrecht – Eine Zwischenbilanz', in *Archiv für die civilistische Praxis*, Vol. 196 (1996), pp. 114 ff.
Trapp, Manfred, *Adam Smith – politische Philosophie und politische Ökonomie* (Göttingen, 1987)
Trapp, Rainer W., 'Politisches Handeln im wohlverstandenen Allgemeininteresse', in Hans-Joachim Koch et al. (eds.), *Theorien der Gerechtigkeit*, ARSP Beiheft 56 (1994), pp. 54 ff. (cited as: 'Politisches Handeln')
Trapp, Rainer W., *'Nicht-klassischer' Utilitarismus: Eine Theorie der Gerechtigkeit* (Frankfurt am Main, 1988; cited as: *'Nicht-klassischer' Utilitarismus*)
Tugendhat, Ernst, *Probleme der Ethik* (Stuttgart, 1984)
Veljanovski, Cento G., 'Wealth Maximization, Law and Ethics – On the Limits of Economic Efficiency', in *International Review of Law and Economics*, Vol. 1 (1981), pp. 5 ff. (cited as: 'Limits')
Veljanovski, Cento G., 'The Coase Theorems and the Economic Theory of Markets and Law', in *Kyklos* Vol. 35 (1982), pp. 53 ff. (cited as: 'Coase Theorems')
Viner, Jacob, 'Adam Smith and Laissez Faire', in *The Journal of Political Economy*, Vol. 35 (1927), pp. 198 ff.
van Aaken, Anne, *'Rational choice' in der Rechtswissenschaft: Zum Stellenwert der ökonomischen Theorie im Recht* (Baden-Baden, 1993)
von Arnim, Hans Herbert, *Wirtschaftlichkeit als Rechtsprinzip* (Berlin, 1988)
von der Crone, Hans Caspar, *Rahmenverträge: Vertragsrecht – Systemtheorie – Ökonomie* (Zurich, 1993)
von der Pfordten, Dietmar, *Rechtsethik* (Munich, 2001)
von Weizsäcker, Carl Christian, 'Was leistet die Property Rights Theorie für aktuelle wirtschaftspolitische Fragen?' in Manfred Neumann (ed.), *Ansprüche, Eigentums- und Verfügungsrechte, Schriftenreihe des Vereins für Socialpolitik*, NF Vol. 140 (1984), pp. 123 ff.
Weigel, Wolfgang, *Rechtsökonomik: eine methodologische Einführung für Einsteiger und Neugieriger* (Munich, 2003)
Weinrib, Ernest J., *The Idea of Private Law* (Cambridge, 1995)
Wicke, Lutz, *Umweltökonomie: Eine praxisorientierte Einführung* (4th edn., Munich, 1993)
Wiesmeth, Hans, *Umweltökonomie: Theorie und Praxis im Gleichgewicht* (Berlin and Heidelberg, 2003)
Williams, Bernard, *Kritik des Utilitarismus* (ed. and trans.), Wolfgang R. Köhler (Frankfurt am Main, 1979); published in English as, 'A Critique of Utilitarianism' in J. J. C. Smart and id., *Utilitarianism: For and Against* (Cambridge, 1973)
Wittmann, Donald A., *Economic Analysis of the Law: Selected Readings* (Malden, 2003)
Wolf, Jean-Claude, *John Stuart Mills 'Utilitarismus': ein kritischer Kommentar* (Freiburg and Munich, 1992)
Zipursky, Benjamin, 'Rights, Wrongs, and Recourse in the Law of Torts', in *Vanderbilt Law Review*, Vol. 51 (1998), pp. 1 ff.

# Index

Printed in the United Kingdom by
Lightning Source UK Ltd., Milton Keynes
138279UK00008B/39/P